TRANSATLANTIC SOCIAL POLITICS

Studies in Democratic Culture

What does it mean to inhabit a democratic culture? This new series examines that question by bringing together innovative studies that advance our understanding of the history and practice of democracy in societies past and present.

The distinctiveness of the series stems from its focus on political engagement, mobilization, and participation. These themes interest us because high levels of political engagement and the existence of formally representative institutions are separable phenomena—undemocratic societies can have high levels of civic engagement whereas democratic societies—such as those in much of Europe and North America today—can be characterized as having low levels of civic engagement. This cannot be explained solely through the study of democratic constitutions or other formal structures; rather, it demands an approach to the study of democracy attentive to wider processes of civic and political engagement, that is to say, to the study of democratic culture. We seek to showcase new work on the history of democratic cultures from early to late modernity, and to offer a home to transnational and comparative—as well as local and national—studies, especially when they address the democratic cultures of Africa, Asia, and South America.

This new series promotes historical work on political engagement, mobilization, and participation while seeking to extend, enrich, and historicize our understanding of "democratic culture" as a concept.

Transatlantic Social Politics: 1800–Present
Edited by Daniel Scroop and Andrew Heath

Transatlantic Social Politics

1800–Present

Edited by

Daniel Scroop

and

Andrew Heath

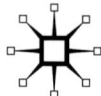

TRANSATLANTIC SOCIAL POLITICS

First published in 2014 by
PALGRAVE MACMILLAN®
in the United States—a division of St. Martin's Press LLC,
175 Fifth Avenue, New York, NY 10010.

Where this book is distributed in the UK, Europe and the rest of the world,
this is by Palgrave Macmillan, a division of Macmillan Publishers Limited,
registered in England, company number 785998, of Houndmills,
Basingstoke, Hampshire RG21 6XS.

Palgrave Macmillan is the global academic imprint of the above companies
and has companies and representatives throughout the world.

Palgrave® and Macmillan® are registered trademarks in the United States, the
United Kingdom, Europe and other countries.

ISBN: 978–1–137–47095–9

Library of Congress Cataloging-in-Publication Data

Transatlantic social politics / edited by Andrew Heath and Daniel Scroop.
    pages cm.
    Summary: "This edited collection, comprising essays by an array of
established and emerging scholars from Europe and the United States,
offers a fresh perspective on the history of transatlantic political networks
and exchanges since 1800. Historians such as Daniel T. Rodgers have
already shown how important such networks were in shaping the politics
of the modern Atlantic world. To date, however, this field has been
dominated by studies of the activities and ideas of progressive reformers,
with a particular focus on the period 1870-1940, an era in which reform
networks coalesced so as to fashion the world of 'social politics' so
brilliantly depicted in Rodgers's path-breaking study Atlantic Crossings
(1998). The contributions gathered here challenge the chronological and
ideological orientation of such work. They do so by collectively proposing a
new periodization of modern transatlantic politics—one demonstrating the
vitality and long-range significance both of early and mid-nineteenth, and
of post-1945 interactions. At the same time, they illustrate the ideological
heterogeneity of transatlantic political exchange, which encompassed a
kaleidoscope of conservative, radical, and populist elements, in addition to
the progressive and liberal currents about which so much has already been
written"—Provided by publisher.
    Includes bibliographical references and index.
    ISBN 978–1–137–47095–9 (hardcover : alkaline paper)
    1. Europe—Relations—United States. 2. United States—Relations—
Europe. 3. Social networks—Political aspects—Europe—History. 4. Social
networks—Political aspects—United States—History. 5. Political culture—
Europe—History. 6. Political culture—United States—History. 7. Europe—
Politics and government. 8. United States—Politics and government.
9. Europe—Social policy. 10. United States—Social policy. I. Scroop, Daniel,
1973– II. Heath, Andrew.

D34.U5T74 2014
306.209182'1—dc23   2014023059

A catalogue record of the book is available from the British Library.

Design by Newgen Knowledge Works (P) Ltd., Chennai, India.

First edition: December 2014

Contents

Acknowledgments

The origins of this volume of essays lie in a workshop on transatlantic social politics held at the University of Sheffield's Humanities Research Institute in September 2011. We are grateful to all the historians who participated in that event. We also thank the University of Sheffield's Centre for the Study of Democratic Culture, which hosted the workshop, and the Leverhulme Trust, which provided funding under the auspices of the three-year international network program on the comparative history of political engagement in Western and non-Western societies.

Happily, the initial workshop spawned a collaboration with friends in Spain, two of whom—Manuel Álvarez Tardío and David Sarias Rodríguez—contributed essays published here. This in turn led to a series of memorable intellectual and gastronomic exchanges between Sheffield and the Universidad Rey Juan Carlos Madrid, though it must be said that in gastronomic terms, the Spanish historians got something of a raw deal. We are especially indebted to our Spanish friends for their hospitality.

We thank all of our authors for their patience, good humor, efficiency, and above all their ideas. It was a pleasure to work with you. And we acknowledge the support of Chris Chappell at Palgrave USA, who backed this project from the outset, his colleague Mike Aperauch, who nursed us through the publication and permissions process, and Deepa John from Newgen for assistance with copyediting and proofs.

Introduction

Daniel Scroop and Andrew Heath

Few works of history written in the last quarter century have been more influential than Daniel T. Rodgers's *Atlantic Crossings: Social Politics in a Progressive Age*.[1] Published in 1998, it brought late-nineteenth and early-twentieth-century transnational reform into the historiographical spotlight, and made the Atlantic world—a field previously dominated by historians of early modern trade, empire, and slavery—into an area of study historians of modern social and political reform could also claim as their own. *Atlantic Crossings* was by no means the first attempt to investigate the reform networks that spanned the North Atlantic in the years between the 1870s and the Second World War. Intellectual historians made significant contributions to the study of modern transatlantic social and political thought as early as the 1950s, mapping ideational currents, charting reform networks, and pinpointing patterns of influence and exchange.[2] But there is little doubt that *Atlantic Crossings* is more comprehensive in coverage, more ambitious in scope, depth, and conceptual design, and more skilful in execution than any other comparable work. Heralded upon publication as a work of rare brilliance, it remains indispensable for any serious student of modern transatlantic reform.[3]

Atlantic Crossings is an innovative work of scholarship, but its great influence arguably stems less from its intrinsic novelty than from the fact that its arrival confirmed and consolidated a historiographical shift that was already well underway. This was particularly true, perhaps, in the United States where for half a century the Cold War bolstered and protected pre-existing exceptionalist tendencies in historical thinking. By the mid-1990s, however, the end of the Cold War and the emergence of new cultural, economic, and political developments associated with globalization combined to make narrowly nation-centered approaches to the study of political and social reform appear decidedly anachronistic. In an age of instant communication, rapid demographic change, and unprecedentedly volatile capital flows, the idea of the United States as a bounded nation more or less impervious to outside influence lost evidential force. Responding to these changed circumstances, historians, unsurprisingly, began asking new sorts of questions about the past.[4]

For many scholars working in the fields of political culture, social change, and political reform, greater acceptance of the notion that the United States was shaped in fundamental ways by foreign ideas proved liberating.[5] No longer in thrall to exceptionalism, they freed themselves from the grip of nation-centered history, and in this way helped to spawn the twenty-first century transnational history boom.[6] Transnational history, its practitioners have noted, is as much a "way of seeing" as a rigid method.[7] The shift in perspective brought hitherto unseen connections into view and revealed what Rodgers calls a "web of global interdependencies."[8] Today, such an approach is well-established, as a quick glance at job listings and journals reveals.[9] But the battle to legitimize transnational history was far from won when *Atlantic Crossings* first appeared. When, in his prologue, Rodgers noted the permeability of all nations' histories no matter how profound their exceptionalist convictions and self-understandings, he was making an important scholarly intervention.[10]

This volume presents a series of essays on the history of transatlantic politics over the past two centuries, all of which respond directly or indirectly to *Atlantic Crossings*. The essays here can be read individually as self-standing pieces that engage on their own terms with Rodgers's work—and with the wider field of transatlantic history—while developing a distinct critique or perspective based on in-depth historical research on a particular topic or subtheme. They can also be read collectively, as an effort to interrogate and to contest some of the core assumptions of *Atlantic Crossings*, as well as to illuminate neglected areas of research. Of course they also testify to the continuing vibrancy in the twenty-first century of transatlantic and transnational intellectual exchange. The contributors to this collection work at universities based across North America and Europe, and range in their national origins from the United Kingdom to the United States, Spain, Germany, and France.

The essays presented here are organized chronologically and are divided into three parts. Part I covers the years 1800–1870, probing the character of transatlantic social politics in the era before Rodgers's study begins. Part II focuses on what might be termed the "classic phase" of transatlantic reform, examining the same period—1870–1940—with which *Atlantic Crossings* is concerned. The studies in this section show that although Rodgers's book was unusually capacious, it was by no means comprehensive, and that its omissions are telling in both historical and historiographical terms. They expand and contest the boundaries of the multiple worlds of reform that animated the late-nineteenth and early-twentieth centuries. Part III explores the post-1945 era, charting the emergence of new transatlantic politics of both the Right and the Left. It develops the theme of programmatic diversity introduced in Part II, expands the geographical range of the volume, and surveys the European reception of American ideas after the United States became a net exporter of policy. Two of the four essays in this section focus on Spain, a nation whose engagement in transatlantic politics is overlooked in *Atlantic Crossings*.

This collection is not the only attempt that has been made in recent times to reflect upon the significance of *Atlantic Crossings*, or for that matter to comment more broadly on the wave of transoceanic and transnational scholarship it helped to spawn.[11] In addition to the initial rush of book reviews and symposia on Rodgers's work that appeared around the millennium, in recent years transnational historians have produced a plethora of impressive methodological and state-of-the-field essays, which have done much to advance our understanding and to enrich our knowledge of what is still a fast-growing historical sub-discipline.[12] The essays gathered here join those debates while also bringing new voices and fresh empirical research to light. More than that, however, the studies in this collection make two distinct intellectual contributions. First, they contest the periodization of *Atlantic Crossings*, demonstrating the vitality of the politics of transatlantic reform both before and after the period (1870–1940) covered by Rodgers. Second, they incorporate work on transatlantic networks operating across the political spectrum, rather than confining themselves to the study of progressives and other historical actors operating on the left and centre-left. The volume includes studies of conservative networks as well as research on modes of progressive and populist politics neglected in *Atlantic Crossings*.

This book stretches the chronological and programmatic parameters of Rodgers's work but it keeps the Atlantic as its geographic setting. Given the "global turn" in historical writing over the last two decades, the Atlantic mooring might appear confining. In the 1990s, a venturesome historian of the Civil War would typically explore the conflict from the vantage point of Europe, but now, transnational scholarship in the field is as likely to look to Egypt and Mexico as the North Atlantic.[13] Global history has sometimes emphasized the worldwide significance of the United States before its rise as a superpower. The Civil War, indeed, is one of the few events to merit a sub-chapter of its own in C. A. Bayly's *Birth of the Modern World*, whereas the English-translation of Jurgen Osterhammel's Braudelian *Transformation of the World*—another monumental study of the long nineteenth century—appears in Princeton University Press's "America in the World" series.[14] Yet by showing how capital, labor, and ideas flowed in multiple directions, global historians have acknowledged, as Bayly puts it, that "[i]t is no longer really possible to write 'European' or 'American' history in a narrow sense."[15] New work on multinational organizations, meanwhile, has further weakened the stranglehold of the national state on historians' imagination. By the middle decades of the twentieth century, institutions like the United Nations and International Labor Organization served as brokers, distributing social policy expertise around the globe, and Cold War rivals vied to imprint their own developmental models onto postcolonial nations.[16] When compared to the predictable currents of Rodgers's Atlantic, the motion can seem dizzying.

In the realm of social politics, however, the North Atlantic retains its utility as a focus for the study of transnational borrowing and exchange. As Rodgers notes, contrast with Europe helped to define the post-independence identity of the United States, but as industrialization undermined Jeffersonian dreams of an Arcadian yeoman's republic, citizens became increasingly aware that their own path to social, economic, and urban modernity bore similarities to the trails being followed in Britain, Prussia, France, and other European nations. Moreover cultural linkages, abetted by rapid and regular travel, brought the national states of the North Atlantic into closer communion. Whether through the Common Law inheritance, the classical curriculum of college education, elite rituals like the grand tour, or the racial politics of what Reginald Horsman has called "Anglo-Saxonism," many nineteenth-century Americans identified with the Old World even if they saw themselves improving on its political organization.[17] A century later, Cold War warriors picked up on these longstanding affinities by pitting a freedom-loving West against a despotic East. Relations between the United States and Europe changed markedly between American independence and the late twentieth century, but without wishing to overstate the continuities, citizens and subjects on either side of the ocean shared enough "common referents" before and after Rodgers's "Progressive Age" to warrant an Atlantic focus.

An element of risk intrudes upon the decision made here to maintain the geographical boundaries of Rodgers's Atlantic while expanding the chronological and programmatic parameters of transatlantic reform. Rodgers's key concept—social politics—has about it a pleasing specificity, which does much to give *Atlantic Crossings* its intellectual drive and coherence. Indeed a merit of his approach is that is treats exceptionalism not simply as a historiographical assumption but also as a historical mindset: a set of beliefs about American difference that changed with the ebb and flow of domestic and international events. He argues that the period 1870–1940 was "different" because in these years, for a peculiar set of reasons, Americans were able and ready to look to, and to learn from, Europe.[18] The emergence of the "social" as a distinct realm of knowledge—a development fostered by US adaptations of British social science associations and German seminar teaching in the decades after the Civil War—provided an intellectual foundation for the study of complex, interdependent phenomena like the modern city.[19] Experts in the new science of society found institutional homes in university faculties and government departments as reform became a professional vocation. Meanwhile, the steamship—that great emblem of late-nineteenth-century globalization—ferried social policy "tourists" back and forth across the ocean. But above all, Rodgers explains, in the decades after 1870, Americans arrived at the realization that the problems of Europe were their problems too. On both sides of the Atlantic capitalist development and the tensions and contradictions it engendered forced reformers to rethink the relationship between state and society, to generate and to trade in new ideas, and, in the broadest terms, to remake the Atlantic so that it became a space of connection in which likeminded brokers of reform operated. Advocates of progressive politics in the Atlantic "moment" came from different backgrounds and embraced eclectic ideas, but as an epistemic community, they were bound together by their interest in answering the questions posed by rapid urban and industrial growth.

Recognition of interdependence, then, was crucial to the emergence of social science, but the main precondition for transnational exchange was the convergence of social experience. Americans ventured abroad, saw fixes for the problems they observed in their own society, and came home eager to apply them. The movement of social policy in this era therefore ran westwards from the Old World to the New, and carried the seeds of modern American liberalism. Routine aspects of contemporary US government—zoning and social security for instance—were borne along on this oceanic current.

Yet according to Rodgers, Americans' "peculiarly open" disposition to foreign ideas, did not last. Having "marched to a more internalist drummer" before the 1870s they retreated in the 1940s to "full volume" exceptionalism. Scarred by its encounters with Fascism and Communism, and increasingly pre-occupied by its Cold War rivalry with the Soviet Union, Europe—in the US imagination at least— became not a storehouse of ideas but a battlefield to be secured. The Cold War's stultifying atmosphere encouraged many ardent liberals to see postwar European welfare states as dangerously un-American: the direction of exchange now reversed as Americans looked to remake the world in their image. Social politics, Rodgers suggested, had little role in this process of reconstruction.[20]

Rodgers, of course, made this argument for America's transatlantic social-political moment at a specific historical juncture. At the close of the twentieth century, his recovery of "a phase of American history and politics we have all but lost" armed US progressives with a usable past to deploy in their battle to defend what remained of the New Deal order.[21] *Atlantic Crossings* appeared four years after the Republican Revolution of 1994 and two years after Bill Clinton signed into a law a welfare reform bill that dismantled part of the 1935 Social Security Act. In this era of liberal accommodation and retreat, embattled defenders of the New Deal order mournfully asked themselves "why Americans hate welfare," effectively reinforcing the conservative line that social democratic politics had never taken root in the United States.[22] Others, while lauding European examples, tried to tie the pursuit of social justice to the responsibilities of citizenship.[23] In contrast, Rodgers showed that in the heyday of American capitalism, foreign models held wide appeal. He did not say so directly in 1998, but the implication was clear: with the Cold War a receding memory and globalization providing a new world of "common referents," the United States might begin again to learn lessons from overseas. He could not have known, of course, that just three years later the terrorist attacks of September 11, 2001 would significantly alter the posture of the United States towards the rest of the world once again, bringing the era of relative openness and opportunity in which *Atlantic Crossings* was written to a close.

Since the publication of *Atlantic Crossings*, the historiographical as well as the historical climate has changed. New work on the nineteenth century is perhaps particularly significant in this respect, not least for the ways in which it begs further questions about Rodgers's periodization of transatlantic reform. It is reasonable to argue that a distinct phase in the history of Atlantic exchange drew to a close sometime around 1800 with the curtailing of the slave trade, the success of independence movements, and a turn to economic nationalism.

Thereafter, from the perspective of many Americans, Europe was a beacon of warning.[24] Anglophobia lingered in the political culture of the new nation, and as Rachel Hope Cleves's work on anti-Jacobinism in the Early Republic has demonstrated, Federalism and abolitionism were infused by fears of revolutionary violence. Yet if Americans tried to steer their ship of state away from revolutionary rocks, the upheavals in France were, for them, "an event of profound local significance."[25] Recent studies of nineteenth-century America show how the earthquakes that shook the Old World reverberated in the New. The aftershocks of the 1848 Revolutions, Italian Risorgimento, German Unification, and Paris Commune were each felt in American society.[26] Often, such moments strengthened exceptionalist conviction, as when Americans celebrated republican hero Louis Kossuth as if he were a new Washington, or when they determined that the French were unfit for self-government. This new scholarship highlights the doubts nineteenth-century Americans harbored about the nation's immunity from world-historical forces, and their anxieties about the compatibility of capitalism, democracy, and slavery.

Americans did not, then, respond passively to European affairs before 1870. Rather, they debated the relevance of developments overseas to their own society and, in many cases, joined the work of transatlantic reform. These early brokers of reform may have shared concerns about their nation's future course, but in other respects they defied easy categorization. They included in their number conservatives who praised the infusion of "life, vigor and patriotism into the stagnation of monarchy," utopian socialists who embraced Charles Fourier's designs for communal living, and abolitionists who took British emancipation as their model. It is notable that all of the aforementioned groups rejected exceptionalism. In the pages of Horace Greeley's influential *New York Tribune*, readers encountered the ideas of the paper's European correspondent, Karl Marx. Before the "Progressive Age" heterodox, schemes for social reconstruction—often forged in Europe but adapted for an American setting—vied for attention, influence, and popularity.[27]

These debates usually took place in a language that would have sounded archaic to the experts of the Progressive era. The first chapter in this volume cover a period prior to the professionalization of social science in which "socioconstitutional" analysis trumped the "socioeconomic."[28] Phenomena that half a century later Americans would explain in sociological terms were blamed in the mid-nineteenth century on maladies afflicting the body politic. But the gulf between what Philip J. Ethington has termed the "political conception of society" and a "social conception of politics" was not unbridgeable, and in the last few years, historians have turned to terms like "social democracy" to describe the varieties of American politics of the era.[29] Although lacking institutional perches in government and education, cosmopolitan reformers before the Civil War did ponder a science of society, proving more willing than is sometimes recognized to look for inspiration beyond the borders of the United States.

New work on the US state and government raises further doubts about Rodgers's framing of the Atlantic moment. *Atlantic Crossings* largely accepts the Progressives' characterization of the American state as a laggard, arguing that the revolutionary generation proved so successful in guarding against aggregations of power that its descendants were left ill equipped to deal with the challenges posed by capitalist expansion. At the turn of the century, he suggests, citizens found themselves forced all of a sudden to begin the work of reconciling themselves to the need for big government. But in light of recent scholarship, the idea of a sharp distinction between a weak nineteenth-century state of "courts and parties" and a strong, efficient twentieth-century state built by Progressives and New Dealers is harder to defend. The origins of Progressive Era statecraft, for example, long predate the Civil War. Similarly, aspects of Early Republican governance continue to shape American politics. That is not to minimize the shift that occurred around 1900 as private interests retreated before public needs; nor is it to deny the shift in the opposite direction that has been such a powerful feature of US history since the 1970s. But scholars have shown that at moments when American government was far from being a model of the rational, bureaucratic state, it nevertheless built infrastructure, waged war, and engaged in projects of large-scale social reconstruction.[30]

Rodgers is surely right that the "core political project" of the decades before the Civil War lay in the "formation of a democratic nation." But if the gulf separating monarchies and republics meant Europe often served as the despotic antithesis to New World liberty, Americans were not always closed to the merits of foreign policies that might strengthen their own political order. The first two chapters in this volume explore two facets of nation-building in which Americans sometimes feared Europeans had stolen a march: education and urban planning. As David Komline shows in the essay that begins this collection, there were dense and consequential transatlantic networks in educational reform over the first decades of the nineteenth century. In the Early Republic, educational reform networks changed in character, shifting from an initial concern with the

adoption of particular pedagogical approaches to a later preoccupa-
tion with educational models and systems. Throughout, however,
the United States remained relatively open to European influence.
"[E]ven before the *Savannah* made the first transatlantic steam-
powered voyage in 1819," he writes, ideas about education flowed
more or less freely across the ocean. Alert to the wider ramifications
of this argument, Komline suggests that *Atlantic Crossings* does not
succeed as an attack on American exceptionalism because it merely
replaces one form of exceptionalism—*Sonderweg*—with another—
Sonderzeit. Andrew Heath's essay, which completes the first part
of the volume, builds on Komline's argument. It shows that ideas
about urban governance borrowed and adapted from the politics of
the French Second Republic and Second Empire influenced debates
over the course of the Civil War-era American city. By the 1860s, US
cities were being re-imagined as sites of intertwined spatial and social
reconstruction. Focusing primarily on Philadelphia, Heath illumi-
nates how, before the 1870s, the French Second Empire contributed
to a new vision of the city as a social policy arena.

The essays in Part II overlap chronologically with *Atlantic Crossings*
while highlighting varieties of transatlantic reform Rodgers neglects.
These chapters build on work undertaken since 1998, which has
shown the varied character of Atlantic politics in the Progressive era.
The protean nature of Progressivism meant the drift of social policy
did not only lead in the direction of modern liberalism. Apartheid,
for example, had a transnational history in a period that "witnessed a
planet-wide proliferation of residentially-segregated cities."[31] Brokers
of exchange, meanwhile, were diverse, encompassing segments of
American society renowned—in some cases unjustly—more for parochialism than for cosmopolitanism. In his chapter on Boston publisher Benjamin O. Flower, Jean-Louis Marin-Lamellet shows that
like other participants in the world of transatlantic social politics, US
Populists could be outward-looking, deeply interested in learning
from European models and experiments, and as keen to be involved
in the formation of social policy as were other so-called progressives.
It is true that there were limits to Flower's cosmopolitanism—in the
pages of Flower's magazine, *The Arena*, it was assumed that European
policies would need to be "Americanized" if they were to succeed on
US soil—but it is equally clear that historians need to rethink the
place of Populism in their accounts of transatlantic politics in the
late nineteenth and early twentieth centuries. Further developing this
point, Daniel Scroop's essay on the travels of two leading populist-
progressives of the early twentieth century—William Jennings Bryan

and Robert M. La Follette, Jr—argues that the stubbornly persistent idea of populism as a fundamentally parochial and inward-looking political tradition has blinded historians to its significance as a constituent element of transatlantic politics. Both Bryan and La Follette, he shows, were embedded in transnational and (in Bryan's case) global networks of reform.

Axel Schäfer's innovative study of the career of Isaac Rubinow brings Part II to a close by highlighting another neglected strand in the intricate latticework of transatlantic reform. His examination of the interface between social policy and migration shows that Rubinow—a man sometimes referred to as the "father of Social Security"—drew on German mutualism in an attempt to create a fresh model of social welfare for the modern age. Seeking a bold, pluralistic approach to social citizenship, Rubinow's powerful redistributive ideas ran aground, Schäfer argues, as a result of the increased bureaucracy and repression that accompanied the First World War. His efforts were further impeded by changing perceptions of Germany as it shifted from being a widely admired source of policy innovation and civilized values to being cast as an essentially barbaric nation. In the age of the Red Scare, there was no place for Rubinow's tolerant pluralism. Schäfer's essay provides a valuable account of an important episode in US social policy while also showing how the historiographies of transatlantic reform and immigration can be connected.

The four essays in Part III of the volume test both the periodization and the programmatic bias of Rodgers's work on transatlantic reform. Jonathan Bell's study challenges the established assumption that US and European liberalism diverged in the aftermath of the Second World War. Deploying evidence drawn from case studies of Australia and New Zealand as well as from Europe, he shows that mid-twentieth-century US liberalism actively sought solutions abroad. Despite the constraints imposed by business antistatism and emboldened anticommunism, the war "widened the parameters of American liberalism," he argues. American liberals and progressives were fascinated, for example, by the reforms of the Attlee government in the United Kingdom but ultimately lacked the ideological resources to exploit the opportunities that arose, notably in the case of the fight for health care reform, in which they were outgunned by their well-organized conservative opponents.

The final three essays of the collection demonstrate that in the post-1945 era transatlantic politics was animated by vibrant right-wing as well as left-wing interactions.[32] Where Parts I and II followed Rodgers in tracing the movement of ideas from east to west, Part III explores how American policy and ideas influenced European debate as the United States exerted its global might. First, Manuel Tardio highlights how the international debate sparked by the publication in 1960 of US sociologist Daniel Bell's classic *The End of Ideology* influenced the thought of two leading technocrats who operated close to the heart of the Franco regime: Laureano López Rodó and Gonzalo Fernández de la Mora. The Bell thesis helped these key figures to elaborate a politics, which legitimized the authoritarian Franco regime in a way that advanced their position as expert administrators and proponents of free market economics. Tardio deftly explains both the peculiarly Spanish context and the wider transnational setting of a moment in which US sociology and Spanish technocracy joined in an unlikely instance of transoceanic intellectual dialogue. The essay that follows, written by David Sarias, picks up on and further develops the theme of US-Spanish ideological exchange. It sketches the emergence and subsequent trajectory of an epistemic community of traditionalist US conservatives whose politics was powerfully influenced by their exposure to European debates in general and to Spanish connections in particular. Political and cultural development in the 1950s and 1960s, he argues, fostered cooperation between US and Spanish conservatives, including those on the far Right of the political spectrum. But as Nick Witham's contribution—the final essay in the collection—shows, it was not only on the programmatic Right that fresh connections were being made in the middle and late twentieth century. Focusing on two publishing initiatives started by Verso Books in 1985—*The Year Left* and *The Haymarket Series*—Witham shows how publishing was an important zone of engagement for the transatlantic Left. Combining elements of cultural and intellectual history, his essay suggests that the declension narratives typically associated with the trajectory of Left politics in the 1980s require some adjustment. It also reminds us that print culture was a powerful agent of transnational interconnection in the late modern Atlantic world, just as it was in the early modern period. The radical internationalists of Witham's study differed in many ways from their forebears, but he shows that long after the classic age of transatlantic political exchange, the Atlantic remained an important nexus of interaction between the European and US Lefts.

Notes

1. Daniel T. Rodgers, *Atlantic Crossings: Social Politics in a Progressive Age* (Cambridge, MA: Harvard University Press, 1998).

2. Examples of this early work include, "British Social Thought and American Reformers of the Progressive Era," *Mississippi Valley Historical Review* 42, no. 4 (March 1956): 672–92; Kenneth O. Morgan, "The Future at Work: Anglo-American Progressivism, 1890–1917," in *Contrast and Connection: Bicentennial Essays in Anglo-American History* eds H. C. Allen and Roger Thompson (Athens, OH, Ohio University Press, 1976); Benjamin R. Beede, "Foreign Influences on American Progressivism," *The Historian* 45, no. 4 (1983), 529–49; and Melvyn Stokes, "American Progressives and the European Left," *Journal of American Studies* 17, no. 1 (1983): 5–28. For a more recent exploration of the politics of Anglo-American reform, see Marc Stears, *Progressives, Pluralists, and the Problems of the State: Ideologies of Reform in the United States and Britain* (Oxford: Oxford University Press, 2002). The outstanding study of the traffic of European and American social and political thought for the period 1870–1920 remains James T. Kloppenberg, *Uncertain Victory: Social Democracy and Progressivism in European and American Thought, 1870–1920* (New York: Oxford University Press, 1986). See also Axel R. Schäfer, *American Progressives and German Social Reform, 1875–1920: Social Ethics, Moral Control and the Regulatory State in a Transatlantic Context* (Stuttgart: Franz Steiner Verlag, 2000). It should be noted that in the 1930s and 1940s African American and Afro-Caribbean historians blazed a trail in the study of transnational networks. See W. E. B. Du Bois, *Black Reconstruction: An Essay Toward a History of the Part which Black Folk Played in the Attempt to Reconstruct Democracy in America, 1860–1880* (New York: Harcourt Brace, 1935); C. L. R. James, *The Black Jacobins: Toussaint L'Ouverture and the San Domingo Revolution* (New York: Dial, 1938); and Eric Williams, *Capitalism and Slavery* (Chapel Hill: University of North Carolina Press, 1944).

3. *Atlantic Crossings* won a number of prestigious prizes, among them the George Louis Beer Prize of the American Historical Association and the Ellis W. Hawley Prize of the Organization of American Historians. It was published in German translation in 2010 and in Chinese in 2011.

4. The scholarly literature on American exceptionalism is vast. For a range of perspectives see Ian Tyrrell, "American Exceptionalism in an Age of International History," *The American Historical Review* 96, no. 4 (October 1991): 1031–55; Michael Kammen, "The Problem of American Exceptionalism: A Reconsideration," *American Quarterly* 45, no. 1 (March 1993): 1–43; Seymour Martin Lipset, *American Exceptionalism: A Double-Edged Sword* (New York: W. W. Norton & Co., 1997); Daniel T. Rodgers, "American Exceptionalism Revisited," *Raritan Review* 24 (fall 2004), 21–47; and Godfrey

Hodgson, *The Myth of American Exceptionalism* (New Haven: Yale University Press, 2010).

5. It should be noted that historians of reform whose research touched on, or engaged with, work in the history of migration, immigration, diasporas, or race relations, were not affected in the same way because these fields were already substantially transnational in their assumptions and core methodologies long before *Atlantic Crossings* appeared.

6. Perhaps the strongest manifesto for a transnational approach to the American past is the collection of essays in Thomas Bender (ed.), *Rethinking American History in a Global Age* (Berkeley: University of California Press, 2002).

7. C. A. Bayly, et al., "AHR Conversation: On Transnational History," *American Historical Review* 111 (2006), 1454.

8. Rodgers, *Atlantic Crossings*, 2.

9. For journals, see for instance *Diaspora: A Journal of Transnational Studies* (established 1999); *Atlantic Studies: Global Currents* (established 2004); and the *Journal of Transnational American Studies* (established 2008). History departments in Europe and the United States now often advertise jobs in transnational history. By 2010, 52.3% of departments in the United States counted at least one world historian among their faculty, an increase of over 30% from 2000. See Lisa A. Lindsay, "The Appeal of Transnational History," *Perspectives on History* 50, no. 9 (Dec. 2012), 48–49.

10. Rodgers, *Atlantic Crossings*, 2.

11. For critical dialogue and a range of perspectives specifically on *Atlantic Crossings* see the "Symposium on *Atlantic Crossings*," in *Historical Research/Historiche Sozialforschung* 25 (2000) and the debate to which Rodgers himself contributes in "Borrowing Policy: A Dialogue on *Atlantic Crossings*," *Comparative Labor Law & Policy Journal* 21 (winter 2000): 371–90. See also Thomas L. Haskell, "Taking Exception to Exceptionalism," *Review in American History*, 28, no. 1 (March 2000): 151–66; Robert Gregg, review of *Atlantic Crossings*, *Social History*, 26, no. 3 (October, 2001): 354–57; and especially the "Review-Symposium" on *Atlantic Crossings* at http://hsozkult.geschichte.hu-berlin.de/rezensio/symposiu/atlantic.htm (accessed May 12, 2014).

12. For a range of perspectives on the development of transnational history over the past quarter century and its implications for U.S. scholarship, see Ian Tyrell, "American Exceptionalism in an Age of International History," *American Historical Review*, 96 no. 4 (October 1991): 1031–55; Michael McGerr, "The Price of the New Transnational History," *American Historical Review* 96 no. 4 (October 1991): 1056–67; David Thelen, "The Nation and Beyond: Transnational Perspectives on United States History," *Journal of*

American History 86, no. 3 (December 1999): 965–75; Thomas Bender, *La Pietra Report: Project for Internationalizing the Study of American History* (New York: Organization of American Historians, 2000); Thomas Bender (ed.), *Rethinking American History in a Global Age* (Berkeley, University of California Press, 2002); C. A. Bayly, Sven Beckert, Matthew Connolly, Isabel Hofmeyr, Wendy Kozol, and Patricia Seed, "AHR Conversation: On Transnational History," *American Historical Review*, 111 no. 5 (December 2006), 1441–64. See also Davide Rodogno, Bernhard Struck, and Jakob Vogel, *Shaping the Transnational Sphere: Experts, Networks, and Issues* (New York: Berghahn Books, forthcoming 2014). For reference consult Akira Iriye and Pierre-Yves Saunier, *The Palgrave Dictionary of Transnational History* (New York: Palgrave, 2009).

13. See for instance Alan J. Rice and Martin Crawford (eds), *Liberating Sojourn: Frederick Douglass and Transatlantic Reform* (Athens: University of Georgia Press, 1999); R. J. M. Blackett, *Divided Hearts: Britain and the American Civil War* (Baton Rouge: Louisiana State University Press, 2001); Sven Beckert, "Emancipation and Empire: Reconstructing the Worldwide Web of Cotton Production in the Age of the American Civil War," *American Historical Review* 109, no. 5 (December 2004): 1405–38; Gregory P. Downs, "The Mexicanization of American Politics: The United States' Transnational Path from Civil War to Stabilization," *American Historical Review* 117, no. 4 (April 2012): 387–409; Patrick J. Kelly, "The North American Crisis of the 1860s," *The Journal of the Civil War Era* 2, no. 3 (September 2012): 337–68.

14. C. A. Bayly, *The Birth of the Modern World, 1780–1914: Global Connections and Comparisons* (Malden, MA: Blackwell Pub., 2004), 161–65; Jürgen Osterhammel, *The Transformation of the World: A Global History of the Nineteenth Century*, trans. Patrick Camiller (Princeton: Princeton University Press, 2014).

15. Bayly, *Birth of the Modern World*, 2.

16. Akira Iriye, *Global Community: The Role of International Organizations in the Making of the Contemporary World* (Berkeley: University of California Press, 2002); Lorenz M. Luthi, *The Sino-Soviet Split: Cold War in the Communist World* (Princeton: Princeton University Press, 2008). See also the articles in Matthew Hilton and Rana Mitter (eds), "Transnationalism and Contemporary Global History," *Past and Present* 218, supplement 8 (2013).

17. Caroline Winterer, *The Culture of Classicism: Ancient Greece and Rome in American Intellectual Life, 1780–1910* (Baltimore: Johns Hopkins University Press, 2002); William W. Stowe, *Going Abroad: European Travel in Nineteenth-Century American Culture* (Princeton: Princeton University Press, 1994); Reginald Horsman, *Race and Manifest Destiny: The Origins of American Racial Anglo-Saxonism* (Cambridge, MA: Harvard University Press, 1981).

18. Rodgers, *Atlantic Crossings*, 4.
19. Thomas L. Haskell, *The Emergence of Professional Social Science* (Urbana: University of Illinois Press, 1977); Lawrence Goldman, *Science, Reform, and Politics in Victorian Britain: The Social Science Association, 1857–1886* (Cambridge: Cambridge University Press, 2002). On the "scientization of the social" in the late ninenteenth century, see Kerstin Brückweh, Dirk Schumann, Richard F. Wetzell, and Benjamin Ziemann (eds), *Engineering Society: The Role of the Human and Social Sciences in Modern Societies, 1880–1980* (Basingstoke: Palgrave Macmillan, 2012).
20. Rodgers, *Atlantic Crossings*, 3–4, 502–8.
21. Rodgers, *Atlantic Crossings*, 7.
22. Martin Gilens, *Why Americans Hate Welfare: Race, Media, and the Politics of Antipoverty Policy* (Chicago: University of Chicago Press, 1999).
23. See for instance Michael B. Katz, *The Undeserving Poor: From the War on Poverty to the War on Welfare* (New York: Pantheon Books, 1989), 238–9; Michael B. Katz, *The Price of Citizenship: Redefining the American Welfare State* (New York: Metropolitan Books, 2001).
24. On dating the end of the Atlantic World, see Donna Gabaccia, "A Long Atlantic in a Wider World," *Atlantic Studies: Global Currents* 1, no. 1 (2004): 7–8.
25. Rachel Hope Cleves, *The Reign of Terror in America: Visions of Violence from Anti-Jacobinism to Antislavery* (Cambridge: Cambridge University Press, 2009). On Anglophobia, see Sam W. Haynes, *Unfinished Revolution: The Early American Republic in a British World* (Charlottesville: University of Virginia Press, 2010); David Sim, *A Union Forever: The Irish Question and U.S. Foreign Relations in the Victorian Age* (Ithaca, NY: Cornell University Press, 2013); John E. Moser, *Twisting the Lion's Tail: American Anglophobia between the World Wars* (New York: New York University Press, 1999). Even in the decades after the War of 1812, however, Anglophobes vied with admirers of Britain. See Elisa Tamarkin, *Anglophilia: Deference, Devotion, and Antebellum America* (Chicago: University of Chicago Press, 2008).
26. Timothy Mason Roberts, *Distant Revolutions: 1848 and the Challenge to American Exceptionalism* (Charlottesville: University of Virginia Press, 2009); Andre M. Fleche, *The Revolution of 1861: The American Civil War in the Age of Nationalist Conflict* (Chapel Hill: University of North Carolina Press, 2012); Paola Gemme, *Domesticating Foreign Struggles: The Italian Risorgimento and Antebellum American Identity* (Athens: University of Georgia Press, 2005); Philip Mark Katz, *From Appomattox to Montmartre: Americans and the Paris Commune* (Cambridge, MA: Harvard University Press, 1998).
27. Charles F. Schmidt, "Monarchies and Republics," *Debow's Review* (February 1867), 156. Frank Prochaska, *The Eagle and the Crown:*

Americans and the British Monarchy (New Haven: Yale University
Press, 2008); Ian Walter Radforth, *Royal Spectacle: The 1860 Visit
of the Prince of Wales to Canada and the United States* (Toronto:
University of Toronto Press, 2004); Carl J. Guarneri, *The Utopian
Alternative: Fourierism in Nineteenth-Century America* (Ithaca, NY:
Cornell University Press, 1994); W. Caleb McDaniel, *The Problem
of Democracy in the Age of Slavery: Garrisonian Abolitionists and
Transatlantic Reform* (Baton Rouge: Louisiana State University
Press, 2013); Adam-Max Tuchinsky, *Horace Greeley's New York
Tribune: Civil War-Era Socialism and the Crisis of Free Labor* (Ithaca:
Cornell University Press, 2009).

28. Martin J. Burke, *The Conundrum of Class: Public Discourse on the
Social Order in America* (Chicago: University of Chicago Press,
1995), 3.

29. Philip J. Ethington, *The Public City: The Political Construction of
Urban Life in San Francisco, 1850–1900* (Cambridge: Cambridge
University Press, 1994), xiv; Adam-Max Tuchinsky, "'The Bourgeoisie
Will Fall and Fall Forever': The *New York Tribune*, the 1848 French
Revolution, and American Social Democratic Discourse," *Journal of
American History* 92, no. 2 (September 2005): 470–97.

30. Daniel T. Rodgers, "An Age of Social Politics," in Thomas Bender
(ed.), *Rethinking American History in a Global Age* (Berkeley:
University of California Press, 2002), 253. On the "state of courts
and parties," see Stephen Skowronek, *Building a New American
State: The Expansion of National Administrative Capacities,
1877–1920* (Cambridge: Cambridge University Press, 1982), 24.
For re-evaluations of state power, see Max M. Edling, *A Revolution
in Favor of Government: Origins of the U. S. Constitution and the
Making of the American State* (Oxford: Oxford University Press,
2003); Brian Balogh, *A Government out of Sight: The Mystery of
National Authority in Nineteenth-Century America* (Cambridge:
Cambridge University Press, 2009); William J. Novak, "The Myth of
the 'Weak' American State," *American Historical Review* 113, no. 3
(June 2008): 752–72.

31. Carl H. Nightingale, "The Transnational Contexts of Early
Twentieth-Century American Urban Segregation," *Journal of Social
History* 39, no. 3 (spring 2006): 668; Kornel Chang, "Circulating
Race and Empire: Transnational Labor Activism and the Politics
of Anti-Asian Agitation in the Anglo-American Pacific World,
1880–1910," *Journal of American History* 96, no. 3
(December 2009).

32. On right-wing exchange in the era, see Richard Cockett, *Thinking
the Unthinkable: Think-Tanks and the Economic Counter-Revolution,
1931–1983* (London: HarperCollins, 1994); Martin Durham and
Margaret Power (eds), *New Perspectives on the Transnational Right*
(Basingstoke, UK: Palgrave, 2010); Daniel Stedman Jones, *Masters*

of the Universe: Hayek, Friedman, and the Birth of Neoliberal Politics (Princeton: Princeton University Press, 2012); Philip Mirowski and Dieter Plehwe (eds), *The Road from Mont Pèlerin: The Making of the Neoliberal Thought Collective* (Cambridge, MA: Harvard University Press, 2009), and Richard Robison (ed.), *The Neoliberal Revolution: Forging the Market State* (Basingstoke, UK: Palgrave, 2006).

Chapter 1

An American *Sonderzeit?* Reconsidering Rodgers in Light of Antebellum Educational Reform

David Komline

In addition to its magisterial treatment of late-nineteenth- and early-twentieth-century reform movements, perhaps the greatest contribution of Daniel Rodgers's *Atlantic Crossings: Social Politics in a Progressive Age* is to set the history of the United States within a global context. Rodgers notes that too often historians focus on "specifying each nation's distinctive culture, its peculiar history, its *Sonderweg*, its exceptionalism."[1] Rodgers's *tour de force*, in contrast, shows that American reformers drew inspiration from similar movements abroad, conclusively demonstrating the importance of foreign influences on US public policy in the Progressive Era.

But while Rodgers denies the possibility of an American *Sonderweg*, he posits instead an American *Sonderzeit*. From the 1870s to the 1940s, he asserts, American politics was "peculiarly open to foreign models and imported ideas."[2] This assessment ignores the extent to which the antebellum era was animated by rich networks of transatlantic exchange and interaction. As we shall see, in the field of education—an area of reform Rodgers neglects in his broader treatment of the interventionist state—European influence on US education from the early 1800s to the early 1840s was substantial. In this period, the United States moved from absorbing European educational *practices* to absorbing European educational *policies*. An interest in European *ideas*—for example Lancasterian and Pestalozzian teaching methods—shifted over time toward a focus on European *models*, particularly concerning the organization of state educational systems.

Many of the most significant educators of the early nineteenth century participated in transatlantic exchange, including Emma Willard, who taught a generation of female teachers, and Henry Barnard, who edited several major educational journals. Some of the reformers who reported on European policies in the 1830s are best known for their activities outside of educational reform, such as the scientist Alexander Dallas Bache and the historian Robert Baird. Others, among them Harriet Beecher Stowe's husband and literary agent Calvin Stowe, are better known now for their famous connections than for their substantive achievements in the world of reform. Of those who took the lead in importing European practices, Thomas Eddy and Francis Lieber stand out. Eddy, a Quaker, helped precipitate the 1828 schism within his denomination through his vigorous support of social reform. Lieber later became one of America's foremost political theorists. A common interest in educational reform, and especially in reforms from Europe, ties together this diverse and impressive group.[3]

Existing scholarship treats the wave of educational reform that washed across the United States in the 1830s in considerable depth but does so chiefly within a national rather than a transnational framework. The standard narrative established by Michael Katz and followed by numerous other scholars emphasizes the economic factors that pushed educational reformers to advocate public schools as the nation's social and organizational life was subjected to systematization and professionalization.[4] This nationally oriented argument may in large part explain why historians have neglected the transatlantic dimension of educational reform before the US Civil War. Local studies of Northern states—and of Massachusetts in particular—played an especially prominent role in shaping the view that the history of educational reform is best understood in terms of the social tensions provoked by industrialization and modernization at the national level. This skewed geographical focus on New England has meant that reports on European education that emerged from other regions of the United States have been overlooked. But even historical studies with a broad remit neglect European influences. The second volume of Lawrence A. Cremin's trilogy, for example, bears the telling title: *American Education: The National Experience, 1783–1876*. The rare works of scholarship on US education that do emphasize Europe focus more often on comparison than on influence.[5]

Long before commercial steamships began regularly traversing the Atlantic in the 1840s, however, and even before the *Savannah* made the first transatlantic steam-powered voyage in 1819, ideas about education flowed freely from Europe to America.[6] Three European ideas became especially prominent, at various points and places, in the early nineteenth century: the Lancasterian system of instruction; gymnastics; and Pestalozzianism.

The Lancasterian system owes its name to Joseph Lancaster (1778–1838), an English Quaker and schoolteacher. In 1798 Lancaster founded a school at Borough Road in his hometown of Southwark, in South London. The school utilized a monitorial system of education that Lancaster himself had invented, according to which one teacher instructed older students, who in turn passed their knowledge on to younger ones. Using this system, Lancaster eventually taught over 1,000 students at a time. Not surprisingly, word of his innovations spread quickly.[7]

In New York, Lancaster's fellow Quaker Thomas Eddy (1758–1827) heard about the Englishman's innovations through correspondence with Patrick Colquhoun, a London lawyer and moral reform advocate. Most of the Eddy–Colquhoun correspondence focused on prison reform, but in 1804 Eddy thanked Colquhoun for sending him Lancaster's pamphlet on education. Eddy was so pleased with Lancaster's treatise that he had 1,000 copies of it printed and distributed in New York and Philadelphia. He hoped that Lancaster's methods would be widely adopted, and he even aimed to implement them himself in a school for the poor that he was planning. Indeed, two months later, Colquhoun wrote to say that the monitorial systems had worked in two schools he had established for paupers. When in 1805 Eddy led a joint effort with other members of the New York elite to found a society supporting a Free School for indigent children, he ensured that the resulting schools used Lancaster's methods. Only with instruction conducted on such a large scale could a charity school survive. In fact the Lancasterian method surpassed Eddy's expectations: it enabled schools in New York not simply to survive, but to thrive.[8]

Lancasterianism soon spread far beyond New York. Philadelphia next experimented with Lancaster's system, opening a similar school under the leadership of the Quaker Thomas Scattergood. With firm roots in these two important American cities, Lancasterianism extended its branches further. In 1818, Lancaster himself visited the United States, delivering lectures and conferring with educational leaders. Impressed with the country, he decided to settle in Baltimore and found a Lancasterian Institute there. By this time, his following had spread beyond the English-speaking world. Books on his methods were published in France, and Lancaster eventually moved to South America, where he established additional schools. Lancaster thus pioneered one of the first transatlantic networks for educational reform.[9]

One of the routes through which Lancasterianism travelled to the United States included a stop in Germany. A two-piece article from 1826 appeared in the *Literarischen Blätter der Börsen-Halle* titled "Über die Lancastrische Lehrweise." Before many Germans had the chance to read the article, however, its author, Francis Lieber (1798–1872) fled the country in search of greater political freedom. He eventually made his way to Boston, brought there by Americans interested in introducing a second foreign element into American education: gymnastics.

The first American gymnasium was founded at the Round Hill School in 1825 by Charles Follen (1796–1840). Follen, who, like Lieber, had escaped from Prussia, would later become Harvard University's first professor of German. Gymnastics was not the only distinctly European element at the Round Hill School. Its founders, George Bancroft (1800–1891) and Joseph Cogswell (1786–1871), modeled their school specifically on the *gymnasiums*–schools that prepared students for university–they had encountered during their pioneering university studies in Germany. Envious of the opportunities available at this Northampton school, Boston's elite soon demanded similar facilities.[10]

In fact, Bostonians tried to hire the founder of gymnastics himself, Friedrich Ludwig Jahn (1778–1852), who was affectionately known as *Turnvater Jahn*. When that failed, their agent in London turned to Lieber. Lieber, who had been in London for several months while searching for work, had managed to make himself popular among polite company, spending time especially with the editor and translator Sarah Austin (1793–1867) and her circle. Another temporary member of this social group, the American author John Neal (1793–1876) of Portland, Maine, was acting as the intermediary for the Bostonians who wanted to hire a gymnastics instructor. Lieber fit the bill: he came with glowing recommendations from Jahn himself. Although it took several months to arrange, Neal finally hired Lieber for the position.[11]

Lieber's early educational endeavors in the United States were not particularly successful. In addition to establishing a gymnastics program in Boston, he opened America's first public swimming pool. The project piqued enough curiosity that President John Quincy Adams visited it; the Massachusetts Humane Society hoped Lieber could use it to teach Boston children how to swim. The pool received high praise in the press, and Lieber wrote several articles advocating physical education. But ultimately he could not turn a profit and so moved on to other ventures.[12] The influence of this foreign import remained somewhat marginal.

By contrast, one other European educational import found a substantial following in American educational circles during the years of the early republic. The methods of the Swiss pedagogue Johann Heinrich Pestalozzi (1746–1827) differed dramatically from those of Lancaster, but this Romantic reformer found his own supporters across the Atlantic. Powerfully influenced by the educational philosophy of Jean-Jacques Rousseau, Pestalozzi stressed learning through activity and responsiveness to nature. Whereas Lancaster's system appealed to American proclivities for industry and efficiency, training many students with few teachers, Pestalozzi's emphasis on personal attention and holistic training appealed to American individualism.[13]

William Maclure, a Scottish-born American geologist (1763–1840) who travelled extensively in pursuit of new objects for scientific study, visited Pestalozzi's school at Yverdon during a European trip in 1804. Impressed with Pestalozzi's pedagogical practices, Maclure invited him to move to Philadelphia to establish a school there. Pestalozzi rejected the proposal, but he recommended one of his students, Joseph Neef (1770–1854), who accepted the job and arrived in the United States in 1806. Neef and Maclure collaborated on several educational ventures. Both published on Pestalozzi's methods, and Neef went on to found schools in several cities. Maclure's most famous project was a Pestalozzian school at New Harmony, Indiana, the utopian community that he established with Robert Owen.[14]

Other Americans also visited Pestalozzi, carrying his reforms back across the Atlantic. Joseph Carrington Cabell (1778–1856), a Virginian travelling in Europe to convalesce in 1805, joined Maclure on his second trip to see Pestalozzi. Cabell must also have been impressed: when he went on to a successful career as a state legislator he ensured that Pestalozzian reforms were instituted in his hometown.[15] John Griscom (1774–1852), who in 1825 introduced Lancasterian instruction at his school in New York, visited Pestalozzi at Yverdon during a European trip in 1818–1819. The two-volume travelogue that he published upon his return, which introduced Americans to European educational methods on a broader scale, mentioned Pestalozzi several times.[16] The travels of individuals such as Griscom, Maclure, and Neal helped lay the foundations for an even larger transatlantic network of educational reform that would soon emerge.

By the late 1820s, then, substantial European influence on American educational methods was visible on several fronts. Further, influential Europeans had begun to express interest in American educational practices. Emma Willard (1787–1870) of New York, who was involved in reforming female education long before the more general educational reforms peaked in the 1830s, offers one example of this early back-and-forth across the Atlantic. Her 1819 book, *A Plan for Improving Female Education*, for example, was read both in the United States and in Europe. When General Lafayette made his 1825 visit to America and stopped by her school in Troy, he and Willard forged a connection that led Willard to specifically international educational endeavors. Lafayette and Willard, who got along spectacularly well, began a correspondence after Lafayette's departure. When Willard visited Europe in 1830, she made sure to call on her friend. Lafayette opened many doors for her, introducing her to prominent educators and helping her gain access to French schools. During her six months in Paris, Willard also befriended Bessie Rayner Parkes Belloc, the prominent advocate for women's rights and education, with whom she visited other schools. When Willard departed for England, Belloc provided her with letters to Maria Edgeworth and other well-to-do women reformers who shared their interest in education. Upon her return to the United States, Willard wrote a volume detailing her trip, *Journals and Letters from Europe* (1833). This book helped introduce Americans to European educational practices, particularly those in France and England and the funds from its sale were donated to establishing in Greece a college for women based on the model of Willard's own school.[17]

It is therefore clear that a number of prominent American educational reformers were interested in European educational practices, but European educational policy had not yet found its way into American laws. Americans, furthermore, were not at this stage particularly interested in how Europeans set up their schools. New Jersey offers a prime example of this early indifference. Robert Baird (1798–1863) is now best remembered for *Religion in America*, a groundbreaking book published in 1844 that introduced Europeans to Christianity in the United States. But in 1828 he had served as an agent for the New Jersey Missionary Society, touring the state and distributing Bibles to all who would take one. Perhaps due to his experience as a principal of a grammar school for half a decade, the rudimentary level of his fellow citizens' education attracted his attention. In fact, it prompted him to begin a crusade to fix New Jersey's schools. He held public meetings across the state, discussing the advantages of a strong system of common schools. He also wrote several essays and newspaper articles for local audiences. Largely because of his work, in 1829 the New Jersey legislature appropriated $20,000 for the support of common schools. Baird's early activity in New Jersey occurred largely without reference to international educational practices. Although he corresponded with people from New York, Pennsylvania, and across New England about the educational systems in their states, there is no record of him looking abroad for inspiration. It was only from the mid-1830s onward that Americans began to engage with European figures on the matter of educational policy.[18]

One final example underlines how American educators missed opportunities to learn more from their European colleagues in the early 1830s. At an 1831 meeting of the New York State Lyceum, a movement emerged to establish a National Lyceum with members drawn from across the Union who would collaborate on introducing "a uniform and improved system of education...throughout the country." The conference attendees had plenty of international experience: John Neal served as the Lyceum's secretary and John Griscom was on the committee of arrangements. But although they proposed surveying different states for their opinions on schools, no discussion of international education arose.[19]

Despite this lack of engagement with educational policy, by the early 1830s Americans were engaging energetically with European ideas and pedagogical innovations. The same journal that reported on the New York meeting also reported on European educational developments. In fact, about half of the articles in that edition from 1831 described educational methods being used across the ocean. Although these articles focused on description, not prescription, they still point to an increased interest in European educational ideas.

One simple reason for the shift in American interest from European educational practice to European educational policy in the 1830s was increased transatlantic travel. Between 1833 and 1835, three significant American educational reformers travelled to Europe. At the time, none of them knew that their European trips would be significant for US education. In 1833 the health of Unitarian minister Charles Brooks (1795–1872) began to fail and he left his post at the Third Church of Hingham, Massachusetts, for a recuperative sojourn in Europe. One year later, Robert Baird, now serving as a missionary, moved to France to evangelize its Catholics. Finally, in 1835, Henry Barnard, a Yale graduate who had served as a Pennsylvania schoolteacher for a year before deciding to study law, travelled to Europe as a delegate to an international peace convention in London. All three became important in the transatlantic educational reform movement in the late 1830s, but when they left America, none of them foresaw the significance of their international journeys.[20]

Changes in the careers of two more future reformers also set them up to take later trips abroad. In the fall of 1832, the Virginian

Benjamin Mosby Smith (1811–1893) entered Union Theological Seminary (now Union Presbyterian Seminary) in Virginia. Smith had taught at a small academy in North Carolina after his graduation from Hampden-Sydney College in 1829. Three years later he returned to the campus of Hampden-Sydney and enrolled in the neighboring seminary. He continued to remain involved in education, however, establishing an Educational Association at the college upon his arrival. One year later, Calvin Ellis Stowe (1802–1886) left the East Coast to follow Lyman Beecher to the opening American frontier, where he took up a position at Beecher's new Lane Theological Seminary in Cincinnati, Ohio. Stowe supported public education from the beginning of his time in Cincinnati. He became especially active in the Western Literary Institute and College of Professional Teachers, originally founded in 1829. The aggressive expansion of this society represents one more sign of the significance of educational reform in this era. Across the country states recognized a need for improved schools.[21]

Another catalyst that introduced specifically policy-oriented discussion to American educational discourse was the published work of Victor Cousin (1792–1867). Cousin is now best remembered as a philosopher whose eclectic appropriation of traditions as diverse as Common Sense realism and Hegelianism imbued his lectures at the Sorbonne with the magnetism to attract enormous crowds, but ultimately left him without an enduring philosophical contribution of his own. Unlike his formal philosophy, however, Cousin's educational reforms proved immensely influential.

Cousin's influence in the United States rests largely on his contributions in the form of a report on Prussia's education. After the July Revolution of 1830 overthrew King Charles X of France, the new government sought to create a state school system. It therefore sent Cousin, already an established professor serving on the Council of Public Instruction, to explore the educational policies in Prussia, which had the most highly regarded educational system in Europe. This state-sponsored trip set him on a path that ultimately led to significant authority over education in France.[22] But his influence also spread far beyond France. Cousin's report on Prussian education was read widely in both Britain and the United States. Americans learned of it almost immediately after its initial publication in France in 1832. The *Edinburgh Review* performed the introduction by publishing an article that many Americans read on "Cousin and German Schools."[23] Eventually, Americans adopted two major innovations found in Cousin's report: the office of a state superintendent for common schools and state-sponsored professional teacher training colleges. Even before the report had been translated into English, knowledgeable and well-connected Americans read Cousin's writings. On January 17, 1834, Francis Lieber wrote to Cousin with a twofold agenda. Lieber noted that Cousin's report had already received "an uncommon attention" in America and that Lieber had even been asked to translate the work. Given their common interest in education, Lieber presented Cousin with a copy of his latest book, hot off the press: *A Constitution and Plan of Education for Girard College for Orphans.* In this work Lieber drew on international sources to inform the pedagogical practices he proposed for this newly established school; his book thus represents another example of Americans drawing on European educational practices that was so prevalent at this time. But Lieber's letter also pushed further, toward specific elements of governmental policy. Lieber noted that Pennsylvania was considering beginning a general school system; he therefore asked if Cousin would send him "such legislation or other papers which have reference to the newly established or establishing school systems in France."[24] Many other educators took up the pattern Lieber had pioneered by looking specifically to Cousin's report for policy proposals about how specific states should organize their own public schools.

Lieber would not translate Cousin into English, however. Only three months after Lieber's letter, Sarah Austin, the same Englishwoman who originally introduced Lieber to John Neal, put the finishing touches on her translation of Cousin's report. This rendition soon found its way across the Atlantic, where John Orville Taylor (1807–1890) republished it in 1835, with a new preface specifically aimed at his American audience. Unsatisfied with the results, he issued an abbreviated version of Austin's translation (which was itself already abbreviated) the next year, allowing Americans even easier access to Cousin's findings.[25]

Taylor was not alone in his admiration for Cousin's report. In fact, his publication of Austin's translation received financial support. James Wadsworth (1768–1844), who had made a substantial fortune in real estate, underwrote the complete cost of its printing so that the book could be sold affordably.[26] Due to the efforts of Taylor and Wadsworth, Cousin's report spread even more quickly through American educational circles.

Others soon read Taylor's publication and used it for their own purposes. As early as the summer of 1835, Eliza Robbins (1786–1853), a well-known author of children's textbooks, wrote a series of anonymous newspaper articles describing the faults in the current common school system and suggesting possible solutions, often appealing to Prussian reforms. The articles were well received and members of the American Institute of Instruction, a group organized in 1830 to discuss educational practices and policies, wrote to the paper and requested that the articles' author give them a more detailed speech. Robbins therefore wrote a lecture and had her friend George S. Hillard, a lawyer and author from Boston, read it before the institute, which did not allow women as members. The arguments were based almost entirely on Cousin's work. When her lecture was later published, a reviewer praised the "neat little volume," which was cheaper than Austin's translation of Cousin, though not very different.[27]

Whereas Robbins focused her efforts on writing, others made even more public appeals on behalf of American schools. A prominent example is Charles Brooks, who first met Victor Cousin during his stay in France in 1834. Education was not yet on his agenda, but later on his trip, at an evening gathering in London, he met Nikolaus Heinrich Julius (1783–1862), a doctor from Hamburg.[28] Julius was on his way to the United States to study its schools, hospitals, prisons, and other public institutions and in 1839 published his findings in the form of a two-volume study entitled *Nordamerikas sittliche Zustände*. Brooks, who was getting ready to return to the United States, discussed Prussian schooling with Julius extensively. The two men roomed together on the transatlantic voyage, during which Julius regaled Brooks with stories about the schools in his homeland. In the course of the journey, according to Brooks, he "fell in love with the Prussian system."[29]

Julius toured America for six months, travelling at least as far south as South Carolina and as far north as Massachusetts. He made the acquaintance of other reformers, including Francis Lieber, with whom he published a pamphlet on the relationship between education and crime. He maintained his friendship with Brooks, whom he visited in Hingham in the spring of 1835. During the visit, Brooks announced to Julius his plan to introduce the Prussian system of state supervision into the Massachusetts educational system. Taylor's first edition of Cousin's report had recently been published and word was beginning to spread about Prussian reforms. Before setting out on his own crusade, however, Brooks arranged for Julius to give a speech to the education committee of the Massachusetts legislature. The address was printed by both Massachusetts and New York, but had no immediate effect.[30] Undeterred, Brooks began an independent campaign for Prussian-style reforms.

Brooks began locally. On Thanksgiving Day, 1835, he delivered a speech detailing the deficiencies of the Massachusetts school system and the advantages that could be won by instituting a system of state sponsored teacher training colleges, like those found in Prussia. In quick succession he delivered three more lectures, each two hours in length, developing his plans in greater detail. A year later, his speeches had made little headway. In November of 1836 he therefore formulated a new plan, advertising a December convention in Plymouth to discuss methods of improving education, specifically in light of the Prussian example. He printed a circular announcing the meeting and had it sent across the state. When the time for the convention came, Brooks finally tasted success: after two days of meetings, convention attendees adopted a series of resolutions endorsing his reforms.[31]

In 1836, then, Brooks laid the groundwork for educational reforms in Massachusetts. His numerous speeches finally generated sufficient attention to warrant a convention supporting his efforts. And Brooks was not alone in making progress on this front. Across the United States, 1836 was a year of preparation: reformers took significant steps that ultimately resulted in new laws from Ohio to Massachusetts.

Despite having married only one week previously, Calvin Stowe attended a teacher's convention in Columbus, Ohio—over 100 miles from his home in Cincinnati—in January of 1836. He brought along his new wife, the former Harriet Elizabeth Beecher, who perhaps heard him deliver his two-part lecture on Prussian schools. Even if she did not, other notables certainly did—the Ohio governor among them. Stowe's lectures were praised, and before the year was out they were published as *The Prussian System of Education: And Its Applicability to the United States.* In addition to outlining eight characteristics of the Prussian system that, if properly adapted, would serve the American context well, Stowe noted the recent public interest in looking abroad for educational inspiration. He especially drew attention to a recent speech by Ohio's governor that "called the legislative attention to the Prussian school system."[32] Stowe's comments demonstrate that Cousin's work had penetrated as far west as Ohio by late 1835.

Stowe's speech increased this interest and accelerated the pace of Ohio's reforms. In March 1836 the Ohio legislature commissioned Stowe, who was already planning a transatlantic trip, to conduct a study of Prussian schools for the state. He set sail on June 1, armed with detailed instructions for preparing a report, including a list of 25 questions about Prussian schools to which local teachers wanted answers. Stowe's interest in Prussian education had permeated the local culture of American educators, but he was not the only American drawn overseas by an interest in European affairs.[33]

Two weeks after Stowe departed, Benjamin Mosby Smith also boarded a ship to cross the Atlantic. Smith had graduated from Union Seminary, but another year there serving as a tutor convinced him that he needed further training, and so he departed for Halle, which was then a prominent center for the study of theology. Despite his theological program, education never strayed far from Smith's mind. Even while on the boat, he spent time, as he called it, "scheming...for old Virginia" and developing a plan to raise "a fund to help poor young men" train for the teaching profession. This line of thinking may have been inspired by Lucian Minor, a lawyer who later taught at William and Mary, who had delivered an address about Prussian education before the Institute of Education at Hampden Sidney College in September of 1835. On arrival in Europe, Smith set about studying the Prussian educational system, keeping a detailed notebook of his observations. He soon realized that he was not the only one examining the local schools. A couple months after arriving, Stowe tracked down Smith in Halle and the two spent several days together.[34]

Back in the United States, one week after Stowe took leave of Smith, Alexander Dallas Bache (1806–1876) received word that he, too, would join US educators abroad in search of foreign inspiration. Bache had become president of Girard College, for which Lieber had earlier compiled an educational plan. Lieber had proposed sending someone to examine educational practices internationally, but it took the school until September 19, 1836, finally to authorize Bache for such a mission. The trustees asked for an examination that was "thorough and practical" and even sent a list of 16 details they wanted to know about each school he visited. Otherwise, his charge was broad, and he was sent without a specific return date. Bache used this opportunity to spend two years travelling Europe, visiting 278 schools.[35]

The groundwork for the coming wave of educational reform was laid, therefore, in 1836, the year in which Brooks began his campaign and in which three US citizens ventured abroad with the intention of studying international education. The following year, a framework of educational policy was erected on that foundation when Massachusetts passed its first substantial reforms, beginning with the inauguration of a state Board of Education.

Brooks's campaign for public education made rapid progress. Although Nikolaus Julius had inspired his initial undertaking, in 1837 he turned to Victor Cousin for further support. On February 16 of that year Brooks wrote the first of at least seven letters to the famous philosopher. He explained that he had delivered summaries of Cousin's report to numerous audiences, including the Massachusetts General Court, and requested additional information to aid in establishing a formal system of elementary education in the United States. Two months later the legislature took a significant step towards fulfilling Brooks's objective: it established the Massachusetts Board of Education and appointed as its secretary Horace Mann, who went on to become one of America's most famous educational reformer.[36]

Massachusetts was not yet finished with its reforms—with Brooks's help, Mann soon introduced others, including a state-sponsored teacher training college—but at the same time that Massachusetts took these steps, inspired by the Prussian example, other states were moving in the same direction. Just as Brooks was speaking to the Massachusetts legislature, Stowe returned to Ohio, where his wife and recently born twin daughters greeted him. He spent that summer preparing his report for Ohio, but the state did not wait to receive it before introducing similar reforms. In March it created a new administrative position, Superintendent of Common Schools, appointing Samuel Lewis (1799–1854) to this important post.

These reforms continued into the next year. Stowe submitted his finalized report to the Ohio legislature in December of 1837, and by April the legislature responded by passing an even more far-reaching educational law that further centralized the administration of the state's schools. But Stowe did not wait for Ohio to take action. Instead, he took his act on the road. In February 1838 he spoke before the Pennsylvania Senate, which printed 3,000 copies of his *Report* to distribute to the public. One thousand of these were printed in German, showing that the Senate hoped the report could reach well beyond educators in Philadelphia. Other states took similar steps. In addition to Ohio, which printed 10,000 copies and sent one to every school in the state, the legislatures of Massachusetts, Michigan, North Carolina, and Virginia also reprinted and circulated Stowe's report.[37]

While Stowe was delivering lectures about German education across the country, the reformers in Massachusetts maintained contact with Cousin, communicating with him about further steps they could take to improve education. Brooks wrote to him throughout 1837, and Cousin sent several packages of pamphlets in return, shipping large packages, as requested by Brooks, to the Brooks Brothers & Co. address in New York (although letters traveled the Atlantic easily, bulky parcels were more difficult to mail).[38] When the American Institute of Instruction, where Robbins had presented her lecture and with which Brooks became very involved, elected Cousin as an honorary member, its secretary, Thomas Cushing, wrote to Cousin with the news.[39] Cousin responded positively, mailing more material directly to the institute.[40] Cousin communicated with others as well, perhaps through Brooks as an intermediary. Both the Massachusetts Governor and Harvard College sent words of thanks to Cousin through Brooks.[41] In addition, Eliza Robbins and Cousin corresponded.[42] Robbins was said to be outgoing in social contexts, but she required the prodding of the leading transcendentalist Orestes Brownson before she wrote to Cousin.[43]

The encouragement these reformers drew from Cousin inspired them to push for a special kind of training in a separate institution for teachers. Brooks traveled throughout the Northeast, from New Hampshire to Pennsylvania, preaching the maxim, "As is the teacher so is the school." In January of 1838 the Massachusetts legislature addressed the demand for a normal school. After listening to both Mann and Brooks, and hearing that a private citizen had donated $10,000 toward the project if the legislature would match the gift, it approved the school's establishment. After accomplishing this goal, Brooks set aside his education work and returned to the pulpit. He occasionally came out of retirement to give a speech or write a response on education, but for the most part he left further reform to Mann and others.[44]

States other than Massachusetts engaged in reform. On returning from his first European trip Henry Barnard was elected to the Connecticut state legislature, where in 1838, after a quiet first year, he defended a bill to establish the Board of Commissioners of the Common Schools. Barnard's speech, described by a contemporary as being of "great power and eloquence," earned him an appointment as Board Secretary. From this position, Barnard ascended to educational leadership in the Northeast. He networked with other reformers, including Brooks and Mann in Massachusetts, Emma Willard in New York, and even Stowe, and also wrote frequently for the board. In fact, the board established a semi-monthly journal, the *Connecticut Common School Journal*, which Barnard edited. This journal found a large audience: more than 60,000 copies of the first 12 numbers were distributed. In addition to smaller articles, the journal distributed larger works such as Stowe's *Report*.[45]

Robert Baird, serving as a missionary in France, also communicated with Barnard. In 1838 the latter engaged Baird to write a piece on teacher seminaries in France. Barnard was not Baird's only correspondent. One year earlier the *American Quarterly Register* signed

him up as a "contributor and correspondent" who would write specifically about European education, a topic in which it aimed to increase
its offerings. When Baird returned to New Jersey in 1838, the state
remembered his previous educational work and asked him to present
a report on how the Prussian system of educational had performed
since its recent introduction to France.[46]

In February of 1839, Brooks summarized recent progress in a
letter to Cousin: "the governments of Massachusetts, Connecticut,
New Hampshire, New-York, Ohio, and New Jersey have each passed
wise laws, and in some states 'Boards of Education' have been established with power to regulate and improve the school system."[47]
Brooks did not even mention Michigan, which had actually introduced Prussian style educational reforms even before Brooks convinced Massachusetts to do so. In that state, reform efforts were led
by Isaac E. Crary (1804–1854) and John D. Pierce (1797–1882),
both of whom had read Cousin but neither of whom, it seems, had
traveled internationally.[48]

A number of states that Brooks did not list were nonetheless examining European examples while they considered their own reforms. In
Virginia the Democratic governor David Campbell asked the recently
returned Benjamin Mosby Smith to compile his educational research
into an official report to submit to the legislature. Smith did so, and
the state published the document in 1839. The report included not
only a description of Prussian schools, focusing on how they all ultimately stood under governmental control, but also an appendix, titled
"Suggestions on the Application of the System of Primary Schools to
Virginia." Smith focused on three improvements: first, the obligation
of both the state and parents to ensure that all children are educated;
second, a general tax on all citizens to support public schools; and
third, following the Prussian emphasis on teacher quality, Virginia,
too, should emphasize teacher quality.[49]

The Virginia legislature took no immediate action on Smith's
report, but the report did not go unnoticed. William H. Ruffner,
who 30 years later became a prominent educational reformer in
Virginia, participated in a debate on the report while he was a college student in 1839. The Graham Society, of which he was a part,
discussed the subject: "Would the cause of education be promoted
in this state, by the adoption of the methods appended to Benjamin
Smith's report on Prussian Schools?" Later in the year the same
society discussed the question "Should a system of District free
schools be established throughout Virginia?" The overwhelming
vote was in favor.[50]

In Pennsylvania, Bache's *Report on Education in Europe, to the Trustees of Girard College for Orphans* was published in 1839. Although problems at Girard College prevented Bache from implementing his findings there, he brought the ideas he encountered in Europe to his next job, as superintendent of Philadelphia's Central High School. The reforms he oversaw in Philadelphia's public schools were deeply influenced by his time abroad.[51]

Transatlantic exchange, and the associated influence of European reforms ideas, continued unabated after the 1830s. The career of Henry Barnard most clearly exemplifies this trend. After moving to Rhode Island, Barnard helped shepherd his own educational bill through the state legislature. The law, which was passed in 1843, established a comprehensive state system of education. Everything from funding to teacher approval came from the state, which ensured uniformity and accountability. In 1852 he returned to Europe for six months, studying education abroad first hand and publishing a book on his findings. From 1855 to 1881 he published the *American Journal of Education*, which frequently featured articles about education abroad.[52]

Others continued the work of introducing European ideas to the United States. Eliza Robbins, for example, visited Europe in 1841, using her credentials as an author of educational books to obtain letters of introduction. John Griscom took his early influences from Pestalozzi with him when he became a superintendent of public schools in New Jersey in 1842. Horace Mann visited Europe to examine its schools in 1843. His famous *Seventh Annual Report*, in which he appealed prominently to the teaching methods he had seen in Prussia, aroused the ire of a group of Boston schoolmasters who insisted that their schools needed little help from abroad, but by this time their protests were in vain. Prussian influences, from the Board of Education that Mann headed to the teacher training colleges that Mann advanced, had secured their place in American education. Transatlantic exchange was now thriving among antebellum educators. At times, this exchange appeared even more important than contacts within the states. In 1840, Horace Mann wrote to Henry Barnard: "If we were on opposite sides of the Atlantic, I think we might hear from each other oftener than at present."[53]

But education is not a *Sonderfall*, an exception to the rule of US isolationism. Whereas educational reform efforts provide one perspective on transatlantic social politics in the antebellum era, even from this vantage point other significant transatlantic reform efforts come clearly into view. Prison reform, for instance, looms large. In the early 1800s, Thomas Eddy frequently discussed prison reform in his correspondence with Patrick Colquhoun; in the 1830s, European interest in American prisons sent both Nikolaus Julius and, of course, Alexis de Tocqueville sailing across the Atlantic. The intensity of the European gaze caused Americans, in turn, to look more carefully at their own prisons: Francis Lieber helped Tocqueville and Beaumont gather their data and later translated and annotated their finished book. During Henry Barnard's first trip to Europe he displayed more concern for European prisons than for European education, and the only bill he introduced during his brief stay in the Connecticut legislature concerned jails.[54] Other types of reform also had substantial transatlantic dimensions. Robert Baird's preaching inspired a Scandinavian temperance movement, and other figures mentioned in this chapter were involved in temperance movements at home.[55] Few of the figures treated here were involved in the abolitionist movement, but it was a vital and historically groundbreaking example of antebellum transatlantic reform.[56] The seeds of transatlantic intellectual, social, and political exchange had been carried back and forth from the shores of Europe to the shores of the United States well before the Atlantic crossings of the Progressive Era that Rodgers finds exceptional. In antebellum America, these seeds had not only been planted, they were flowering.

Notes

1. Daniel T. Rodgers, *Atlantic Crossings: Social Politics in a Progressive Age* (Belknap Press of Harvard University Press, 2000), 2.
2. Ibid., 4.
3. For scholarship focusing on these figures' work in areas beyond education, see: Joan D. Hedrick, *Harriet Beecher Stowe: A Life* (New York: Oxford University Press, 1995); Hugh Richard Slotten, *Patronage, Practice, and the Culture of American Science: Alexander Dallas Bache and the U.S. Coast Survey* (New York: Cambridge University Press, 1994); Sydney E. Ahlstrom, "The Problem of the History of Religion in America," *Church History* 39, no. 2 (June 1, 1970): 224–35; H. Larry Ingle, *Quakers in Conflict: The Hicksite Reformation* (Knoxville: University of Tennessee Press, 1986); Frank Burt Freidel, *Francis Lieber, Nineteenth-Century Liberal* (Baton Rouge: Louisiana State University Press, 1948).
4. Michael B. Katz, "The Origins of Public Education: A Reassessment," *History of Education Quarterly* 16, no. 4 (December 1, 1976): 381–407; Stanley K. Schultz, *The Culture Factory: Boston Public Schools, 1789–1860* (New York: Oxford University Press, 1973); Samuel Bowles and Herbert Gintis, *Schooling in Capitalist America:*

Educational Reform and the Contradictions of Economic Life (Albany: SUNY Press, 1976); Alexander James Field, *Educational Reform and Manufacturing Development in Mid-Nineteenth Century Massachusetts* (New York: Garland Publishing, 1989); Ward A. McAfee, *Religion, Race, and Reconstruction: The Public School in the Politics of the 1870s* (Albany: SUNY Press, 1998).

5. For strong local studies, see Sidney L. Jackson, *America's Struggle for Free Schools: Social Tension and Education in New England and New York, 1827–42* (Washington, D.C.: American Council on Public Affairs, 1941); Michael B. Katz, *The Irony of Early School Reform: Educational Innovation in Mid-Nineteenth Century Massachusetts* (Cambridge: Harvard University Press, 1968). Two books with a national focus are Carl F. Kaestle, *Pillars of the Republic: Common Schools and American Society, 1780–1860* (New York: Hill and Wang, 1983); Lawrence A. Cremin, *American Education: The National Experience, 1783–1876* (New York: Harper & Row, 1980). For a comparative perspective, see Charles Leslie Glenn, Jr., *The Myth of the Common School* (Amherst: University of Massachusetts Press, 1988).

6. On the early history of steamships in the Atlantic, see N. R. Bonsor, *North Atlantic Seaway: An Illustrated History of the Passenger Services Linking the Old World with the New in Four Volumes*, vol. 1, 4 vols (New York: Arco Publishing, 1975).

7. Joseph Lancaster, *Epitome of Some of the Chief Events and Transactions in the Life of Joseph Lancaster: Containing an Account of the Rise and Progress of the Lancasterian System of Education; and the Author's Future Prospects of Usefulness to Mankind* (New Haven, CT: Baldwin & Peck, 1833).

8. Samuel Lorenzo Knapp, *The Life of Thomas Eddy: Comprising an Extensive Correspondence with Many of the Most Distinguished Philosophers and Philanthropists of This and Other Countries* (New York: Conner & Cooke, 1834), 163, 206–208; David Nasaw, *Schooled to Order: A Social History of Public Schooling in the United States* (New York: Oxford University Press, 1979), 19–21; John Franklin Reigart, *The Lancasterian System of Instruction in the Schools of New York City* (New York: Teachers College, 1916). For two primary sources on how the Lancasterian system was implemented in New York, see John Griscom, *Monitorial Instruction: An Address, Pronounced at the Opening of the New-York High-School, with Notes and Illustrations* (New York: Mahlon Day, 1825); *Manual of the Lancasterian System, of Teaching Reading, Writing, Arithmetic, and Needle-Work, as Practised in the Schools of the Free-Society, of New York* (New York: Samuel Wood and Sons, 1820).

9. Charles Calvert Ellis, "Lancasterian Schools in Philadelphia" (PhD diss., University of Pennsylvania, 1907); Alexandre De Laborde, *Plan D'éducation Pour Les Enfans Pauvres, D'après Les Deux Méthodes Combinées Du Docteur Bell Et De M. Lancaster*, 2nd ed. (Paris: Chez L.

Colas, 1818); Domingo Amunátegui y Solar, *El Sistema De Lancáster En Chile I En Otros Paises Sudamericanos* (Santiago: Imprenta Cervantes, 1895); Sir Edgar Vaughan, *Joseph Lancaster in Caracas, 1824–1827: And His Relations with the Liberator Simon Bolivar: With Some Accounts of Lancasterian Schools in Spanish America in the Nineteenth Century and Some Notes on the Efforts of the British and Foreign Bible Society to Distribute the Scriptures in Spanish in the Same Territory* (Sutton, Surry: Edgar Vaughan, 1986).

10. Freidel, *Francis Lieber, Nineteenth-Century Liberal*, 50; Joseph Green Cogswell, *Outline of the System of Education at the Round Hill School: With a List of the Present Instructers [sic] and of the Pupils from Its Commencement until This Time, June 1831* (Boston: N. Hale, 1831), 50.

11. Freidel, *Francis Lieber, Nineteenth-Century Liberal*, 49–50.

12. Ibid., 58–60; "Teachers of Gymnastics," *American Journal of Education* 1, no. 11 (November 1826): 699–701; "Gymnasium," *American Journal of Education* 2, no. 5 (1827): 316; "Book Review: A Treatise on Calisthenic Exercises; The Elements of Gymnastics," *American Journal of Education* 2, no. 8 (1827): 487–91; "Review: A Treatise on Gymnastics, Taken Chiefly from the German of F. L. Jahn," *American Quarterly Review* 5 (March 1828): 126–50.

13. For the best recent introduction to Pestalozzi, see Daniel Tröhler, *Johann Heinrich Pestalozzi* (Stuttgart: UTB, 2008).

14. Frederick M. Binder, *The Age of the Common School: 1830–1865* (New York: Wiley, 1974), 26; Will S. Monroe, *Joseph Neef and Pestalozzianism in America* (Boston, s.n.: 1894). Maclure wrote several articles in the *National Intelligences* in 1806; Neef published his major treatise in 1808: Joseph Neef, *Sketch of a Plan and Method of Education, Founded on an Analysis of the Human Facilities, and Natural Reason, Suitable for the Offspring of a Free People, and for All Rational Beings* (Philadelphia: Printed for the Author, 1808).

15. William Arthur Maddox, *The Free School Idea in Virginia Before the Civil War* (New York: Teachers College Press, 1918), 119–20; Alexander Brown, *The Cabells and Their Kin: A Memorial Volume of History, Biography, and Genealogy* (New York: Houghton, Mifflin and Co., 1895), 263–67.

16. John Griscom, *A Year in Europe. Comprising a Journal of Observations in England, Scotland, Ireland, France, Switzerland, the North of Italy, and Holland. In 1818 and 1819*, 2 vols (New York: Collins and Co., 1823).

17. John Lord, *The Life of Emma Willard* (New York: D. Appleton and Company, 1873), 124–34; Paul Monroe, *Founding of the American Public School System: History of Education in the United States*, vol. 1 (New York: Macmillan, 1940), 236.

18. Henry Martyn Baird, *The Life of the Rev. Robert Baird* (New York: A. D. F. Randolph, 1866); *A Statement of the Proceedings of the Princeton*

Corresponding Executive Committee of the New-Jersey Missionary Society (Princeton: Hugh Madden, 1830); John Maclean, *A Lecture on a School System for New Jersey: Delivered, January 23, 1828, in the Chapel of Nassau-Hall, Before the Literary and Philosophical Society of New Jersey* (Princeton: Princeton Press, 1829), 23.

19. *American Annals of Education and Instruction* 1, no. 6.2 (June 1831).

20. Edith Nye MacMullen, *In the Cause of True Education: Henry Barnard and Nineteenth-Century School Reform* (New Haven: Yale University Press, 1991), 34–40. MacMullen provides far and away the best biography of Barnard. Earlier biographers have often claimed that this trip was undertaken specifically to study European education—a motive that would later send others across the Atlantic. MacMullen shows that this is not the case. The fact that people would assume that it was, however, testifies to the fact that these types of transatlantic journeys were becoming more frequent.

21. William G. Caperton, "Benjamin Mosby Smith and the Common School Education in Virginia" (MA thesis, Radford, VA: Radford College, 1971); Francis Rosebro Flournoy, *Benjamin Mosby Smith, 1811–1893* (Richmond: Richmond Press, 1947); John Harker, "The Life and Contributions of Calvin Ellis Stowe" (PhD diss., Pittsburgh: University of Pittsburgh, 1951), 38; Newton Edwards, *The School in the American Social Order: The Dynamics of American Education* (Boston: Houghton Mifflin Co, 1947), 335.

22. Doris S. Goldstein, "'Official Philosophies' in Modern France: The Example of Victor Cousin," *Journal of Social History* 1, no. 3 (April 1, 1968): 259–79; Walter Brewer, *Victor Cousin as a Comparative Educator* (New York: Teachers College Press, 1971).

23. Robbins to Cousin, August 16, 1838. Bibliothèque de la Sorbonne (Paris), MSVC 246. A French translation of this letter is available in Jules Barthélemy-Saint Hilaire, ed., *M. Victor Cousin: Sa Vie Et Sa Correspondance* (Paris: Hachette and Alcan, 1895), 422. These articles themselves are: "Cousin on German Schools," *The Edinburgh Review: Or Critical Journal* (July 1833): 505–42; "National Education in England and France," *The Edinburgh Review: Or Critical Journal* 63, no. 117 (October 1833): 1–30.

24. Francis Lieber to Victor Cousin, January 17, 1834. Bibliothèque de la Sorbonne (Paris), MSVC 237. For a French translation, see Barthélemy-Saint Hilaire, *M. Victor Cousin: Sa Vie Et Sa Correspondance*, 399–400.

25. Paul D. Travers, "John Orville Taylor: A Forgotten Educator," *History of Education Quarterly* 9, no. 1 (April 1, 1969): 57–63; "Obituary: John Orville Taylor," *New York Times* (New York, January 19, 1890).

26. Cousin, *M. Victor Cousin: Sa Vie Et Sa Correspondance*, 423.

27. Adam Waldie, "Instruction in Prussia," *Waldie's Select Circulating Library: The Journal of Belles Lettres* (1836).
28. Charles Brooks to Victor Cousin, February 16, 1837. Bibliothèque de la Sorbonne (Paris), MSVC 220.
29. John Albree, *Charles Brooks and His Work for Normal Schools* (Medford, MA: J.C. Miller, Jr., 1907), 10–17.
30. William Ogden Niles, "The Prussian System of Education," *Niles' Weekly Register* (Baltimore, April 11, 1835), 89; J. Orville Taylor, "Seminaries for Teachers," *American Railroad Journal and Advocate of Internal Improvements* 4, no. 12 (March 28, 1835): 187–88; Francis Lieber and Nicolaus Heinrich Julius, *Remarks on the Relation between Education and Crime: In a Letter to the Right Rev. William White, D.D. to Which Are Added, Some Observations* (Philadelphia Society for Alleviating the Miseries of Public Prisons, 1835); Ellwood Patterson Cubberley, *Public Education in the United States: A Study and Interpretation of American Educational History; An Introductory Textbook Dealing with the Larger Problems of Present-Day Education in the Light of Their Historical Development* (New York: Houghton Mifflin, 1919), 277.
31. Albree, *Charles Brooks and His Work for Normal Schools*, 17–23.
32. John A. Walz, *German Influence in American Education and Culture* (Philadelphia: Carl Schurz Memorial Foundation, 1936), 17–20; Harker, "The Life and Contributions of Calvin Ellis Stowe, 39–41.
33. Harker, "The Life and Contributions of Calvin Ellis Stowe," 45, 128–31.
34. Caperton, "Benjamin Mosby Smith and the Common School Education in Virginia"; Flournoy, *Benjamin Mosby Smith, 1811–1893*, 23–24, 29–30, 34; Lucian Minor, *An Address on Education: As Connected with the Permanence of Our Republican Institutions: Delivered before the Institute of Education of Hampden Sidney College, at Its Anniversary Meeting, September 24, 1835, on the Invitation of that Body* (Richmond: T. W. White, 1835). Some specific details come from the Diary of Benjamin Mosby Smith, vol. 1. Union Presbyterian Seminary Library. Available on microfilm. See especially p. 13 for details about Smith's departure and pp. 186–92 for description of his time with Stowe.
35. Alexander Dallas Bache, *Report on Education in Europe, to the Trustees of the Girard College for Orphans* (Philadelphia: Lydia R. Bailey, 1839), iii–vii, 1–7.
36. Charles Brooks to Victor Cousin, February 16, 1837. Bibliothèque de la Sorbonne (Paris), MSVC 220.
37. Harker, "The Life and Contributions of Calvin Ellis Stowe," 118–39.
38. Charles Brooks to Victor Cousin, July 28, 1837, October 28, 1837, July 14, 1838. Bibliothèque de la Sorbonne (Paris), MSVC 220.

39. For more on Brooks and the American Institute of Instruction, see *The Introductory Discourse, and the Lectures Delivered Before the American Institute of Instruction, at Worcester, (Mass), August, 1837, Including a Journal of Proceedings and List of Officers* (Boston: James Munroe & Co., 1838); Robert Ulich, *A Sequence of Educational Influences, Traced Through Unpublished Writings of Pestalozzi, Fröbel, Diesterweg, Horace Mann, and Henry Barnard* (Cambridge: Harvard University Press, 1935), 50–60; Charles Northend, *The Annals of the American Institute of Instruction: Being a Record of Its Doings for 54 Years, from 1830 till 1883* (New Britain, CT, 1884). The Ulrich volume reprints several lectures, the manuscripts of which are in the Harvard University Library.

40. Cushing wrote to Cousin at least twice. Brooks discussed the honorary membership in his October 28, 1837 letter to Cousin.

41. Brooks to Cousin, February 5, 1839. Bibliothèque de la Sorbonne (Paris), MSVC 220.

42. Robbins's letter to Cousin survives: Sorbonne Letters, Robbins to Cousin, August 16, 1838. Bibliothèque de la Sorbonne (Paris), MSVC 246. Cousin's response does not, but he mentioned writing to Robbins in a letter to Orestes Brownson, implying that he did respond. See Theodore Maynard, *Orestes Brownson: Yankee, Radical, Catholic* (New York: Macmillan., 1943), 104.

43. For a description of Robbins, see Parke Godwin, *A Biography of William Cullen Bryant: with Extracts from His Private Correspondence* (New York: D. Appleton and Company, 1883), 338–39. For her letter, see Cousin, *M. Victor Cousin: Sa Vie Et Sa Correspondance*, 422–29.

44. Albree, *Charles Brooks and His work for Normal Schools*, 25–27.

45. MacMullen, *In the Cause of True Education*, 45–72.

46. Vincent P Lannie, ed., *Henry Barnard, American Educator*, Classics in Education 50 (New York: Teachers College Press, 1974), 46; B. B. Edwards, "Preface," *The American Quarterly Register* IX (1837): 4; *Memorial to the Legislature of New Jersey on Public Instruction* (New York: S. W. Benedict, 1838), 16. For Baird's writing on European education, see Robert Baird, "The University of Paris," *The American Quarterly Register* IX (August 1836): 17–58; Robert Baird, "Literary Institutions in France," *The American Quarterly Register* IX (February 1837): 238–63.

47. Brooks to Cousin, February 5, 1839. Bibliothèque de la Sorbonne (Paris), MSVC 220.

48. Cubberley, *Public Education in the United States*, 273–74.

49. Flournoy, *Benjamin Mosby Smith, 1811–1893*, 23–29; Caperton, "Benjamin Mosby Smith and the Common School Education in Virginia," 39–40. The report may be found in Benjamin Mosby Smith, *The Prussian Primary School System as Seen by a Virginia Traveler a Century Ago with Suggestions as to Its Application to the State of Virginia* (Staunton, VA: McClure Co., 1936).

50. Caperton, "Benjamin Mosby Smith and the Common School Education in Virginia," 16–17.

51. Bache, *Report on Education in Europe, to the Trustees of the Girard College for Orphans*; Hugh R. Slotten, "Science, Education, and Antebellum Reform: The Case of Alexander Dallas Bache," *History of Education Quarterly* 31, no. 3 (October 1, 1991): 323–42.

52. Edith Nye MacMullen, *In the Cause of True Education: Henry Barnard and Nineteenth-Century School Reform*, 96–120, 187–98. For more on the journal, see Richard Emmons Thursfield, *Henry Barnard's American Journal of Education* (Baltimore: The Johns Hopkins Press, 1945). See especially Chapter 4, "The *Journal* as a Record of European Education."

53. Kenneth Walter Cameron, "Emerson, Transcendentalism, and Literary Notes in the Stearns Wheeler Papers" (1973): 73; John H. Griscom, *Memoir of John Griscom, LL. D.: Late Professor of Chemistry and Natural Philosophy; With an Account of the New York High School; Society for the Prevention of Pauperism; the House of Refuge; and Other Institutions* (New York: Robert Carter and Brothers, 1859); Horace Mann, *Seventh Annual Report: Together with the Seventh Annual Report of the Secretary of the Board* (Dutton and Wentworth, 1844); Lannie, *Henry Barnard, American Educator*, 50.

54. MacMullen, *In the Cause of True Education*, 50.

55. Franklin D. Scott, "American Influences in Norway and Sweden," *The Journal of Modern History* 18, no. 1 (March 1, 1946): 37–47.

56. See for example Alan J. Rice and Martin Crawford, eds, *Liberating Sojourn: Frederick Douglass and Transatlantic Reform* (Athens: University of Georgia Press, 1999).

Chapter 2

Paris, Philadelphia, and the Question of the Nineteenth-Century City

Andrew Heath

In 1870, the *Penn Monthly*—a journal the Philadelphia Social Science Association soon adopted as its official organ—carried two letters from a US native in the capital of Second Empire France. "Paris, with American eyes" explained how Imperial power had rebuilt the city after Louis Napoleon's coup in 1851. The correspondent guided his audience down the fashionable promenades, but he urged readers to look beyond the radial avenues and understand the city's social as well as spatial reconstruction. His analysis roamed widely, touching on religion, labor, and temperance, but he saw in the Second Empire a systematic approach to urban reconstruction that had brought France prosperity "beyond conception." Debt-financing, public works, and command over space had turned a viper's nest of insurrectionists into one of the most beautiful and wealthy cities in the world. Revolutionaries, he argued, had dwindled in number to a few hundred; republican critics to a few thousand, as "love and reverence" for the Emperor "predominate." Leading his readers from questions of state security to urban improvement, he arrived at a striking conclusion. Baron Haussmann's wide streets, he claimed, "show how completely the question of building the city of the nineteenth century has been met—how nearly it has been solved."[1]

The writer appreciated how heretical his doctrines must have sounded to an audience reared on republicanism. "The American visitor leaves his home with preconceived ideas of both men and things outside of the Republic," he warned "and in nine cases out of ten he brings back with him the same opinions." Second Empire France to these visitors seemed little more than a despotism of church and state. His attempt, as he put it, to "unsettle the mind of the American as to all he is to expect to see in Paris," was, as he well understood, not easy in the era.[2] The Old World, Daniel T. Rodgers argues in *Atlantic Crossings*, seemed to Americans before the 1870s the antithesis of New World liberty. With "the republican understanding of America" depending "utterly on its contrast with an imagined Europe," citizens in the United States found themselves happily marooned on "an island of world historical immunities," and had little reason to heed developments elsewhere. Only when Gilded Age class conflict and mass urbanization "formed a world of common referents" did policymakers become "peculiarly open to foreign models." The plea in the *Penn Monthly* for Americans to "admit our deficiencies" and draw lessons from abroad might be seen in this regard as an unlikely early example of transatlantic borrowing.[3]

The *Penn Monthly*'s correspondent, though, may have overstated his readers' exceptionalist convictions, for since the work of reconstruction commenced in 1853, American city builders paid close attention to the experiment underway in Paris, using it to evaluate the merits of activist government in their own urban centers. They did so because the question of building the city of the nineteenth century long predated the Gilded Age. The coincidence of riots and strikes in the 1830s and 1840s, coupled with growing inequality, undermined faith in the exceptional course of the American city, and led radicals and conservatives to look elsewhere. The two letters in the *Penn Monthly* were not so much an abortive beginning of the "transatlantic moment" as the continuation of an ongoing debate over the legacy of both the Second Republic (1848–1852) and the Second Empire (1852–1870).

Historians who have explored the impact of French urbanism in the US have tended to focus on later periods. Alan Lessoff and Howard Gillette have shown how, in an atmosphere of heightened nationalism, Washington DC's postbellum-era boosters turned to heavy borrowing and authoritarian government to rebuild the nation's capital. The head of the Metropolitan Board of Works, Alexander Shepherd, emerges in this literature as Haussmann's closest American cousin prior to the planners of the City Beautiful Movement of the early twentieth century. In domesticating the Second Empire, Lessoff argues though, Americans misunderstood it, for where imperial urbanism ultimately aimed to buttress the authority of the state, the US urban tradition viewed activist government as the handmaiden of private interests.[4] Few historians have examined the debates Second Empire city building provoked in the heyday of local boosterism, which in northeastern cities extended up to the Civil War. David

Scobey's *Empire City*, which explores bourgeois New Yorkers' search for "an American Haussmann," marks a rare exception, showing how elements of Bonapartist politics shaped urban ambitions.[5] Interest in Paris may be unremarkable in relation to Washington, the Union's capital and biggest city; the French capital's relevance to city building in Civil War-era Philadelphia, however, is perhaps more surprising. The most influential study of the midcentury metropolis, Sam Bass Warner's *The Private City*, portrays a parochial civic culture marred by a myopic commitment to an individualist ethic.[6] As a portrait of nineteenth-century urbanism, Warner's interpretation has proved enduring: Rodgers's depiction of the American metropolis prior to the Gilded Age borrows heavily on Warner's concept of "privatism", a synonym, its coiner later conceded, for a capitalism hostile to community endeavor.[7] But contrasts between prewar privatism and Progressive era municipalization can be overdrawn. We now know, for instance, that the nineteenth-century city was a highly regulated environment in which governments willingly exercised their police power to regulate for the common good.[8] In Civil War-era Philadelphia, indeed, the reconstruction of Paris between 1848 and 1870 offered a set of lessons for thinking through what Rodgers, writing of the Progressive Era, calls "the clash between private property rights and public needs."[9]

That struggle was also about the nature of democracy. The postwar retreat in North as well as South from an expansive commitment to democratic rights is so well documented that it is hard to believe it had no antebellum antecedents. Historians indeed have located lingering suspicions of popular sovereignty in Whig thought into the 1850s and cast the Nativist movement as a back-door route to suffrage restriction.[10] We should not be surprised, then, when some Philadelphians expressed their admiration for elements of Napoleon III's authoritarian system, or their horror at the "social republic" of 1848: a form of government that had many radical admirers in the United States. The Emperor's apparent ability to master men as well as the metropolis could make him an attractive, if divisive, figure.

The Urban Frontier of American Exceptionalism

By the 1840s, US citizens eagerly followed developments in other "great cities." Mayor Alexander Henry in Philadelphia fielded correspondence from Europe about aspects of Philadelphia's local government.[11] Fact-finding missions, though far less frequent than in the Progressive Era, were not unheard of either, as citizens ventured abroad to explore, for example, gas lighting and park design.[12] More Americans, however, learned about goings-on across the Atlantic through journalism and travel writing: the bigger dailies carried front-page letters from Paris and London, and if the news tended to focus on political and diplomatic developments, correspondents often delved into urban affairs. Papers in Philadelphia soon took for granted readers' knowledge of the reconstruction work in Paris, whereas cosmopolitan radicals followed European developments in clubs and newspapers of their own. The brokers of urban planning then were not the credentialed social scientific experts of the Progressive Era, but politicians, journalists, travelers, and political exiles who either observed European urban reform at first hand or translated others' understanding of it for an American audience.

By the mid-1840s, most agreed that American "great cities" bore an ever-increasing resemblance to their European counterparts. Though the metropolitan centers of the New World still lagged behind London and Paris in sheer size, the extraordinary rate of their growth suggested they would soon catch up. The pull of commerce and industry and the push of the Irish famine swelled New York's population by 200,000 over the 1840s. Philadelphia county grew by 150,000. With growth came disorder. In 1828, 1834, 1836, 1838, 1842, 1843, 1844 (twice), and 1849 riots ravaged Philadelphia.[13] Leaders of crowd violence tended to see themselves as conservatives rather than revolutionaries, targeting the out-groups who posed a threat to the moral order of the community. Abolitionists, African-Americans, and Catholics were each on the receiving end of the mob's ire. Into the 1830s, "gentlemen of property and standing" sometimes joined the fray, but collateral damage to property and the state hardened bourgeois hostility to mobs, and in 1844, after a summer in which Nativists torched churches and homes and engaged in an artillery duel with state militiamen, many of the city's leading citizens vindicated the decision of the militia captain to fire on the crowd.[14] Critics, on the other hand, compared the transformation of the metropolis into a garrison town to European despotism. Philadelphia, one put it, had become "St. Petersburg," and by turning military force on the crowd, the city government would meet the fate of Charles X in 1830. In France, he warned, "they have fired upon the mob, till they have so accustomed them to the whistling of bullets, that in Paris, they are as bold and sometimes as good soldiers as the king's troops."[15]

The comparisons to Paris seemed apt in the 1840s, for as Philadelphia grew, it looked less and less American. In the decade that followed the riots, citizens began to plot the society and space of the

European city onto their own urban form. Comparisons abounded between American urban violence and the French Revolution.[16] Like the Parisian mob of 1792, the argument went, Philadelphia's rioters sprung from inscrutable suburbs. Moreover, they were often Irish Catholics, who, ethnologists insisted, were from the same tempestuous branch of the Celtic race as Parisians. Inhabitants of courts and alleys became the "canaille," riots "emeutes," and radical workingmen "red republicans."[17] Morton McMichael's *North American* especially recognized the political capital to be gained from comparing New and Old World cities: superimposing the social relations of one on the other provided a powerful impetus for state intervention. Surveying the "purlieus of Philadelphia," his paper declared that "all great cities" contain a *"canaille"* who, in Paris, had "always been the most formidable body in the revolutions of which that city has been the scene." Without the "most strenuous exertions to alleviate" their "necessities," the paper concluded, "they will—they must—make the orderly portion of society their prey."[18] Others went beyond identifying un-American people and places in the city to generalize about transatlantic similarities more broadly. After a summer of violence in 1849, for instance, one of the paper's correspondents—who would go on to become a gushing admirer of the Second Empire—insisted "The American and French people have many characteristics in common." Each were "armed, brave, impulsive, and disposed to offer forcible resistance to real or fancied wrongs." The United States was "free from the crushing burthens" of "crowded populations," but civil authorities in the New World lacked "the means of military resistance in popular insurrection." A riot could escalate into a rebellion, he suggested, without a strong police to nip it in the bud.[19]

Even critics who questioned the parallels drawn between European and US cities accepted the merits of the comparative method. "In this roomy land of ours," wrote one Philadelphian after 1844, no "mob proper" existed; those who thought it did were mistranslating a European "text" in a New World context.[20] In 1851, the *Public Ledger* contrasted European riots with troubles in Philadelphia, and concluded that whereas "class" lay behind the former, the latter had never owed to "social differences of condition." Yet even the *Ledger* could not say the same for New York: a metropolis Philadelphians assailed for its glaring economic divisions, its burgeoning immigrant population, and its impudence in claiming the mantle of Empire City. There, "insolent pretension and brutal envy" led to "terrible and bloody riots."[21] Tentatively, then, bourgeois Philadelphians began to map their nation's urban frontier with concepts and categories borrowed from Europe.

Radical social critics of the midcentury city did not mind the comparisons. For Philadelphia's socialists, reformers, and militant journeymen, the riots of 1844 were a catastrophe, fracturing bonds of solidarity forged in the flush times of the mid-1830s. Yet from the ashes they began to rebuild. Just before midcentury, craft unions, land reform clubs, Fourierist associations, and a host of other organizations with overlapping memberships flourished in the city's lyceums, while a revolutionary newspaper, the popular novelist George Lippard's *Quaker City*, circulated widely. Although they were hardly the *canaille* bourgeois reporters had in mind, radicals happily raised the banner of French "Red Republicanism." Leaders like Lippard and the Irish Chartist emigrant John Campbell offered fulsome praise to the regicides of 1793. All the terrorists wanted, Campbell argued, was to ensure producers received the full value of their toil. Lippard urged the "Workers of the World" to unite against a transatlantic bourgeoisie who lived off producers' labor. The current of internationalism reflected radicals' conviction that the obstacles they faced were not uniquely American. The *Quaker City*, for instance, called poverty a "pestilence," which, having "ravaged the old world," had now "crossed the ocean" to New York and Philadelphia.[22]

Radicals helped open a conceptual space for discussion of the social. Philip Ethington's study of political culture in San Francisco charts the transformation over the course of the Civil War decades from a "political conception of society" to a "social conception of politics." Others have noted the shift in a similar period from a "socioconstitutional" to "socioeconomic" language of class.[23] Such movements closely parallel the decline of republicanism and the rise of liberalism. A good republican knew that inequality owed to bad laws and bad men. A good liberal, in contrast, understood that politics pitted rival interests against one another. The postwar science of society tried to understand those interests rather than sniffing out, as the antebellum American might have done, the stench of political corruption.[24] In the 1840s and 1850s, though, advocates of republican and liberal frameworks jostled with one another. Exceptionalists followed the *Ledger*'s line by arguing that class conflict was a foreign problem, or read European revolt as American-made remedies for diseased body politics. Radicals, though drawing inspiration from the Founding Fathers, had less time for purely political explanations. They pointed to the material foundations not just of Old World revolutions (the downfall of Louis Phillippe, Lippard claimed, owed to "eighteen years of social, more than constitutional, evil") but also of the inequality engrafted into the built environment of American cities.[25] Producers' dead labor found real form in the "palaces" and "mansions" of the bourgeois city, they insisted, while high rents confined living labor to "some dirty, narrow court, lane, or alley." Radicals rarely prescribed purely political solutions to the problems the metropolis encountered, reasoning instead from a structural analysis of society: "The world is now divided between two antagonistic powers," wrote a "Mechanic" in a journal edited by a former leader of the citywide General Trades' Union: "the power of capital and the power of labor."[26]

The social resemblance radicals noticed between European and American cities enabled transatlantic borrowing a generation before Rodgers's Progressive reformers. In 1848, after the downfall of the July Monarchy, French liberals formed a precarious alliance with Paris's working class. As the junior partner in a revolutionary coalition, the capital's craftsmen and laborers were able to extract concessions from the Second Republic, not least of which was the establishment of National Workshops. From February, the Ministry of Public Work organized the ranks of unemployed into labor brigades, and by June, more than 100,000 Parisians—about half the city's male working class—had enrolled. The policy offered little satisfaction to any party. Moderate republicans resented the cost of what was tantamount to a public dole; workers complained about the pitiful wages they received. When conservatives closed the workshops in June, however, the unemployed resorted to the barricades. After three days of bloody fighting, followed by a wave of arrests and summary executions, the government defeated the insurrectionists. But the rise and fall of the National Workshops illustrates, as David Harvey puts it, how the "question of work lay at the heart of the Parisian workers' movement of 1848."[27] The same could be said for radicals in the United States, who shared their French counterparts' conviction that labor was the source of all value.

The Second Republic's labor policy provided US radicals with a model for the social reconstruction of their own republic. Philadelphia's workingmen had called for make-work schemes after the Panic of 1837, and in the lean years that followed reformers often looked to growth politics for salvation. The future Radical Republican William D. Kelley, for instance, began to lobby for construction of a federally funded Pacific Railroad, whereas Edward A. Penniman, like Kelley an erstwhile craft unionist, backed local railroad-building schemes as a means to absorb surplus labor.[28] But where these projects rested on the use of the state as a stimulus to private enterprise, others advocated more radical projects. The Irish Chartist Campbell, who had come to the United States from Manchester as a political refugee after the failure of a general strike in 1842, advocated the socialization of private property just as news of the French Revolution arrived in the United States. "The nation must become the employer as well as it has become the landholder, and the banker," he argued in calling for the creation of national workshops. In state-owned enterprises, workers would deposit "all kinds of goods," and receive in exchange notes equivalent to the full value of their toil. Campbell dedicated his *Theory of Equality* to the leaders of the Provisional Government in Paris.[29]

The most systematic attempt to translate the Second Republic's social policy for an American audience, though, came in Thomas Dunn English and George G. Foster's hastily compiled *French Revolution of 1848*, which appeared in April, soon after news of the monarchy's fall reached the United States.[30] Despite serving as city editor on McMichael's conservative *North American*, Foster embraced utopian socialism in the late 1840s, and portrayed Philadelphia's "bourgeoisie" and "proletaries" in his sketch journalism. He later compared his writing on cities to the work of Henry Mayhew in London, but his take on the Second Republic indicates his debt to French socialism as well as British reform. English and Foster read the 1848 Revolution as the culmination of a historical conflict between idle capitalists and productive workers. "Capital arrayed itself against labor," the authors argued, until the "working class...in this final struggle...emancipated itself from the chains of the bourgeoisie." If the French Revolution had social origins, then, it also had social consequences, and here the National Workshops stood as exemplars. The Second Republic's founding promise to guarantee work marked "a new and momentous principle." "These are the most important and pregnant lines ever published by a government to a people," English and Foster declared. In their chapter on the "The Labor Question," they doubted that the "new state of things in France" would receive a fair hearing in the bourgeois American press, but they tried to address the misinformation by giving over several pages to Louis Blanc's design for state-funded cooperatives. In the "pledge of work and existence to the laborer," the Provisional Government had expressed "the hopes, the aspirations, the destiny of the age." "Behold the problem of the Nineteenth Century!" the authors exclaimed.[31]

In raising the cry for social as well as political democracy, Philadelphia's radicals upended bourgeois readings of the 1848 Revolutions. Rather than Europe embracing American republicanism, they insisted, the United States needed to learn from Europe. As English and Foster put it:

> Instead of the cruel, cold-blooded dogma that "the world is governed too much," which leaves labor helpless and weaponless to struggle and die beneath the grasping pressure of capital and combination, the new government of France boldly inculcates the warmer and more hopeful truth – "the world is wrongly governed."

The state, they argued, had an obligation to protect citizens "not only in their barren and theoretical political rights, but also in their right to labor and reward, as the means of life." The French, by acknowledging *laissez-faire* was a thin euphemism for class power, had proved more willing than Americans to admit government was not "some dangerous monster whose claws it is necessary to keep well trimmed."[32]

There would be no Second American Republic in 1848 but the legacy of cosmopolitan social politics of that year is easy to underestimate. Lippard, Campbell, and other radical leaders forced Philadelphia's economic elite onto the defensive. At a vast meeting on Independence Square to celebrate the overthrow of Europe's crowned heads, wealthy Whigs and Democrats found themselves vying for the stage with socialists and reformers who assailed the regulation of wages through supply and demand and lauded the principle of "associated labor." The officers retaliated by striking any endorsement of "fraternity" from the meeting's resolutions, only for abolitionists and radical reformers to organize another gathering in protest a few weeks later. The end of slavery in France's colonies, universal suffrage, "and the earnestly endeavored organization of industry," the second meeting agreed, "reveals the sentiment of our own Revolution in all its deep significance."[33] Attempts to Americanize the social meaning of 1848 could not go unchallenged. The *North American*, whose owner, McMichael, had spoken at the initial gathering on Independence Square, questioned English and Foster's "fiery, Fourierish" account of affairs in France, and complained that "the bourgeoisie appears as a kind of monster whom they berate, and buffer, and torment," despite the class in "all countries" having "great respect for the rights of property." Others fought back against the "stupendous idea" of government as the "sole employer." In the violence of the June Days, conservative opinion sided firmly with the state, and blamed socialists for the bloodshed. But even critics of the "social republic" agreed that "the emancipation of labor is the great question which claims the attention of the philanthrophists and statesmen of this age."[34] Here, the labor question arrived in the United States with the 1848 Revolutions, well before the Paris Commune.

These early lessons of Paris led Philadelphia's economic elite to pay careful heed to socialist movements. They did so despite the ebbing of the radical tide. As a freshet of reaction washed over Europe, the millenarian promise of 1848 gave way to disillusionment. William Elder, who had welcomed the downfall of the Orleanist monarchy and urged reform in the United States as "men must choose between that and revolution," admitted his "ardent hopes" had been "disappointed," after "the model nation of the world" voted a Bonaparte into office. The other labor question—whether the Union could endure half-free and half-slave—split white reformers into sectional camps, with Campbell and his followers taking an ultra-proslavery stance.[35] Meanwhile, the influx of gold from California after 1849 spurred an economic boom that, for a time at least, brought close to full employment without a visible state stimulus. Even as the radical threat receded, however, the iron manufacturer Stephen Colwell called socialism "one of the greatest events of the age," and urged citizens to acquaint themselves with its teachings and "watch its movements." Colwell, who read widely in European political economy, saw socialism as a misguided but understandable response to the misdeeds of church and state.[36] Addressing his lengthy polemic to American Protestants, he prescribed Christian charity as an antidote, but his concerns about a turbulent working class almost certainly fed into his support for strengthening city government in the 1850s.

Drawing on what Martin Burke calls the rhetoric of "reconcilable class conflict," radicals argued that revolution would come to American cities too if the state failed to address the social rights of labor.[37] Either side of midcentury, as the "great cities" of the New World began to look ever more like their counterparts on the other side of the Atlantic, their prophecy acquired a measure of plausibility. Bourgeois papers like the *North American* had little difficulty in seeing Chartists, Red Republicans, and Jacobins running amok in the warren of streets and alleys that ran behind the straight lines of Philadelphia's gridiron. The city's real socialists, they feared, might stir up class envy and direct the crowd's ire against the rich. In future, it might not be the abolitionists, blacks, or Catholics that the mob turned on, but—egged on by radical demagogues—property itself. The 1848 Revolutions therefore did not reinforce American exceptionalism.[38] Rather they suggested that the world's great metropolitan centers obeyed similar laws of cause and effect.

Paris and the Panic of 1857

The Panic of 1857 gave Philadelphians the opportunity to apply lessons from Paris in 1848 to their own city. With thousands thrown out of work by the slump, bourgeois Philadelphians braced themselves for a recurrence of the urban crises of the 1840s. One citizen, fearing "popular tumult," expected vigilance committees or martial law would be required to maintain the peace, whereas John C. Bullitt, who went on to a career as a postwar municipal reformer, anticipated "robberies, riots and crimes of all kinds." McMichael too warned of the "terrors that must follow" if the crisis was not met by quick government action. But the traditional response to hard times lay in retrenchment, and within weeks, the City Councils, struggling to honor their own warrants, called for austerity. Though critics warned such measures would create "a panic among the laboring men" they found themselves a small minority.[39]

Workingmen, in contrast, demanded the expansion of government spending. At a series of mass meetings, foreign and native-born laborers asked for the "immediate employment of those out of work by the civic, State, and Federal authorities." Calls for new parks, bridges, and streets soon followed. By November, citizens were petitioning the municipal authorities to issue $4m in small notes as a legal currency. This idea, which some councilmen had already raised while municipal warrants floated at a heavy discount as emergency paper, caught on. A committee of unemployed told the Mayor "We will loan our labor—and our labor is capital—if you will assure us that the scrip of this city…will be taken for…necessaries of life." Later in the month, the *North American* reported, the leaders of the movement were asking local government to borrow $50m for "improving property in the precincts of this great city." This figure was about three times the existing funded debt, and would have paved the way for reconstruction on a Haussmannesque scale. In actuality, though, the amount was probably a misprint—$5m, cited elsewhere, seems far more probable—but the support the proposal won indicates that the radicals embrace of an activist state in 1848 lived on almost nine years later.[40]

Leaders of the unemployed movement in 1857 did not refer directly to the National Workshops of the Second Republic but the shadow of 1848 hung over the debate. The early 1850s saw a changing of the guard in radical leadership. Campbell's proslavery apostasy isolated him from radical circles whereas Lippard died in 1854. Many of the leaders of the unemployed movement, however, had cut their teeth in

the labor conflicts of midcentury, and would almost certainly have
been familiar with the rise and fall of French make-work schemes.
They sensibly couched their appeals to the city government in senti-
mental homilies about the sanctity of family life and their duties as
men to provide for their dependents, leaving the threat of violence
to speakers at the mass meetings, but their proposals suggest a keen
appreciation of the possibilities of urban political economy. The call
for securing public debt through labor, for instance, bore echoes of
the radical producerism in Campbell's *Theory of Equality*, yet held
appeal to city builders eager to erect an imperious urban form. Such
demands, however, fell on deaf ears. Just as Gilded Age conservatives tried to undermine strikes by raising the specter of the Paris
Commune, bourgeois Philadelphians rarely missed an opportunity to
compare the unemployed movement of 1857 to the Parisian crowd of
1848. The press condemned "worn out French barricade Passwords"
and "Red Republican agrarian doctrines." "To open public workshops
as in Paris on the public credit," one paper warned, "would only end
as these have done, in universal anarchy, fraud, and the destruction of
the public credit." Reporting on one of the meetings in Philadelphia,
the *New York Times* came to the conclusion that the "communism"
of the "the barricades of Paris" had crossed the Atlantic.[41]

When executive power held out hope to the unemployed, though,
the Second Empire rather than the Second Republic seemed to offer
a more fitting analogy. Under Haussmann's direction between 1853
and 1869, the state cut wide boulevards through old neighborhoods,
tightly regulated new construction to ensure architectural harmony,
and gave the city a new infrastructure of water, sewerage, and gas.
"Old, narrow streets disappear," reported a conservative New York
paper in 1854, and new spacious and elegant avenues take their
place."[42] Radicals, having witnessed Louis Napoleon's dismember-
ment of republican government, had little sympathy for the Emperor's
designs and no faith in his plebiscites.[43] Still, the reconstruction generated jobs, and in New York during the Panic, Mayor Fernando Wood
supported demands from the unemployed for a program of public
works, which included the construction of model housing. Hitherto
regarded as one of the "best men," Wood was not forgiven for his
treacherous course by wealthy New Yorkers, who soon abandoned
him at the polls.[44] Philadelphia's chief magistrate, Richard Vaux—
like Wood a "gentleman Democrat"—had also made sympathetic
noises to workingmen. Both figures came under suspicion as "demagogues," and after Vaux vetoed Councils' nonbinding austerity reso-
lution one of the members accused him of "acting Napoleon the III"

by "pandering to a feeling which existed among certain classes of our people, that the Government must furnish them with bread."[45]

In 1857, then, critics of the unemployed movement searched for indigenous alternatives to a program that reeked of Paris. The *Press*, a conservative Democratic journal, warned that providing work to the "dangerous classes" mirrored the wayward course of the Emperor. Instead of "forced employment" in cities, it argued, workers in New York and Philadelphia ought to pursue a course of "voluntary emigration." Before the closing of the National Workshops, the Provisional Government toyed with a program of dispersing the Parisian poor through military enlistment, agricultural colonies, and railroad building, but in 1857, the frequent calls for outmigration offered a distinct American solution to over-concentration, via the safety valve of western land. As a social policy, indeed, the dispersal of population out of the "great cities" had a long history in the United States, and stood in stark contrast to the program of French metropolitan centralization. The course of revolution and reaction after 1848, though, strengthened conviction in the principle. Paris's capacity to dictate to France—which McMichael's paper in the days of the Second Republic had compared to absolute monarchy—troubled citizens. But rather than scattering the dangerous classes across his empire, Napoleon III's city building drew laborers to the capital. By 1859, the *North American* observed how "A vast army of *ouvriers* has girdled itself around the whole of Paris, altogether, or in a great measure, dependent for their employment and daily bread upon the public works of the capital." Once the reconstructions stopped the Empire would find it had brought into being its own gravediggers.[46]

The common distinction between French centralization and American dispersal comforted exceptionalists in the 1850s and 1860s. But the response to the unemployed movements of 1857 indicated that bourgeois Americans were already struggling to reconcile a powerful state with an expansive commitment to democratic rights. Paris under both republic and empire served as a warning of what would happen when the masses ran amok. Even before the financial crash, indeed, the *North American* recommended disfranchising Pennsylvania's dependent poor on the grounds that "some future Louis Napoleon may induce paupers, with bread, to force a perpetual despot upon a nation, poisoned at the root by poverty, vice and idleness. "Present elections," it reminded readers, "are actually controlled by the corruption of a caste who have no higher views than their own interests."[47] Read in this light, the objection to the proposals of the unemployed rested less on the policy itself—indeed McMichael and others suggested some make-work programs of their own in 1857—and more on who proposed it. Under the control of "best men," strong government was fine, but if elite control could not be guaranteed, it was better to rein in what the state could do.

This question of who controlled whom in Paris framed bourgeois responses in the United States to the city's reconstruction. But the answer was by no means obvious. At the height of the Panic the conservative diarist Sidney George Fisher received a letter from his cousin in Paris. Fisher's relative noted the "unparalleled magnificence" of the improvements underway in the city, but reminded him that they offered the capital "defence and security" as well as "ornament." Paris "can never again be controlled by a mob," Fisher wrote, and "order is perfect for the time." Fisher's own views on Bonapartism seesawed. Incapable of conceding to the French the capacity for self-government, he saw empire as almost inevitable, but with his preference for the mixed government of constitutional monarchy, he attacked the "despot" and "tyrant" who sat on the throne. Still, France for him, like much of monarchical Europe, was "ably governed" by rulers who represented "educated opinion; social amelioration, industrial progress, the arts of peace," and "the well being and happiness of the masses." Here the Old World, where "wise and prudent measures" soothed fears of "civil discord," presented a chastening contrast to the New, in which "just fears of revolution and national destruction are from time to time excited." "I think we are likely to prove, instead of an alluring example, a beacon to warn other nations against the evils of democracy," Fisher concluded in 1857.[48] Like radical calls for a Second American Republic, Fisher inverted the familiar juxtaposition of New World progress and Old World decadence, though this time for antidemocratic ends. From 1852 to 1869 others from his class would follow him, reading Napoleon III and the transformation of Paris not as a mirror of Wood and Vaux's demagoguery, but rather as a modern program of social reconstruction imposed from the top down. The lessons drawn from Paris in this regard were very different from the socialist reading of 1848 or conservative fears of an ascendant mob in 1857.

"Paris of America"

The possibility that Napoleon III was not a creature of the crowd but its master made the Second Empire far more palatable to bourgeois northern conservatives. Some wealthy citizens certainly offered fawning praise for imperial government. One Philadelphian, who had previously noted the similarities between the French and American people, called for an armed police under the head of one man, and advocated the centralization of municipal power, argued from Paris just weeks before the firing on Fort Sumter that Napoleon III ruled "with a strong hand, but with consummate ability." Over the previous years, the emperor had been "astonishing the world with the power and wisdom of his rule," and had elevated France in "wealth, power and grandeur." Observing the man himself at close quarters at the theater, the correspondent traced the contours of a large, well-developed head "with an overwhelming mass of brain in the frontal or intellectual region." "If I had not known who it was," he wrote, "I am sure I should have looked upon him as a man of genius." "You may think, by my high encomiums, that I have fallen in love with the man and his system," he told his republican audience, but while he considered Bonapartism ideal for France, he did not want a similar regime in the United States, "excepting for the seceding part."[49] That caveat was telling. For what might be read as a fantasy of dictatorship in a moment of national emergency provided a revealing insight into why Second Empire urban policy intrigued the Civil War-era bourgeoisie. In the un-American spaces of their own cities, they argued, despotic power might be necessary to bring about not just physical but also a social and political reconstruction. Just as Republicans began to toy with the extension of Federal power to regenerate the South—measures their critics charged smacked of Bonapartism—urban reformers imagined a similar use of municipal power to regenerate the city.[50] Ultimately, they recognized that Haussmann's methods were too much at odds with traditions of limited government to employ on a grand scale, but they continually used the rebuilding of Paris as a template for their metropolitan design.

Napoleon III's success, his admirers insisted, owed to his elevated perch above the fray of democratic politics. Reading their own desires into the reconstruction of Paris they cast Haussmann as an enlightened expert sheltered from the passions and prejudices of an ignorant electorate. Outside moments of crisis like the Panic of 1857, indeed, his administration seemed to offer a model for the kind of commission government that would become an increasingly common feature of US cities in the Gilded Age and Progressive Era. Frustrated by the perceived failings of their own municipal governments, and eager to blame myopic partisan politicians and the voters who sustained them at the polls, they looked enviously across the Atlantic. "The French government desires to place, in the direction of its affairs, men who will see for themselves," McMichael's *North American* argued, while the United States thrusts "high incompetents" into office. *The Philadelphia Inquirer*, meanwhile, praised the "perfection" of Paris's "municipal system," which had supposedly made corruption all but impossible by giving the reins of power to the best men: "The Municipal Council is composed of sixty gentlemen, appointed by the Emperor himself, from the mercantile ranks, and every member is a man of the highest personal character." When McMichael served a term as postwar mayor he confided to a friend that the "admirable management," "excellent police," "perfect pavements," and "general order and security" he had observed in Europe far surpassed anything Philadelphia's government could achieve. Bourgeois reformers saw themselves in Haussmann and longed for a measure of his power.[51]

In Philadelphia, the transformation of Paris bolstered the case for strengthening executive authority over the society and space of the city. Bourgeois Philadelphians yearned for what David Scobey has called a "heroic" city builder even before Haussmann's appointment.[52] "Oh that we had among our prominent citizens, and especially among our Councilmen, *one* that had the prescience to see our future, and the philanthropy and nerve requisite to do battle for its right direction," wrote a citizen in 1852.[53] News of the rebuilding underway in France bolstered the case for interventionist government. In November 1853, McMichael's paper juxtaposed the "magnificent works" in the French capital to the "small ideas" prevalent in the United States, and expressed the wish "some of the energetic spirit of enterprise and progress displayed in the works of Louis Napoleon...could be infused into our citizens and our municipal councils." Two months later it asked for a "comprehensive arrangement for the improvement of the suburbs" under an "enlightened" civil engineer.[54] Over the course of that period, McMichael led a committee of merchants, manufacturers, and professionals charged with the responsibility of drawing up a new city charter, and although the impact of Haussmann's work on its labors is necessarily conjectural, it is striking how what was originally intended as an extension of police coverage over inner suburbs became in the space of a few months a more ambitious reform, annexing the entire county, creating a Board of Surveys, and giving the municipal authorities the responsibility of providing parks and public space. McMichael certainly believed the Consolidation Act, as it became known, would enhance the power of the mayor and grant government the money and power to widen streets, plan suburban extensions, and bring order to turbulent faubourgs. Haussmann did much the same when he extended the borders of Paris a few years later.[55]

But advocates of stronger municipal government in the United States, Lessoff argues, ultimately saw the state as the servant of private interests rather than their master.[56] Certainly the Second Empire's American admirers sometimes read Napoleon III as a Gallic incarnation of Henry Clay. The *North American*, Philadelphia's most enthusiastic exponent of debt-financing city—and railroad building, reprinted the Emperor's claim that the improvements to Second Empire Paris would bear a "productive result," in contrast to the supposedly useless make-work schemes of the Second Republic.[57] State-supported growth politics did provide one solution to the high unemployment of the 1840s, and it might not be surprising, that several Philadelphians who had either embraced or engaged with socialist ideas around mid-century—notably William Elder, Stephen Colwell, and William D. Kelley—gravitated to the boosterish political economist Henry Carey. Carey and his followers, though fierce critics of French centralization, admired Bonapartist economic nationalism, which they saw as a way to harmonize the interests of labor and capital.[58] McMichael's paper became a mouthpiece for their political economic vision, but added a spatial dimension by urging the transformation of Philadelphia into the Paris of America. In 1860, it concluded that Bonapartist urbanism—in its amalgam of reform, expansion, and reconstruction—was "the way to advance a town." "Let the expenditures be within the city's visible means of immediate, or at least, prospective payment," it argued, and a metropolis could be made "accessible, convenient, orderly, healthy, and in every way attractive."[59]

For those who looked to the Second Empire for inspiration, indeed, Haussmann's debt-financed reconstruction offered a way to bring dynamism, order, and beauty to cities. Under what Scobey calls elite "stewardship," a good plan promised to resolve the contradictions of growth, by enabling rapid expansion without the social and spatial crises that had menaced Philadelphia in the 1840s.[60] The retrofitting of Paris provided an instructive model. "That great metropolis," one postwar planner argued, "originally built at hap-hazard, without any plan, a complicated and confused network of narrow, tortuous, and obstructed streets, has been rendered not only the most elegant but the most convenient city in the world, a triumph of engineering and art." No one seriously countenanced the transformation of any American urban center on such a scale. "Paris, with the vast revenues of a wealthy and powerful empire at command, and used despotically at the behest of a single man," McMichael's paper conceded, "can of course achieve works to which the finances of a single city like Philadelphia must at present be unequal." Yet the gulf in political and financial capital between the two metropolises could not disguise common fears and wants.[61]

The civil wars raging on the streets of American cities either side of the Civil War provided an alarming contrast to Napoleon III's apparent success in subduing insurrection. Police reform and the extension of municipal authority over the suburbs brought a precarious peace to Philadelphia after midcentury, but anxiety about radicalism and riot lingered. Comparing US democracy to Louis Napoleon's coup, the *North American* called for Philadelphia's "Red Republicans" to be "put down" in 1852, though it proposed the ballot box rather than the bayonet as the weapon of counter-revolution. This might be dismissed as an attempt on the part of a Whig paper to tarnish its Democratic opponents as un-American, but in private too conservatives feared a resurgence of Old World street fighting on their side of the Atlantic. Doubts about exceptionalism resurfaced when draft resistors torched Manhattan in July 1863. The *Evening Bulletin*, applying the logic of the Second Republic in the June Days and the American Republic in 1861, advocated retribution: "What though a score or a hundred of the rioters should fall? The supremacy of the laws must be maintained at any sacrifice." Despite the profound differences between the racial pogrom that unfolded in New York and the revolutionary violence of Paris in 1848, conservatives saw each event as alarmingly similar, and having mapped US cities with the markers of class-riven Europe, it made sense for them to look to Second Empire France for possible solutions.[62]

Meanwhile Philadelphia's plan stood in need of radical overhaul. The gridironed streets may have looked much more orderly than the winding lanes of Medieval Paris, but their seventeenth-century dimensions left them similarly ill-suited to the demands of the nineteenth century. In the French capital, Napoleon III's new thoroughfares linked railroad termini to the business core, offering wide arteries for commerce and playgrounds for the bourgeoisie. Lacking, as one paper put it, a "Louis Napoleon who can order and execute the widening of the streets," Philadelphia's boosters turned to the two avenues on their plan, which already boasted Haussmanesque dimensions: Market and Broad. The former, running east to west from the Delaware to the Schuylkill and beyond, they envisaged as a channel for commerce, carrying the western trade of the Pennsylvania Railroad to waterfront warehouses; the latter, running north to south through the center of the old city proper, they pictured as a fashionable promenade, lined with stately mansions and bourgeois institutions. Both streets, though, defied expectations. Provision sheds, patronized by the city's working class, clung like an "incubus" to the eponymously named Market, whereas coal and lumber yards—drawn by cheap land and access to railroads—mocked Broad's pretensions as Philadelphia's Rue de Rivoli. Campaigners for the "improvement" of each avenue contrasted Haussmann's energy to American inaction, laughed at the idea of Napoleon III erecting market halls along his "far famed boulevards," and linked urban embellishment to national unity. "What would France be without Paris? What would Paris be without its boulevards?" asked one citizen at a meeting for the improvement of Broad Street soon after the Civil War. "Were the Baron in Philadelphia," an ardent admirer of the Second Empire said of Haussmann in 1868, "he would make short work of Broad street." Eventually, though, bourgeois schemes to augment merchant and cultural capital succeeded, with the municipal government authorizing loans to fund the removal of the provision sheds (1858) and the boulevarding of sections of Broad (1871).[63]

As social policy, however, the improvement of Market and Broad offered minimal benefits. Beyond the creation of a few patronage jobs in construction and the prospect of greater private investment and public revenue, most Philadelphians saw scant rewards. Critics, not without reason, attacked each scheme as a public subsidy for a privileged class. When opponents raised the cry against "mercantile aristocrats" and "boulevard people" they echoed critiques of urban inequality from the 1840s.[64] Yet advocates of state-led reconstruction in Philadelphia envisaged the social transformation of the city. Some reformers believed that authoritarian power acquired a measure of legitimacy when it was applied to Americanize the city's foreign spaces: the immigrant and working-class enclaves in which "Jacobins" and "Red Republicans" supposedly lurked. Calls for clearing "infected districts" of the city actually predated the Second Empire. The Anglo-American legal tradition gave government the power of eminent domain alongside the right to regulate for the common weal, so when the *Public Ledger* urged municipal authorities to buy up much of the property in riotous Moyamensing in 1847 and rebuild the suburb, the novelty lay in the scale of the proposal rather than the principle.[65] By 1867—the high watermark of support for a radical reconstruction of Philadelphia's urban space—the *Evening Star* suggested that "If the city would purchase the district from Fifth to Seventh and from Lombard to Fitzwater streets, and "reconstruct" it, the "health of the city would improve, the peace and quiet of the city would be promoted, the police force could be materially diminished, and no doubt the business of the city would increase." Such calls grew more common through the era: "Financially, it would pay the city or capitalists to buy up all the property in the neighborhood of this plague spot and destroy it entirely," the *Inquirer* wrote of the Bedford Street vicinity. By 1874, the Board of Health was pushing for the demolition of the same neighborhood, claiming the "public health demands the abandonment of these pest-spots."[66]

In calling for demolition and reconstruction of the city's borderlands, few invoked the example of the Second Empire. Where Haussmann cut new avenues through the old neighborhoods, consigning most of the old residents to the periphery, advocates of razing the likes of Bedford Street envisaged selling land acquired to reputable private developers. Although the *North American* briefly supported an improbable plan for a "new and magnificent system of diagonal avenues" stretching outwards from the intersection of Broad and Market, calls for demolition rarely went hand in hand with designs to override the grid.[67] Instead, rebuilding would widen narrow streets, condemn unsanitary housing, and if necessary remove undesirable people.

But Bonapartist urbanism almost certainly influenced advocates of urban reconstruction in the United States who came to see Paris as an experiment in social policy. Urban historians have tended to argue that causal links between environment and behavior were not drawn with any regularity until the 1890s. They have shown how the growing awareness from that decade onwards that grim surroundings led to a host of social problems provided an intellectual foundation for professional city planning. At midcentury, in contrast, a degraded built environment was more a symptom than a cause of moral wretchedness, and the route to uplift lay through the reformation of a neighborhood's inhabitants: either voluntarily, through evangelical reform, or coercively, via the power of new police forces. Work on park and cemetery design has challenged this periodization somewhat, and by the 1850s, the idea that the built environment exerted a determinative force in shaping character had gained ground.[68] Just as political corruption threatened republics, environmental corruption menaced physical and moral well-being. The miasmas that emanated from morbid spaces polluted body and mind, threatened social contagion, and ultimately ate away at the body politic. Take for instance the *North American.* "In common wretchedness and filth," it argued on the eve of the Panic of 1857, "human creatures forfeit their character as responsible and respectable beings." Eventually, these "outcasts naturally consider the decent and respectable as their enemies, and the property of the better classes as their fair prey." "The day of crowded and unhealthy courts and lanes is past," the paper hoped. The paper's depiction of a "Pariah race" inhabiting the "narrow and crowded purlieus of our towns" probably owed more to the English writer Mayhew than French social thought; its prescription—outward migration to a suburban frontier—localized the American reformer Horace Greeley's invocation to "Go West."[69] Yet the sense that environmental disorder spawned social and political threats spurred interest in Napoleon III's reconstruction. US critics decried the depraved luxury of the Second Empire, but many Americans believed the emperor had pacified the city through environmental uplift, and not just a large standing army.

The idea of Haussmann's Paris as a laboratory of reform proved surprisingly influential. For the *Penn Monthly*'s correspondent, "the squalid misery, the unclad or drunken women, child or man, the evidently idle and dissipated, always to be found somewhere in our American cities…are hidden from the closest inspector." Where he attributed this to Bonapartist political economy, a Midwesterner writing for the *New York Times* saw "the moral physiognomy of the city" as a product of physical reconstruction. Second Empire urbanism, he argued, compared favorably to the quixotic labors of American temperance reformers, whose moral suasion offered little without physical transformation. "A man will do in a narrow, dark and dirty street what he will not do in a wide, open clean street," he insisted, and thanks to Haussmann's rebuilding, "Paris is the cleanest, the healthiest, and the most moral-looking city in the world." Investigating the "renovation of cities," the *Public Ledger* reported that "whole nests and quarters where vileness and pollution reigned in their worst forms" have been "converted into palatial residences and streets of the greatest magnificence." To the paper, Napoleon III had "proved a model reformer to the world." Even critics conceded the environmental merits of Second Empire urbanism. The *Sunday Dispatch*, for instance, talked of the Prefect's designs for "moralizing and elevating" Paris's poor, observing how new streets encouraged cleanliness and temperance.[70]

Haussmann's admirers were not oblivious to the authoritarianism and cost of such designs but they agreed that a combination of hard and soft power had quashed the revolutionary fervor of the capital's population. On the eve of the New York Draft Riots, the *Press* praised an "astute and thoughtful" leader, noting how since he began his reign, there had "not been one *émeute* in Paris." In a city that, as another Philadelphian put it, had "made insurrection a science," this was no mean achievement. Under his administration, the most "fractious, turbulent and ungovernable people in the world" had channeled their riotous energies into commerce and manufactures.[71] Skeptics attributed the pacification of the Parisian crowd to the bread and circuses of imperial pageant, the opening of strategic ways for the massing of artillery, and the presence of a large standing army, but apologies for authoritarian government became more common through the 1850s.[72] The emperor "assumed power in the midst of anarchy," McMichael's paper argued, "and brought the ship of State safely into harbor." One Philadelphian, an ardent supporter of strengthening his own city's municipal government, admired how a "fierce, turbulent, and disorganized people" had been elevated under the guiding hand of a wise ruler.[73] Bourgeois reformers were already accustomed to seeing urban reconstruction as a way to safeguard the state. Eli Kirk Price, McMichael's chief ally in the movement for a new charter, had peered "into futurity" in 1851, reckoned with the interests of "one great community," and urged the municipal authorities to carefully plan suburban extensions. Doing so, he argued, would impress citizens "with the belief that their welfare is best cared for by those whom they elect to govern," enlist them "on the side of government, and "teach them to respect objects of ornament and taste." But after 1853 Second Empire Paris offered an example of such designs in action.[74]

   In an era of urban and national unrest in the United States, the apparent success of Haussmann's experiment was unlikely to go unnoticed. Social and sectional conflict undermined confidence in republican government well before the labor troubles of the Gilded Age. Just as radicals sometimes misread the intentions of the Second Republic, conservatives often misunderstood the principles and practices of Second Empire city building, but the likes of McMichael's *North American* outlined the contours of a systematic program that used credit and power to transform the built environment into an engine for capital accumulation and moral uplift. Rebuilding space became a means to reform society. Wherever markets or morals had failed—and wherever a supposedly barbarous poor appeared incapable of self-government—a strong state might intervene in the name of the public good. This may help explain why supporters of urban reconstruction were often among the strongest backers of the use of Federal government power in the South, and drew on similar environmentalist principles: once the state had swept away the miasmas of the plantation, they insisted, a new society would take root. That is not, however, to equate the democratic reforms of Radical Reconstruction with Bonapartism. As scholars have recently shown,

Napoleon III had more friends among southern Confederates than northern Republicans, but his use of consolidated power—most visibly in the reconstruction of Paris—provided a model for Americans contemplating the rebuilding of their own cities and nation.[75]

The Urban Retreat from Reconstruction

Surveying the public works underway in the city in 1871, the correspondent of the suburban *Germantown Telegraph* declared that "Haussmann must have emigrated to Philadelphia." Across the North, the preceding two decades were marked by innovation in municipal government. With one or two exceptions—the reclamation of Boston's Back Bay in the late 1850s, for instance, and Shepherd's postbellum improvements in Washington D.C.—few of these measures mimicked the grand manner of Napoleon III's Paris. Yet within a decade or so of Appomattox, Philadelphians could watch the erection of a vast City Hall in the Second Empire style, visit the immense grounds of Fairmount Park, and promenade along a boulevarded Broad Street. None of these measures came cheap, and municipal borrowing, already inflated by the need for defensive works and bounty funds of the Civil War, ballooned as a result. Between the consolidation of the city and county in 1854 and 1875, the funded debt increased from about $16m to $55m. For wary tax payers, comparisons to Paris could prove troubling given its association with Haussmann's "apocalypses of modern finance"; Paris was "wonderful and beautiful" the *Daily Age* had observed in 1864, "but at the same time very costly."[76]

Like the Panic of 1857, then, Reconstruction focused bourgeois attention on the political and financial risk of city building. Haussmann, whose powers had been reined in by angry real estate owners, was fired in 1869. The *Inquirer* found revelations of the extent of the Prefect's borrowing "absolutely startling," whereas other papers called him a "spoiled child" who had "used and abused Paris wholly according to his pleasure." Even the *North American*, which had so often lauded the work of the Second Empire, cooled in its admiration. Haussmann, it argued, ignored private rights and public convenience, rode roughshod over the city's past, and replaced a streetscape rich in historical association with "wearisome splendor," all through a "confused and outrageous system of financial management." The French capital had become "the Paris of aristocrats, who want to see nothing but luxury—not a capital of a nation, but the capital of a class." As in 1857, though, it was more common to see Napoleon III as a demagogue, an enlarged reflection of the political bosses whose power in American cities had grown commensurately with the extension of municipal power and democratic rights. Towards the end of the 1860s, bourgeois New Yorkers turned on William Tweed and his Tammany Hall machine, whereas bourgeois Philadelphians, frustrated with city and state Republicans, called for retrenchment. In this climate, the Bonapartist system looked less like a model of elite commission government, and more like boss rule run amok.[77]

When, in 1870, the *Penn Monthly*'s correspondent argued that Napoleon III had all but solved "the question of building the city of the nineteenth century," he was fighting a rearguard action, explaining a system of debt-financed municipal improvement that wealthy Americans feared their city governments had followed too closely over the preceding years. Soon after Haussmann's dismissal, the rapid collapse of the Second Empire in the Franco-Prussian War and the brief career of the Commune appeared to confirm prophesies that imperial government would prove short-lived. The naysayers who warned that the reconstruction of Paris had merely dispersed the revolutionary poor to the periphery saw the dispossessed reclaim the city.

The Commune renewed fears of radicalism in the New World, and as in the June Days, most of Philadelphia's bourgeois press supported the suppression of the "raving maniacs" who held the city from the newly proclaimed Third Republic. Under the banner of the "social republic," lawless men and woman had committed crimes against humanity, and "the world in general" would breathe a sigh of relief at the "good riddance of so much bad blood." Yet the Commune, a conservative paper argued, taught an "important lesson not only to France but to the world," by demonstrating the need to resist Communism. Without action, a minister in Philadelphia warned, "another Paris will be at our very doors." For a time, citizens consoled themselves that the Commune could not happen in their city at least, because Philadelphia was a "Paradise of Workingmen" in which employer and employee shared a harmony of interests. But such confidence hinged on permanent economic growth and municipal government extending improvements outward to working-class suburbs. Thus when the Panic of 1873 sent the city's economy into a tailspin that would last for much of the rest of the decade, the threat of disorder loomed large once more, and though Philadelphia largely escaped street fighting in the Great Strike of 1877, memories of France in 1871 shaped the bourgeois response. "Let us not borrow from the Frenchmen their fashions in politics," the *Evening Bulletin* wrote at the height of the unrest, "[b]ut if this railroad war is an American form of French communism, we may at least adopt the Paris fashion of knocking it in the head." A year later, a speaker at the American Philosophical Society offered advice on how to reclaim a city from a mob. "Some occasions have arisen in the recent past" when such actions were necessary, he told his audience, "and may occur in the future." The question of city building remained as alive in the Gilded Age as it had been in the 1840s but the argument had come full circle. Just as in the riots of 1844, citizens were turning to a militarized response.[78]

But in the decades that separated the violence of the Jacksonian city from the turbulent postbellum metropolis, the Second Republic and Second Empire offered alternatives that radicals and conservatives, though often skeptical of foreign models, tried to Americanize. In different ways the program of each placed collective needs ahead of individual interests: an enticing proposition in American cities in which many citizens had come to recognize the limits of privatism. Those who looked across the Atlantic to France had come to the conclusion that US urban centers, if not yet identical to their Old World counterparts, were tending towards the same course. Once that step had been made Paris became not just a stop on the grand tour or an un-republican Other, but a testing ground in the science of governance. The results, as the *North American* acknowledged in 1856, were not easy to predict. Napoleon III, it wrote then, had apparently found a "social policy" for France that worked. But the paper said the "great question" of whether "a *real* solution has been found" or whether "an apparent one only has been forced and bound down upon the neck of the people by the overpowering influence of an iron will" remained. Throughout the next decade and a half Americans continued to ponder that conundrum.[79]

Rodgers argues that the Progressive era planners who looked to the streets of Paris for lessons "struggled to discern the city's core meaning" amidst a cacophony of "deeply mixed messages." Ultimately, he suggests, the "question the city was to raise in all those who fell in love with it" was whether such a metropolis could be erected without imperial power? This question, though, was not new to the "age of social politics." A generation before, not all Americans "shivered in recoil from Haussman's work," nor from the radical schemes of social reconstruction which preceded it.[80] Many observers then endeavored to make sense of experiments that jarred with their inherited political traditions. For the French capital was nothing if not perplexing. Americans had to decide how to classify a republic that claimed to be an advance on the principles of 1776, a crowned head who claimed authority from universal suffrage, and an authoritarian regime that in its urban policy at least seemed more modern than their own democracy. In numerous ways, therefore, the "social republic" of 1848 and the Empire that destroyed it challenged American beliefs. Many US observers read events in France through a lens shaped by faith in the superiority of their own political and social order, but others, troubled by their own civil wars, used the transformation of Paris to imagine alternatives.

Notes

1. R. B., "Paris, with American Eyes", *Penn Monthly* 1 (July 1870), 274–75, 278.
2. R. B., "Paris", 264, 267.
3. Daniel T. Rodgers, *Atlantic Crossings: Social Politics in a Progressive Age* (Cambridge, MA: Harvard University Press, 1998), 3–4, 35; R. B., "Paris," 268.
4. Alan Lessoff, *The Nation and Its City: Politics, "Corruption," and Progress in Washington, D.C., 1861–1902* (Baltimore: Johns Hopkins University Press, 1994),1–3, 68–71; Howard Gillette Jr., *Between Justice and Beauty: Race, Planning, and the Failure of Urban Policy in Washington, D.C.* (Baltimore, MD: Johns Hopkins University Press, 1995), 62; Judd Kahn, *Imperial San Francisco: Politics and Planning in an American City, 1897–1906* (Lincoln: University of Nebraska Press, 1979).
5. David M. Scobey, *Empire City: The Making and Meaning of the New York City Landscape* (Philadelphia, PA: Temple University Press, 2002), 170, 189–91. See also Michael Wallace and Edwin Burrows, *Gotham: A History of New York City to 1898* (Oxford: Oxford University Press, 2001), 829.
6. Sam Bass Warner, Jr., *The Private City: Philadelphia in Three Periods of Its Growth* (Philadelphia: University of Pennsylvania Press, 1968), x, 98, 102, 157.
7. Rodgers, *Atlantic Crossings*, 113–14, 117; Bruce M. Stave, "A Conversation with Sam Bass Warner, Jr", *Journal of Urban History* 1 (November, 1974), 93.
8. William J. Novak, *The People's Welfare: Law and Regulation in Nineteenth-Century America* (Chapel Hill: University of North Carolina Press, 1996), 2–3.
9. Rodgers, *Atlantic Crossings*, 48.
10. Daniel Walker Howe, *The Political Culture of the American Whigs* (Chicago, IL: University of Chicago Press, 1979), 76–77; Bruce Levine, "Conservatism, Nativism, and Slavery: Thomas R. Whitney and the Origins of the Know-Nothing Party", *Journal of American History* 88 (2001), 455–88.
11. See for instance Mayor of Salzburg to Alexander Henry, June 1, 1859, box 1, folder 2, Alexander Henry Papers, Coll. 278, Historical Society of Pennsylvania.

12. Samuel Vaughan Merrick, *Report, Upon an Examination of Some of the Gas Manufactories in Great Britain, France, and Belgium* (Philadelphia: Printed by Order of Councils, 1834); Domenic Vitiello, "Engineering the Metropolis: The Sellers Family and Industrial Philadelphia" (PhD, University of Pennsylvania, 2004), 306; Russell Thayer, *The Public Parks and Gardens of Europe: A Report to the Commissioners of Fairmount Park* (Philadelphia, PA: Gillin & Nagle, 1880).

13. Elizabeth M. Geffen, "Violence in Philadelphia in the 1840s and 1850s", *Pennsylvania History* 36 (1969), 381–410.

14. Michael Feldberg, *The Turbulent Era: Riot and Disorder in Jacksonian America* (Oxford: Oxford University Press, 1980), 32, 34, 111; Michael Feldberg, *The Philadelphia Riots of 1844: A Study of Ethnic Conflict* (Westport, CT: Greenwood Press, 1975); Leonard L. Richards, *Gentlemen of Property and Standing Anti-Abolition Mobs in Jacksonian America* (Oxford: Oxford University Press, 1970).

15. *Street Talk about an Ordinance of Councils, Passed the 11th July, 1844, Organizing a Military Force for the Government of Philadelphia* (Philadelphia, n.p. 1844), 7, 19.

16. Diary entry, May 8, 1844, volume 7, Thomas P. Cope Diaries, MS Coll 975c, Haverford College Special Collection; diary entry, May 15, 1844, in Nicholas B. Wainwright (ed.), Sidney George Fisher, *A Philadelphia Perspective: The Diary of Sidney George Fisher, Covering the Years 1834–1871* (Philadelphia: Historical Society of Pennsylvania, 1967), p. 168.

17. Diary entry, July 24, 1844, 33, Sidney George Fisher, Diaries, 1834–1871, Coll. 1462, Historical Society of Pennsylvania (hereafter Fisher Manuscript diary); North American and United States Gazette. Philadelphia; 1854 February 22; *New York Herald*. 1844 November 13; *Pennsylvanian*. Philadelphia; 1857 November 11; Mechanic, letter to *Spirit of the Times*, December 22, 1849; North American and United States Gazette. Philadelphia; 1852 March 2. On the use of foreign terms to make sense of the American city in the period, see Elizabeth Kelly Gray, "The World by Gaslight: Urban-Gothic Literature and Moral Reform in New York City, 1845–1860", *American Nineteenth Century History* 10 (June 2009), 137–61.

18. *North American and United States Gazette*, February 22, 1854.

19. C., letter to *North American and United States Gazette*, October 3, 1849.

20. *Street Talk*, 20.

21. *Public Ledger*, August 4, 1851.

22. Bruce Laurie, *Working People of Philadelphia, 1800–1850* (Philadelphia, PA: Temple University Press, 1980), 161–68; Andrew Heath, "The Producers on the One Side, and the Capitalists on the Other": Labor Reform, Slavery, and the Career of a Transatlantic Radical", *American Nineteenth Century History* 13 (June 2012), 199–227; John A. Campbell, *A Theory of Equality; or, The Way to*

Make Every Man Act Honestly (Philadelphia, PA: John B. Perry, 1848), 92; *Quaker City*, April 7, November 24, 1849.

23. Philip J. Ethington, *The Public City: The Political Construction of Urban Life in San Francisco, 1850–1900* (Cambridge, UK: Cambridge University Press, 1994), 206; Martin J. Burke, *The Conundrum of Class: Public Discourse on the Social Order in America* (Chicago, IL: University of Chicago Press, 1995), 1–3.

24. Thomas L. Haskell, *The Emergence of Professional Social Science* (Urbana: University of Illinois Press, 1977), 15.

25. *Quaker City*, March 3, 1849.

26. See for example, Campbell, *Theory of Equality*, 60; Mechanic, letter to *Spirit of the Times*, December 22, 1849.

27. David Harvey, *Consciousness and the Urban Experience: Studies in the History and Theory of Capitalist Urbanization* (Baltimore, MD: John Hopkins University Press, 1985), 108. On the workshops, see William Fortescue, *France and 1848: The End of Monarchy* (London: Routledge, 2005), 107–15.

28. *Town Meeting* (n.p., n.d., 1838), collection of Library Company of Philadelphia; *Public Ledger*, December 24, 1846, May 2, 1849.

29. Campbell, *Theory of Equality*, 111–13.

30. Neither author is remembered as a radical. English, a man of letters who later served in the Democratic party, is probably best known for a fistfight with Edgar Allan Poe, whereas Foster's urban sketches have drawn more attention than his politics. Jeffrey Meyers, *Edgar Allan Poe: His Life and Legacy* (New York: Charles Scribner's Sons, 1992), 191; Stuart M. Blumin (ed.), *New York by Gas-Light and Other Urban Sketches* (Berkeley: University of California Press, 1990).

31. G. G. Foster and Thomas Dunn English, *The French Revolution of 1848: Its Causes, Actors, Events and Influences* (Philadelphia, PA: G. B. Zieber & Co., 1848), 9, 44, 115, 172–80.

32. English and Foster, *French Revolution*, 177–78.

33. *Public Ledger*, April 25, May 18, 1848. On social reform and 1848 in the United States, see Timothy Mason Roberts, *Distant Revolutions: 1848 and the Challenge to American Exceptionalism* (Charlottesville: University of Virginia Press, 2009), 81–104.

34. *North American and United States Gazette*, May 5, 1848; Publius, letters to *Public Ledger*, May 4, 5, 1848; Roberts, *Distant Revolutions*, 29–30.

35. William Elder, *Periscopics; or, Current Subjects Extemporaneously Treated* (New York: J. C. Darby, 1854), 243–44.

36. Stephen Colwell, *New Themes for the Protestant Clergy* (Philadelphia, PA: Lippincott, Grambo & Co., 1851), 359–60.

37. Burke, *Conundrum of Class*, 76–107.

38. Roberts argues the 1848 Revolutions challenged, but ultimately affirmed the exceptional trajectory of the United States. See Roberts, *Distant Revolutions*, 15.

39. Diary entry, October 1, 1857, Wainwright (ed.), *Sidney George Fisher*, 279–80; John C. Bullitt to Midred Bullitt, October 19, 1857, box 2, folder 17, Furness-Bullitt Family Papers, Coll. 1903, Historical Society of Pennsylvania; *Press, October 10, 1857. North American and United States Gazette*, October 16, 1857; *Pennsylvanian*, October 20, 1857. On the Panic, see James L. Huston, *The Panic of 1857 and the Coming of the Civil War* (Baton Rouge: Louisiana State University Press, 1987); Kenneth M. Stampp, *America in 1857: A Nation on the Brink* (New York: Oxford University Press, 1990), 213–38.

40. *Public Ledger*, October 28, 1857; *Pennsylvanian*, October 20, November 11, 1857; *Press*, November 12, 1857; *North American and United States Gazette*, November 12, 1857.

41. *Pennsylvanian*, October 30, 1857; *Public Ledger*, November 6, 1857; *New York Times*, October 27, 1857.

42. *North American and United States Gazette*, July 1, 1854. On Haussmann's work, see David P. Jordan, *Transforming Paris: The Life and Labors of Baron Haussmann* (New York: Free Press, 1995).

43. See for instance *Fincher's Trades' Review*, August 27, 1864.

44. Burrows and Wallace, *Gotham*, 849–51.

45. *Pennsylvanian*, November 6, 1857.

46. *Press*, October 24, 1857; Fortescue, *France and 1848*, 108; *North American and United States Gazette*, July 17, 1848, January 7, 1859.

47. *North American and United States Gazette*, January 31, 1857.

48. Sidney George Fisher, diary entries, November 28, 1857, 180; February 7, 1860, 38, Fisher Manuscript diary.

49. C., letter to *Inquirer*, April 17, 1861. See also C., letters to *North American and United States Gazette*, October 3, 23, 1849.

50. On links between city and nation building, see Scobey, *Empire City*, 19–23; Lessoff, *Nation and Its City*, 1–14; Margaret E. Farrar, *Building the Body Politic: Power and Urban Space in Washington, D.C.* (Urbana: University of Illinois Press, 2008), 40–42; Barbara Berglund, *Making San Francisco American: Cultural Frontiers in the Urban West, 1846–1906* (Lawrence: University Press of Kansas, 2007), 10–11.

51. *North American and United States Gazette*, January 14, 1859; Ajax., letter to *Inquirer*, January 12, 1861; Fisher Manuscript diary, December 2, 1869.

52. Scobey, *Empire City*, 189.

53. J. B. O., letter to *North American and United States Gazette*, March 12, 1852.

54. *North American and United States Gazette*, November 8, 1853, January 13, 1854.

55. On Philadelphia's new charter of 1854, see Howard Gillette, "The Emergence of the Modern Metropolis: Philadelphia in the Age of Its Consolidation", in Cutler, William W., III and Jr. Gillette (ed.), *The*

Divided Metropolis: Social and Spatial Dimensions of Philadelphia, 1800–1975 (Westport, CT: Greenwood Press, 1980), 3–25. On the annexation of Paris's suburbs, see Jordan, *Transforming Paris*, 288–89.

56. Lessoff, *Nation and Its City*, 10–11, 68–71.
57. *North American and United States Gazette*, June 7, 1853.
58. See for instance William D. Kelley, *The National Prospects: An Interview With Hon William D. Kelley* (Philadelphia: Henry Carey Baird & Co., 1877), 7.
59. *North American and United States Gazette*, July 27, 1860.
60. Scobey, *Empire City*, 54.
61. [William Russell West], *Broad Street, Penn Square, and the Park* (Philadelphia: Jno. Pennington & Son, 1871), 5; *North American and United States Gazette*, July 16, 1860.
62. *North American and United States Gazette*, October 30, 1852; *Evening Bulletin*, July 14, 16, 1863.
63. *Evening Bulletin*, July 26, 1867; Lambda., letter to *North American and United States Gazette*, December 30, 1859; *North American and United States Gazette*, March 21, 1867; C., letter to *Public Ledger*, August 12, 1868.
64. *Sunday Dispatch*, November 28, 1858.; *Evening Bulletin*, March 15, 1866;
65. *Public Ledger*, May 14, 1847. For a similar plan, see *Public Ledger*, August 30, 1854. In both cases, the paper noted the legal and moral right of public purchase and demolition.
66. *Evening Star*, September 18, 1867; *Inquirer*, August 4, 1871; Philadelphia. Mayor., *Second Annual Message of William S. Stokley* (Philadelphia: E. C. Markley & Sons, 1874), 356.
67. *North American and United States Gazette*, October 29, 1870.
68. For the older view, see Paul S. Boyer, *Urban Masses and Moral Order in America, 1820–1920* (Cambridge, MA: Harvard University Press, 1978), 221. Works that date "moral environmentalism" somewhat earlier include Stanley K. Schultz, *Constructing Urban Culture: American Cities and City Planning, 1800–1920* (Philadelphia, PA: Temple University Press, 1989) and David Schuyler, *The New Urban Landscape: The Redefinition of City Form in Nineteenth-Century America* (Baltimore, MD: Johns Hopkins University Press, 1986).
69. *North American and United States Gazette*, September 4, 1857.
70. R. B., "Paris", 271; Malakoff, letter to *New York Times*, May 9, 1868; *Public Ledger*, March 22, 1866; *Sunday Dispatch*, November 3, 1867.
71. *Press*, June 23, 1863; *Evening Bulletin*, July 16, 1863; letter to *North American and United States Gazette*, Octobr 6, 1856.
72. See for instance the *Evening Bulletin*, September 2, 1853; Letter to *Sunday Dispatch*, September 23, 1866.

73. *North American and United States Gazette*, May 7, 1855; C., letter to *Inquirer*, April 17, 1861.
74. E. K. P., letter to *North American and United States Gazette*, October 28, 1851.
75. On Confederate enthusiasm for the Second Empire, see Patrick J. Kelly, "The North American Crisis of the 1860s", *Journal of the Civil War Era* 2 no. 3 (September 2012), 337–68; Andrew Heath, "'Let the Empire Come': Imperialism and Its Critics in the Reconstruction South", *Civil War History* 60 no. 2 (June 2014), 152–189.
76. Penn., letter to *Germantown Telegraph*, March 29, 1871; letter to *North American and United States Gazette*, October 6, 1856; letter to *Daily Age*, December 21, 1864. The figures on funded debt are collated from annual reports of the mayor. On postwar urban reconstruction, see Howard Gillette, "Philadelphia's City Hall: Monument to a New Political Machine", *Pennsylvania Magazine of History and Biography* 97 (1973), 233–49; Schuyler, *New Urban Landscape*, 102–108; Russell F. Weigley, "The Border City in the Civil War", in Weigley, Russell F. (ed.), *Philadelphia: A 300-Year History* (New York: Norton, 1982), 363–416.
77. *Inquirer*, July 29, 1868; *Evening Bulletin*, June 15, 1869; *North American and United States Gazette*, June 29, 1869. On the bourgeois retreat from Reconstruction in a northern city, see Sven Beckert, *The Monied Metropolis: New York City and the Consolidation of the American Bourgeoisie, 1850–1896* (Cambridge, UK: Cambridge University Press, 2001). On municipal reform movements in Philadelphia, see Peter McCaffery, *When Bosses Ruled Philadelphia: The Emergence of the Republican Machine, 1867–1933* (State College, PA: Pennsylvania State University Press, 1993), chapter 3.
78. *Public Ledger*, May 18, 1871; *Inquirer*, May 15, June 5, July 2, 1871; *Evening Bulletin*, July 25, 1877; Russell Thayer, "Movements of Troops in Cities in Cases of Riot or Insurrection," *Proceedings of the American Philosophical Society* 18 (July to December, 1878), 89. A few months later, the Fairmount Park Commission sent Thayer to Europe to report back on park design. On the American response to the Commune, see Philip Mark Katz, *From Appomattox to Montmartre: Americans and the Paris Commune* (Cambridge, MA: Harvard University Press, 1998); Beckert, *Monied Metropolis*, 180–81.
79. *North American and United States Gazette*, October 6, 1856.
80. Rodgers, *Atlantic Crossings*, 167–68.

Chapter 3

"Acquainting America with Work in Foreign Experiment Stations": Benjamin Orange Flower and *The Arena*: A Case Study in the Transatlantic Circulation of Ideas

Jean-Louis Marin-Lamellet

"To the old Arena Family—the contributors who gave the magazine an international standing among the world's great reviews of opinion."[1]
Benjamin O. Flower, *Progressive Men, Women, and Movements of the Past Twenty-Five Years*

In 1914, looking back on his career, Boston reformer Benjamin O. Flower dedicated an entire chapter of his memoir of the Progressive movement to the mission he assigned himself of "acquainting America with work in foreign experiment stations."[2] At the heart of this mission was Flower's monthly magazine, *The Arena*, which he edited between 1889 and 1909. This study is an examination of *The Arena* and its cosmopolitan "family" in the context of the circulation of ideas between Europe and the United States in the late nineteenth and early twentieth centuries. From the beginning, Flower defined *The Arena* within a cosmopolitan context, choosing contributors who were "the ablest and boldest thinkers of America and Europe."[3] His aim was to give "readers the important results of progressive political, social, and economic movements in foreign lands."[4]

Flower is an example of "how men of this era thought in strange theoretical combinations"[5]—he was a Christian reformer, a student of both scientific *and* psychical phenomena, a champion of moral uplift and of schemes fostering social harmony, a patron of realist writers and, at the end of his life, an anti-Catholic fanatic.[6] *The Arena*, his "multiple-crusade magazine of general circulation,"[7] was a "journal of protest"[8] produced by a man who, until 1896, "set a standard for the radical publisher in America."[9] Flower's Arena Publishing Company published "serious books for the 'thought-molders of the nation'[10] that commercial houses would not risk."[11] The books on Europe were few but important.[12] In the magazine, articles about European experiments were a regular feature; they grew exponentially with time, especially after 1900, when Flower frequently wrote editorials about transatlantic issues.

Flower and his contributors represented Europe in terms of a pedagogy of progress: the magazine highlighted the "object-lessons"[13] it delivered, dealing with many countries, most notably Switzerland, Great Britain, Germany, and, beyond Europe, New Zealand.[14] This transatlantic (and indeed transpacific) arena was the scene of many experiments in terms of social policy. At the turn of the century, the term social policy implied much more than social security and poor relief, or what came to be known as the welfare state.[15] *Arena* reformers used a broader definition: for them, social politics meant redesigning the political machinery in order to eliminate "root evils" and organize society along more efficient and moral lines. For Flower, that meant implementing "fundamental reforms," such as direct democracy, public ownership of utilities and cooperation. What he called "palliative" reforms, like charity, welfare benefits, or housing reforms, dealt in contrast with the consequences of social ills. They were meant to soothe the collateral damage of a brutal and unfair society. Flower thought it necessary to treat the social body "while preaching and working for the advent of the new democracy and for the reign of justice and fraternity," but for him social politics first and foremost meant finding a cure and reaching social harmony by *fundamentally* altering the system.[16]

In the 1880s and 1890s, critics of *laissez-faire* who were advocates of alternative modernities such as Henry George, Edward Bellamy, and the Populists, were frequently dismissed as "cranks."[17] This fact posed a challenge to Flower and his circle as there was a real danger that their sympathy toward European social policy experiments might lead to them being tarred, however unfairly, with the brush of utopian eccentricity. Flower understood that the reception of European experiments in the United States was colored by such prejudices.[18] In fact, even sympathizers considered Flower's magazine to be "sometimes mad."[19] His aim was therefore to show that "the golden age of the crank"[20] was actually a new era of "practical idealists,"[21] whose policies would solve real social problems. In pursuit of this purpose, *The Arena* served as an interface between homegrown panaceas and implemented social improvements in Europe. For Flower, a "crank" was not a cog in the *laissez-faire* system; it meant the lever to be operated in order to make the social machinery work more efficiently, notably by eliminating political machines.[22] The United States, whose "mechanical civilization" was unmatched, remained, for him and his contributors, ethically backward: their role was to crank up their tinkering with the system.[23]

Flower's approach combined elements of scientific method and high moralism. Citing "authorities"—a regular strategy of his—he strove to "convince the reason and arouse the conscience."[24] Foreign experience was used as a rhetorical tool to demonstrate the practicability of new social policies and to give them legitimacy and the authority of precedent.[25] In the pages of *The Arena,* Europe also functioned as a means of outraging American readers; it was used to mark a contrast between its successful problem-solving schemes and the chaotic, unfair, violent, and degrading social conditions in the United States. Articles about transatlantic social politics were consequently a mix of dull statistical reports and flights of lyrical prophecy or triumphant utopia.

Flower considered that it was necessary to teach progress due to the prevailing ignorance about Populism, direct legislation, and public ownership, especially in the early 1890s. Retrospectively, he described his periodical as a "pioneer."[26] Exploring these new frontiers, which, he claimed, were "denied a free hearing in current periodical literature,"[27] meant looking beyond the Atlantic. Studying foreign examples was, he believed, the prerequisite for social reorganization.[28] The "object-lessons" were given not only by middle-class experts, such as Frank Parsons, William D. McCrackan, or Eltweed Pomeroy, but also by politicians from the Populist hinterland or from Britain and New Zealand. What then did Flower and his "authorities" teach their readers? What were "social policies" for them? Their studies of society took them on a tour of Europe and Australasia. What did they learn from these journeys? Let us follow them on their transoceanic travels.

Reading about Europe: The Populists' Transatlantic Schoolroom

Flower sympathized with the Populists.[29] Like them, he allied the "zeal of missionaries with a sensible method."[30] He opened the pages of his magazine to leaders and supporters of the movement.[31] Flower recalled:

> Naturally enough, this magazine had appealed to the leaders of the people's movement. (...) "We always had *The Arena* with us," he [a Populist] said. "It being a great magazine, numbering among its contributors many of the leading authoritative thinkers of America and Europe, and being published in Boston, its utterances carried great weight with the people, many of whose ancestors had come from Massachusetts, and in its pages were facts, clearly, tersely, boldly stated—just such facts as we needed to awaken and convince the people. We took it with us everywhere and clinched our arguments with its quotations."[32]

Populist leaders wrote in the magazine and some even used it as "the textbook of the Populist movement."[33] Ordinary farmers read it too, even though, in the age the illustrated 10-cent monthlies, a 50-cent monthly chiefly targeted a well-off middle class.[34] Farmers' Alliances subscribed to the journal and ordered books published by The Arena Publishing Company.[35] Subscribers wrote congratulatory letters to Flower: "the magazine is high-priced for farmers about here," wrote one such correspondent, "but we feel it ought to be read."[36] "[I]n dropping the *Atlantic* to make place for this new claimant upon our favor (for we tillers of the soil in this region can illy [*sic*] afford more than one of the leading periodicals), we have taken a long stride in advance."[37] *The Arena*, therefore, was a bridge between east and west, between William Jennings Bryan and his followers[38] (it was the only periodical in the east to support Nebraska's "Great Commoner"), and Boston reformers, between reform-minded farmers in the South and West and urban progressives.[39] In this way it could be construed as an early example of Hofstadter's conception of the Progressive movement as an "alliance between agrarians and the urban middle class."[40] However, although the cliché about Populists as provincial, irrational hayseeds clinging to a pastoral past and unable to adapt to a modern America persists, testifying to Hofstadter's descriptive powers and literary skill, current scholarship for the most part discounts his perception of the agrarian crusade as a species of "cranky pseudo-conservatism."[41] Even Lawrence Goodwyn, who saw in the Populists' cooperative movements the emergence and the tragic demise of a protest culture, characterized the farmers as tradition-oriented.[42] As Charles Postel in particular has shown, the agrarian rebels were modernizers who embraced progress, business methods, and scientific ideas.[43]

In *The Arena*, few articles by Populists are directly about Europe, though one paper does use the policies of the Bank of France as a working example for government loans to farmers.[44] Notwithstanding the argument made by Daniel Scroop in the following chapter of this volume, few Populists traveled to Europe. That does not mean, however, that they were not outward-looking. Populists read *The Arena*, so they read about European experiments, even though they were filtered through a particular Bostonian lens. This correlation suggests a more or less seamless—or at least a connected—world of ideas reaching from Kansas in the US Midwest to the great cities of Europe. One Populist contributor, Carl Vrooman, argued that it was the Populists' detractors who were steeped in narrow-minded isolationism. He condemned "self-styled 'better classes'" who considered Populism to be "the product of wild-eyed, unwashed fanatics," comparing them to selfish frogs ignorant of everything outside their puddle. On the contrary, he maintained, the greatest thinkers and statesmen in *world* history had advocated the principles of the People's Party and Populists, unlike their enemies, *did* know about foreign ideas.[45] Far from being "cranky," they described themselves as part of an international vanguard of economic and social theory. In his essay "A Kansas Populist Abroad," Vrooman "aimed to turn the tables on his GOP foes by identifying them, rather than the reformers, as the true retrogressive enemies of sophistication."[46]

Populists used European case studies to legitimize both their overall agenda and specific policy ideas. An example of the latter is government control of railroads. One of the most successful books Flower published was Marion Todd's *Railways of Europe and America*.[47] A remarkable woman, Todd was the first woman to pass the California bar. She lectured in the Midwest for the Farmers' Alliance.[48] Thoroughly "modern," she was an American educated professional who studied European solutions for American problems. An advertisement in the magazine announced "the Best Authorities of Europe and America on Railroad Profits and Methods. Facts, not Theories."[49] Populist leaders wrote reviews of the book: John Davis, a Representative from Kansas; James Field, the Vice-Presidential candidate in 1892 and Ignatius Donnelly, the perennial reformer, writer, and Congressman.[50] They emphasized Todd's use of European publications. The official, reliable figures were intended to demonstrate that government ownership worked. Europe functioned here as a reservoir of precedents in American debates. In particular, these Populists admired Todd's discussion of the "admirable system of pensions and insurance for the wage-workers" in Germany and "the admirable zone system of Austria and Austro-Hungary."[51] The "zone system" eliminated "rebates" and discrimination, which, according to farmers, impoverished them at the expense of monopolies. It made rates uniform, whether for a poor Kansas farmer or Standard Oil. Standardization would also eradicate free passes to legislators and lawyers, who were both bribed into favoring corporations. The kind of social politics envisaged here, therefore, meant that every citizen, rich or poor, should be able to have equal opportunities to compete on a level playing field. Populists were also concerned by labor troubles and extreme poverty. Pensions and insurance would provide a solution. Sure enough, urban progressives would later take up the cause.

Populists' main concerns—transportation, currency, land reforms, and direct democracy—shaped their electoral platforms and set the research agenda that the *Arena* contributors would study in the laboratories of Europe. At the end of the 1890s, the middle class realized that Populists had not been that cranky after all. As Daniel Rodgers pointed out, the "discovery of the octopus" by urban progressives effectively "stripped the radical veneer of Populism" from the word "People."[52] That *Arena* contributors—most of them middle-class Easterners—took up the cause of direct legislation in the early 1890s is testimony to the pioneering legitimization process at work in the pages of the magazine.

Direct Legislation: "Swiss Solutions of American Problems"[53]

The United States was, to Flower's mind, a "Pseudo Republic."[54] Government *by* the people was just rhetoric; in Switzerland, it was a fact thanks to direct legislation. John Sullivan and William McCrackan made that discovery in their independent travels there: they publicized the referendum, the initiative, and the recall in the pages of *The Arena* and came to be regarded as experts on the question. Sullivan went to Switzerland twice, founded the first state Direct Legislation League in 1892 and a newspaper, the *Direct Legislation Record*, in 1894. McCrackan, who was known as "Mr. Referendum" in Boston reform circles, had spent the first 14 years of his life in Switzerland.[55] Hamlin Garland, a fellow contributor at *The Arena*, remarked that his cosmopolitanism was rather exceptional: "as a reformer, he stood out in notable contrast to the throngs of us who knew only our own country, and not very much of that."[56] Flower recruited him, along with a University of Geneva Professor, Charles Borgeaud.[57] He then used *The Arena* to advance the cause of direct legislation.[58] Careful observation in the field was, for Flower, a prerequisite to acquire expertise and enjoy the status of "authority." In 20 years, they wrote more than 50 papers. McCrackan, in the early 1890s, described the Swiss system in detail, explained the different procedures according to the *canton* and traced its origins to Landsgemeinden (open-air legislative assemblies).[59] Switzerland became a model Republic for *Arena* writers. It was the remedy for what the United States had become—"a government of corporations, by corporations, for corporations."[60]

No social engineering was possible, these writers believed, as long as "the trinity of death"—that is, of bosses, party machines, and corporations—could profit from it.[61] Social politics was impossible so long as corrupt politicians held society captive. The precondition for improving society was the purification of politics, and it was Switzerland that provided "the governmental machinery for a thorough redemption of our own republic."[62] History proved it. Before the introduction of the referendum in 1848, Switzerland had been plagued with the same evils as the United States. Peace and the public ownership of means of communication and transportation then replaced civil war and monopolies. Paupers and millionaires disappeared.[63] *Arena* writers wanted to repeat this idealized version of Swiss history in America. They had faith in "the common sense of the great common people."[64] Paradoxically, they advocated direct democracy by the common man while praising complex electoral apparatuses managed by experts. As members of the middle class, they distanced themselves from the dangers of "class interests," from "money-controlled machines," and the corrupt rich on the one hand to "mob-rule" by poor workers on the other.[65] The ideal of purity meant that "the people" were an abstract construction that imagined that "the people's will was one: a general will, changeable but never permanently divided."[66]

For Flower, social politics was impossible unless good men and women were in power. Policies were thus reduced to a question of character. Direct legislation deterred legislators from corruption as the people could veto laws against their interests, bypass their legislative power, and recall them. It pressured lawmakers into choosing the right policies. Politicians thus became the administrators of the people's policies; government was "based on a business principle," McCrackan wrote.[67] Policy measures came first and were not stymied by politicking. If for William James, college education "should help you to know a good man when you see him,"[68] for direct legislation advocates, the people had common sense enough to see for themselves. Direct legislation was therefore a way of doing away with corrupt politicians and focusing on social improvements, which were regarded as *people's politics*, not *social politics*. Flower and McCrackan, then, were social tinkerers, "self-taught experts working on the intellectual margins of imperfectly professionalized fields."[69] In this world of amateurs, the sociological concept of "society," which developed in universities, did not obtain. This was not top-down social engineering by government agents, nor, for that matter, did it resemble James's professionalization of moral sentiment.

According to Flower and his circle, the Swiss used "a machine, mobile, swift and efficient, by which they could work reforms and effect changes."[70] With such a "fundamental reform," citizens were given the tools to help themselves and to introduce their own "palliatives." They rarely used the referendum and generally introduced conservative measures: openness, confidence and stability could then lead to progress.[71] With the initiative, they put forward wise laws they had fully discussed beforehand. Direct legislation was perceived as American common sense adapted to an industrialized society.[72] Face-to-face discussions were no longer possible in huge modern cities; Swiss methods supplied "the solution to one of the great political problems of the ages: how to enable great masses of people to govern themselves directly."[73] Democratic purity and self-government then logically brought about social innovations for Flower. The Swiss were said to be the happiest people in Europe and Brookline, Massachusetts, a town run with the "Swiss method," provided a functioning American imitation.[74] It demonstrated that, once people ruled, social policies followed. Brookline provided facilities, such as public baths, a library, and better schools, as well as benefits for its citizens, like less taxation and old-age pensions for public servants.[75]

That social and political improvements took place in a Massachusetts town was no surprise as "the initiative simply adapts this well-established principle of the New England town-meeting to a larger and a more complex civilization."[76] Contrary to the legislation overload in the US Congress, which pointed to "the vast productivity of a low organism whose offspring are weak; and most of them useless and destroyed," with direct legislation laws were produced by "a high organism whose offspring are few, highly developed; and most of them live."[77] The Spencerian language naturalized, and thereby legitimized, what its opponents disparaged as a "cranky" innovation that would lead to social disorder.[78] Direct democracy was part of the *natural evolution of America* from simplicity to complexity.[79] This legitimization process also shows that borrowing from abroad did not preclude exceptionalism. Reformers took pains to demonstrate that direct legislation was *natural*, containing no alien elements. It had long been used in New England with its town meetings, and the "local option," whereby citizens voted for the kind of policy they wanted regarding liquor, was also widespread in many states. Direct legislation was "not un-American."[80]

After the individual pioneer work of the 1890s, reformers moved into an organizational phase. Eltweed Pomeroy, for example, took up the task of agitating through *national* organization. A follower of Bellamy, a Populist and a factory-owner sharing profits with his workers, he succeeded Sullivan as editor of *The Direct Legislation Record* and had been the president of the National Direct Legislation League since its formation in 1896.[81] Pomeroy's history of the movement in an 1896 article shows that the phase of discovery had come to an end.[82] In nine in-depth articles between 1896 and 1908, he explained the success of direct legislation in Switzerland, hammering home arguments in favor of its importation. The 1900s saw the popularization of direct legislation on a national level. From 1907 onward, each issue of *The Arena* featured a couple of pages about "Initiative and Referendum News" by Ralph Albertson, the Secretary of the Massachusetts Referendum League. Together with Flower's editorials, they expounded the progress of the crusade in Europe and the United States. McCrackan had supplied reformers with the weapon of knowledge; Pomeroy and Albertson waged the campaign.

To publicize direct legislation, reformers were compelled to Americanize European ideas, or at least to Americanize their names. An exceptionalist framework conditioned the reception of European imports. The referendum and the initiative had to be translated into an acceptable American idiom. As Pomeroy recorded, speaking of John Sullivan:

> ...one of his best contributions to the movement has been the popularization of the name, Direct Legislation. At first it was generally known as Initiative and Referendum which have an alien sound. Direct Legislation is more comprehensive, including the town meeting as well, and it expresses the meaning of the movement better.[83]

Only the optional referendum, in which people did not vote on all laws but only when sufficient numbers signed a petition, could adapt to American soil.[84] The process of acculturation was complete toward the end of the 1900s when articles by and about the Oregon statesman William U'Ren discussed direct legislation in that state without any reference to Switzerland.[85]

With direct legislation, government belonged to the people; they could control and modify social organization. The question of ownership was therefore central.[86] Municipalities took it over.

Curing American Cities with European Remedies: Public Ownership

In the 1900s, social politics centered primarily on the public ownership of utilities, streetcars, telegraph, and telephone services. Frank Parsons, the President of the National League for Promoting the Public Ownership of Monopolies and of the National Referendum League, was the specialist who collaborated with Flower on these matters. Like most *Arena* contributors, Parsons believed in the symbiotic relationship between public ownership of utilities—"industrial democracy"—and the "public ownership of government," by which he meant direct democracy.[87] After an engineering and legal training, he became a lecturer at Boston University. His articles combined Social Gospel motivations with an accumulation of facts and figures, or what he called "mutualism" and "scientific industrialism."[88] This mixture of conscience and reason could not but appeal to Flower.[89] Parsons wrote more than 50 papers for *The Arena*. Along with a committee of experts, he was sent to Europe to study public ownership by The National Civic Federation, an association of business and labor leaders who wanted to foster moderate progressive reform. The commission was "a Progressive-era construction, a fact-finding commission, assigned to comb both sides of the Atlantic for experience and information."[90] Parsons was a member of the committee of four—two advocates and two opponents of the reform—who wrote the final report.[91] He typified the turn-of-the-century shift to the university-based, scientifically trained expert writing brief-like articles to plead a cause to the public and to fellow specialists. Amateurs met professionals in Flower's magazine. University degrees systematically followed the names of contributors. Whereas Flower's tone was that of a prophet using facts to lend force to a moral vision, Parsons' was less uncompromising. He praised the National Civic Federation report as a balanced assessment of the situation. For his editor, it was a "fairy-tale in the interests of private-ownership."[92] *Arena* experts were college-educated but did not hold positions of power nor did they administer their reforms—they agitated for ideas in order to influence public opinion into pressuring authorities to act. They also condemned corporations, and their plans were tainted by their ties to radical politics—Parsons, like Carl Vrooman and other *Arena* contributors, taught at the Populist-backed Kansas Agricultural College in the 1890s, an institution that closed when Republicans came back in power.[93] They were not yet part of the policy-oriented, institutionalized partnership among big business, federal government, and higher education that would "engineer and manage a new America."[94]

As in other areas of social policy, foreign experiences of municipalization were deployed in *The Arena* to build a reservoir of arguments for use in American debates. Germany, for example, cautiously tested both private and public ownership but preferred the latter.[95] Parsons used many official, and therefore authoritative-sounding, documents such as legislative hearings and US Consular reports to demonstrate the superiority of public ownership. British cities, and in particular Glasgow, came to be seen as ideal social organizations.[96] From 1904 onward, Parsons' matter-of-fact analyses were regularly counterpointed by Flower's triumphant editorials.[97] After 1907, Ralph Albertson kept writing about the "splendid record" of municipalization in his monthly "Public-Ownership News." Parsons used his specialized knowledge to bring out the facts about British cities' successes: once they were presented to people, he believed, the superiority of public over private ownership was self-evident, plain enough for everybody to see.[98] Parsons strove to bridge the gap between common sense and expertise that, arguably, would be severed in the twentieth century with, for example, the ideas of Walter Lippmann about "public opinion," and by the conflicts over progress and evolution exemplified in the 1925 Scopes Trial. For Parsons, only corruption and greed could account for the refusal of industrialists and politicians to adopt public ownership. Even opponents were won over by public ownership after visiting Europe.[99] F. C. Howe, the famous cosmopolitan reform journalist, was at first strongly opposed to public ownership but facts as he encountered them forced him to change his views.[100] Some members of the Commission sent by the National Civic Federation to Europe also became converts to the cause.[101]

European precedents confirmed to Flower and likeminded reformers that the advantages, indeed, were many. For consumers, the service was better and cheaper. Working conditions were improved. With inexpensive rates, workers could move out of slums, commute and live in the "wholesome atmosphere of the country."[102] With economies of scale, operating costs were reduced and the profits could be reinvested in the improvement of the city. Finally, the "public service corporation," which was "the fountain-head of corruption," was eliminated.[103] There was no need to bribe politicians to get profitable franchises or to charge extortionate rates to pay dividends on watered stocks. A nonpartisan municipal government replaced bosses with men from the professions who worked in the public interest. Public ownership meant "a *change of purpose* from *dividends for a few* to *service for all*," or in other words, a change from corrupted politics to social politics by technocrats and good men—the two being synonymous for Parsons.[104]

The city, that repository of vice, was turned into a healthy environment "for the people."[105] Clara Colby's article about Glasgow, which was "widely copied and commented on," vulgarized Parsons' complex articles.[106] She described municipal ownership as the extension of city improvement. Sanitation (thanks to public baths) led to inspections of private buildings by the city, then to municipal lodgings, then to the municipalization of utilities and street railways. Parsons concurred. The savings resulting from the coordinated work were used to buy slum areas and build "wholesome dwellings to be rented to the poor at moderate rates."[107] Public ownership was a catch-all term that encapsulated the multiple reforms necessary to solve all the problems that plagued American cities.

Mirroring reformers, opponents of municipal ownership fought side by side, irrespective of nationalities, on both sides of the ocean. *Laissez-faire* advocates also explored Europe for data to be used as rhetorical tools in American debates. Attorneys for the Boston lighting trust were sent on a "mission to England to make a brief against municipal-ownership."[108] *The Arena* recorded the debate. It regularly featured symposia propounding divergent opinions. Parsons also presented "the defendant's brief"—for example a Western Union pamphlet denouncing public ownership as a failure in Britain and an "un-American policy"—before defending the reform.[109] In 1902, the magazine also exposed the London *Times'* transatlantic "crusade against municipal ownership" financed by the Industrial Freedom League, an Anglo-American Pierpont Morgan-financed group that, according to the *Daily News*, existed "to Americanize our municipal methods and traditions." Transatlantic ideological controversies were superimposed on nationalistic feelings.[110]

The transatlantic circulation of ideas therefore flowed both ways. The city of Glasgow, for example, sent a committee to study the underground system of Washington D.C.[111] But still, *Arena*'s contributors insisted upon American backwardness[112]—the United States was "far outstripped" by the rest of the "civilized world."[113] They never used the phrase "transatlantic community" but rather "the civilized world."[114] As "civilization" meant applying the

Golden Rule to social politics, the expression implied that the cosmopolitan community saw itself as a Christian community.[115] It also showed the influence of late-nineteenth-century anthropology. Informed by vulgarized evolutionary ideas, it established a hierarchy of countries according to their degree of "barbarism" or "civilization." Public ownership, for example, was to be found everywhere but in Cuba, Hawaii, Honduras, Cyprus, Bolivia, and the United States, which prompted this remark by Parsons: "how do you like the company, Uncle Sam?"[116] American identity itself, its degree of "civilization"—with its racialist overtones—was at stake. Progressive social policies meant national pride and, if reformers imported ideas from European countries, it was only to beat them in a scramble for "civilization."

Advocating innovative social policies was therefore patriotic. As Parsons put it: "true patriotism wide awake demands for America all that is good, whether it originates in Europe or the Feejee [sic] islands."[117] American democratic mythology was a way of acculturating supposedly newfangled social policies. Monopolies meant that corporations could set prices without users being able to have a say—it was, for Parsons, "taxation without representation." Public ownership was simply the American Revolution *redux*. Even Uncle Sam—personified as the voice of the people in his *Arena* avatar—concurred: "I stopped taxation 'thout representation in '76, an' I'm goin' tew stop it now."[118] Carl Vrooman also tried to prove that "Jefferson Favored Government Ownership of the Means of Transportation."[119] Europe was a necessary detour to regenerate the American spirit. Progressive methods were necessary to preserve American identity, and that is why importing foreign social policies was described as both conservative and radical. Parsons even made fun of critics' claim that America's "different foundations" made imitation impossible:[120] "We must not wear overcoats or neckties or trousers, the Germans do that."[121] Borrowing from abroad thus did not threaten America's exceptionalism.[122] The same law of progress applied on both sides of the Atlantic but it was based on different initial conditions.[123] It was just a question of being in harmony with the "drift of the age," in other words with the extension of government intervention to solve increasingly complex problems.[124] However, if municipalization was more readily accepted because it kept a local character, Parsons, Flower, and other contributors feared ever-larger trusts and nationalization and its Russian-like bureaucracy. The age of bigness threatened the individualism they cherished.

Beyond Municipalities: European (and Antipodean) Paths into the World of Bigness

"The keynote of the present age is union, combination, or co-operation." Flower.[125]

"Combination is evolution. Organization is civilization." Parsons.[126]

Arena writers did not want to return to Wilsonian smallness as the "old competitive system" was nothing less than the "spirit of warfare."[127] Like many other Progressives, they accepted bigness as long as individuals could control the system.[128] For instance, taking up the railroad question where Populists had left it, they argued that government ownership was the only solution. After visiting nine European countries, Parsons came to the conclusion that public ownership was inevitable in both Europe and the United States.[129] In *The Arena*, Carl Vrooman published some of the conclusions of a "systematic investigation of the railway question, traveling extensively over the United States and spending two years in England and on the Continent." His articles were instrumental in publicizing the need for railroad regulation. In the final months of the *Arena* in 1909, he was also its "foreign editor."[130] Bigness—with its savings offered by coordinated services and its improved working conditions for employee—did not jeopardize individualism if it was tempered with direct legislation, which was why it was "easy to nationalize" in Switzerland.[131]

New Zealand, for Flower and Parsons, provided another example. The country was part of their informal network. Parsons exchanged many letters with Edward Tregear, its Secretary of Labor, and Tregear in turn presented his government's policies in *The Arena*.[132] Organizing people's welfare—whether compulsory arbitration, progressive taxation, accident compensation, an eight-hour day, and safe workplaces for workers—implied the extension of government intervention. There was no danger, however, of degeneration into freedom-destroying bureaucracy; as Flower pointed out: "the government of New Zealand is not Paternalism but Fraternalism. Government help is self-help, the partners using the firm to do their work."[133] The government was seen as a collection of co-workers, not as something exterior to the recipients of aid. For example, the state gave employment, through public works, to the jobless to preserve their "self-supporting manhood." New Zealand's scheme was Mayor Hazen Pingree's idea of making poor people cultivate Detroit's vacant lots on a national scale.[134] The country also fostered property ownership thanks to government loans and government-built cottages. Contrary to Germany, old-age insurance was not compulsory, so there was no danger of "heartless" bureaucratic policies that made "the poor keep the poor."[135] *Arena* contributors' essentialist vision of America as the land of freedom and self-reliance shaped their response to foreign experiments, hence their interest in voluntaristic schemes. Social politics, New Zealand taught America, was government-assisted self-help.

Cooperation, however, was *the* policy that perfected the union of individualism and collectivism. New Zealand, arguably, was considered by *Arena* reformers as a cooperative organized by the government on a national scale. Cooperation purified bigness, removed the state from the equation and synthesized all the other reforms: it coordinated direct legislation (cooperators made their own decisions) and public ownership (they shared profits); it also removed the suspicion of radicalism attached to Populist cooperatives. A naturalistic and necessitarian framework reinforced these arguments: cooperation was "simply the manifestation of that fundamental tendency to integration which Herbert Spencer has shown to be a part of the law of progress."[136] Large-scale organization was accepted but translated into a moral idiom—"fraternal cooperation" was "combination" moralized.[137] Cooperation was "a huge trust with all the marvelous mechanism of a trust, but without the soullessness of a trust."[138] Advocates of the "People's trust" were typical Progressives in that their rhetoric denounced monopolies, exalted efficiency, and longed for social cohesion.[139] Flower's vision of government as "Fraternalism" as well as a "firm" used by "partners" provides another example of the virtues of cooperation, which was based both on centralized efficiency and small-scale business principles.

Cooperation was a revelation for Parsons. As he toured Europe, he realized it would solve unemployment by eliminating its cause, competition, and by guaranteeing a "right to work."[140] It represented the ideal of self-made social politics. Cooperatives could build decent homes for their members or further the Garden City movement for instance. The English Rochdale Pioneers' Cooperative Society was a case in point—workers provided for their own welfare. They set up their own educational and recreational facilities as well as their own insurance companies that gave sick pay for example. The mythical tale of its origins and triumph was told and retold by American and European contributors alike. It was accompanied by a litany of Europe-wide successes in articles by John Gray, the General Secretary of the Coöperative Union of Great Britain, as well as in Flower's editorials and, after 1907, in Ralph Albertson's monthly news about the progress of the reform.[141]

In this vision of progressive social politics, it was assumed that the United States ought to duplicate European accomplishments. American imitations, Bradford Peck's Cooperative Association of America in Lewiston, Maine, and Walter Vrooman and George Washburn's Western Cooperative Association People's Trust, showed how cooperation could foster beneficial social policies. For Washburn, European cooperation, "plodding to the active, nervous American mind and hand," had to be modified "to adapt it to our industrial soil" and to the American character.[142] Peck gave four weeks of paid holidays to his cooperators and shared the profits with them. Washburn, after touring Europe to study cooperation, set up his "People's Trust" in Trenton, Missouri. He also shared profits with his cooperators but reinvested in the nearby Ruskin College—a "college for the people"[143]—so that cooperators could get a progressive education.[144] For Flower, this was a sign that Americanized cooperation was more advanced.[145] Both imitated the European idea of bulk purchases, profit-sharing and the reinvestment of profits to finance factories and homes for cooperators. They also translated the European cooperation-as-solidarity formula into an American idiom focused on business-like wealth creation. Washburn's plan was to merge local stores into an arcade to make business "more compact, centralized, facilitated, economized." Experts would then supervise the modernization of the marketing process. Profits would increase and with them the welfare of cooperators. Cooperation was therefore translated as a modernizing scheme: efficiency replaced waste and expertise supplanted the common sense of individuals. As Washburn claimed: "just as we modernize *methods*, so also do we modernize *men*."[146] Cooperation, for Peck, also meant modernization, and, *therefore* social cohesion—he explained that, with "just economic conditions under cooperation," the gap between consumers and producers and between capital and labor would disappear. Everybody would profit from a sound business practice that diffused wealth throughout a pacified society. Peck owned a successful department store that he bequeathed to his cooperative. He wrote a utopian novel, *The World a Department Store*, to convey his vision of an ethical economic and social system—cooperatives were consumption-driven "practical Christian organizations" that would eliminate poverty and social "evils" like slums.[147] His vision also implied that European experiments were mere commodities to be tailored to American consumers' tastes. For the two merchants, cooperation meant individuals organizing large-scale money-making commercial ventures that would foster mutual help and prosperity. The best social politics for them was to create the conditions to make a "welfare state" unnecessary.[148] Social politics would not make individuals the recipients of paternalistic benefits by the government. Cooperators' independence and "manhood" would thus be maintained. Both Peck and Washburn's Americanized cooperation could be seen as an early grassroots version of what came to be known as welfare capitalism. Social politics was made by cooperators and managed with modern methods—it was People's politics modernized, a "People's Trust"; it was self-made welfare capitalism, in other words a utopian dream. Peck's Cooperative Association was dissolved in 1912 and the department store became a prosperous family business.[149] Washburn's social ideals eventually worried Trenton's inhabitants. Cooperators planned to do all the business in town, which prompted a *New York Times* journalist to claim that they wanted to "buy the town outright."[150] In spite of their failure, their cooperative ventures "remain an interesting link between the middle-class literary Utopianism of Edward Bellamy and the middle-class reform ferment of the early Progressive Era."[151]

"Contrary to what seem[ed] to be the usual order of progress," Europe was the locus of innovative cooperation, not the United States.[152] For *Arena* reformers, it was a more advanced place, but also a rhetorical device that they might use to shame Americans into accepting progressive social policies. Humiliation was the dominant feeling when they looked beyond the Atlantic.[153] Reformers everywhere could see "the government of the United States falling from the high position of moral leader of the progressive peoples to that of a camp follower among the nations."[154] Admittedly, they promoted reforms inspired by the European model but their goal was to reestablish the natural order of progress. In their jeremiad, America was a "laggard." For Flower, the country had lost the spirit of experimentation that had turned the early Republic into a model for the decaying countries of the Old World, and the Civil War had ushered in an era of "conventionalism" and "commercialism" that had hindered its progress. European experiments—cooperation, direct democracy, income and inheritance tax, postal savings banks, government ownership of means of communication and transportation, municipal ownership of natural monopolies, and "numerous other salutary reforms have been successfully introduced across the Atlantic"—were not only "completely in harmony with the spirit that dominated the nation at its birth" but they were also a necessary detour to get back to American roots and put an end to "the melancholy spectacle of that Republic (...) falling behind monarchies and other foreign States in the march of progress."[155] The United States, in short, was not up to its definition as an exceptional country—it had to learn but should teach.[156] Because of "her Heaven-sent mission as the leader of civilization's vanguard," the country should be a city upon a hill to be watched by Europe, not the contrary.[157] Flower's optimism, however, made him believe that "what England [had] done, America will do" but better.[158]

"Taking Over the Waters"[159]

Underwater telegraph cables crossing the Atlantic connected reformers together. Modern means of communication, by shrinking the world either side of the "pond," enlarged their community of discussion. Flower's "intellectual hospitality" was a way for him to be part of this world.[160] The cables linked an informal and interpersonal network of like-minded progressives who were interested in many reforms at the same time. Flower's magazine exemplifies "the national and thematic ubiquity of reform and reformers." It also suggests that, far from being separate entities, Populism and Progressivism merged more or less seamlessly into one another across the last decade of the nineteenth century and the first of the twentieth. Accordingly, *The Arena* imagined and helped practically to forge a transatlantic world within which, from California to Germany, reformers could cull from a vast and eclectic reservoir of ideas.[161] J. Heniker Heaton, a British M.P., exemplified the cosmopolitanism of *The Arena*. In an article denouncing the "cable kings'" monopoly, which in his view hampered transatlantic commerce and communication, he proposed that they be taken over jointly by the US and British governments.[162]

In the pages of *The Arena*, social politics chiefly meant giving people back the tools and the facilities, such as a cheap and reliable telegraph system, to produce their own welfare. Reformers remained idealistic: they grudgingly accepted "palliatives" but what they ultimately wanted was to refashion society to reach harmony. No wonder then that they favored cooperation: with this scheme of organization, citizens would create their own brotherly system.[163] Although Parsons tended toward a professionalized, pragmatic approach to social policies, Flower, McCrackan, Pomeroy, Peck, and Washburn still belonged to an age of amateurs. *The Arena* reflected the transition from impassioned amateurism to technocratic social politics. For its editor however, agitation, not implementation, remained the priority. His main focus was individualism, hence his fascination for cooperation and New Zealand's government-assisted self-help.

European borrowings had to be legitimized, notably with the aid of functionalist arguments—according to Flower's evolutionary framework, social experiments were necessary "to meet changed conditions and the increasing demands of the complex social organism."[164] The Old World had adapted to changes; the United States must now follow suit. However, exceptionalism continued to frame the terms of the discussion. It was assumed that policies that had been implemented with success in Europe would have to be Americanized before they would work on US soil. The *Arena's* reformers relied on "foreign experiment stations" to amass arguments and to accumulate case studies, but the boundaries of exceptionalism were not fundamentally shifted. Flower and his acolytes belonged to a cosmopolitan progressive world but this did not stop them from harboring nationalistic feelings. According to Flower, they had to take over the waters, explore Europe, bring back successful policies, and, by adapting them to the American environment, recapture its lost position as the "moral leader" of "civilization." Transatlantic discussions about social politics were but one aspect of a "civilization-molding struggle" between conservatism and progress.[165] Flower did not think about divisions in geographical but in moral terms. He stilled transatlantic exchanges by casting them as a gigantic eschatological battle, the endless, ahistorical re-enactment of a Morality Play featuring moral progressives and immoral reactionaries, "a warfare of darkness against light."[166] *The Arena* was its gallant knight.

Notes

1. Benjamin Orange Flower, *Progressive Men, Women, and Movements of the Past Twenty-Five Years* (Boston, MA: The New Arena, 1914), 5.
2. Flower, *Progressive Men*, 134.
3. Flower, "Notes on Current Events," *The Arena* 12 (May 1895): lxxxi. Hereafter, unless otherwise stated, all Flower's writings are from *The Arena*.
4. Flower, *Progressive Men*, 134.
5. Robert H. Wiebe, *The Search for Order, 1877–1920* (New York: Hill and Wang, 1967), 153.
6. For biographical information see Ralph E. Luker. "Flower, Benjamin Orange," *American National Biography Online*, accessed June 10, 2011 http://www.anb.org/articles/15/15-00227.html.
7. Frank Luther Mott, *A History of American Magazines, Volume IV: 1885–1905*, (Cambridge, MA: Belknap Press of Harvard University Press, 1957), 410.
8. Ibid., 415. Hamlin Garland, *A Son of the Middle Border* (New York: Penguin Books, 1995), 329.

9. Roger Eliot Stoddard, "Vanity and Reform: B.O. Flower's Arena Publishing Company, Boston, 1890–1896. With a Bibliographical List of Arena Imprints," *Papers of the Bibliographical Society of America* 76, no. 3 (1982): 279.

10. This was Flower's own phrase.

11. Stoddard, "Vanity and Reform," 279.

12. Ibid., 315, 318, 325. Out of 206 imprints, seven books dealt with European social policies—three books by William McCrackan, three by Frank Parsons and one by Marion Todd.

13. See for example Flower, "Object-Lessons in Municipal Ownership Offered by Two American Cities," 25 (April 1901): 447.

14. Rodgers, in *Atlantic Crossings*, includes Australasia in his Atlantic Community. On the history of the concept: Bernard Bailyn, "The Idea of Atlantic History," *Itinerario*, 20, no. 1 (March 1996): 39.

15. For an analysis of the phrase "social policy" see Daniel Rodgers, *Atlantic Crossings : Social Politics in a Progressive Age* (Cambridge, MA: Belknap Press of Harvard University Press, 1998), 29.

16. Flower, "The Story of a Victorious Social Experiment," 29 (June 1903): 623.

17. For historiographical elements: Richard L. McCormick, "Public Life in Industrial America" in *The New American History, Revised and Expanded Edition*, Eric Foner, ed. (Philadelphia: Temple University Press, 1997), 117–20. For a description of the period: Nell Painter, *Standing at Armageddon : The United States, 1877–1919* (New York: W. W. Norton, 2008), 36–140.

18. John Thomas, *Alternative America: Henry George, Edward Bellamy, Henry Demarest Lloyd, and the Adversary Tradition* (Cambridge, MA: Belknap Press, 1983).

19. William T. Stead, *Review of Reviews* 4 (July 1891): 51.

20. Carlos Schwantes, *Coxey's Army: An American Odyssey* (Moscow, ID: University of Idaho Press, 1994), 47.

21. Flower uses this phrase recurrently in his writings.

22. Schwantes, *Coxey's Army*, 47.

23. Frank Parsons, "The Railway Experience of Germany. Part II. The State-Owned Railways of Germany," *The Arena* 37 (March 1907): 250. Alan Trachtenberg, *The Incorporation of America: Culture and Society in the Gilded Age* (New York: Hill and Wang, 1982), 38–69.

24. Flower, "How England Averted a Revolution of Force. A Lesson for the Present," 24 (October 1900): 378. Flower used the rather vague term "authorities," frequently. See for example this advertisement for *The Arena*: "The leading progressive review of the world," 4 (November 1891), back matter, unnumbered page; Flower, *Progressive Men*, 22.

25. Lyman Abbott, "Postal Telegraphy," *The Arena* 15 (January 1896): 243.

26. Flower, *Progressive Men*, 62–63, 111.

27. Ibid., 17.
28. Flower, "A Suggestion to Reformers," 37 (March 1907): 300–301.
29. John Hicks, *The Populist Revolt: A History of the Farmers' Alliance and the People's Party* (Lincoln: University of Nebraska Press, 1961), 404.
30. Kazin, *The Populist Persuasion: An American History* (Ithaca, NY: Cornell University Press, 1998), 46.
31. Garland, *A Son of the Middle Border*, 338–40. Between 1891 and 1897 Populists wrote more than 80 articles in *The Arena*.
32. Flower, *Progressive Men*, 99–100.
33. Mott, *A History of American Magazines*, 407.
34. Ibid.,596. H.F. Cline "Flower and the Arena: Purpose and Content", *The Journalism Quarterly*, 17 (September 1940): 248.
35. Nebraska Farmers' Alliance Papers. Microfilm (roll 1–998), July 13, 1894, Nebraska State Historical Society.
36. Flower, "Notes and announcements," 7 (January 1893): xxix.
37. Ibid.
38. Strictly speaking, Bryan was not a Populist, even though he was on the Populist ticket for the 1896 election and had many Populist sympathizers. For a discussion of this question see Lawrence Goodwyn, *The Populist Moment: A Short History of the Agrarian Revolt in America* (Oxford; New York: Oxford University Press, 1978), 335; Charles Postel, *The Populist Vision* (Oxford; New York: Oxford University Press, 2007), 21; Michael Kazin, *A Godly Hero: The Life of William Jennings Bryan*, reprint (New York: Anchor Books, 2007), 78.
39. In this paper, Progressive with a capital "P" refers to the historical term whereas "progressive" is used to indicate support for social reform.
40. Richard Hofstadter, *The Age of Reform: From Bryan to F.D.R.* (New York: Alfred A. Knopf, 1955), 239.
41. Ibid., 20. Worth Robert Miller, "A Centennial Historiography of American Populism," *Kansas History: A Journal of the Central Plains* 16 (Spring 1993): 54–69.
42. Goodwyn, *The Populist Moment*, 7.
43. Postel, *The Populist Vision*, 9.
44. C. C. Post, "The Sub-Treasury Plan," *The Arena* 5 (February 1892): 342–53. Postel gives many examples of Populists using European examples in *The Populist Vision*: 148–49, 152–54.
45. Carl Vrooman, "International Populists and Populism," *The New Time*, 2 (June 1898): 372–74. The list of "proto-Populists," here incomplete, reads like a literary, religious, political, economic, and intellectual hall of fame: Plato, Aristotle, Bacon, Moses, Aquinas, Thomas More, Ruskin, Carlyle, Hugo, Dickens, Tolstoy, Zola, Morris, Mazzini, Cavour, Fichte, Hegel, Bismarck, Gladstone, Franklin, Greeley, Pope Leo XIII, Willard, Carlisle, McKinley, Mill,

Toynbee, many university professors from Oxford, the United States (Ely, Commons, Parsons, Bemis), and Berlin (Smoller, Wagner). Carl Vrooman was a Kansas Populist, from a family of prominent social reformers who became a Regent at the Kansas State Agricultural College, taught at Ruskin College, supported William Jennings Bryan, and participated in many Progressive era reforms. In 1913 he became the senator from Illinois and then Assistant Secretary of Agriculture for President Wilson. In 1924 he turned down an offer to be the running mate of John W. Davis, who won the Democratic Party nomination. Vrooman opposed the New Deal and died in 1966 at the age of 93.

Flower, *Progressive Men*, 117–18; "The Divine Quest (Number Four.) Fundamental Fraternal Movements of the Present," (January 1903): 31–47; "A Conversation with George F. Washburn, General Manager of the People's Trust of America, on How To Meet the Trust Problem Through Co-operation," 28 (October 1902): 410; Cornelius C. Regier, *The Era of the Muckrakers* (Chapel Hill: The University of North Carolina Press, 1932), 34; Thomas Frank, "The Leviathan with Tentacles of Steel: Railroads in the Minds of Kansas Populists," *The Western Historical Quarterly*, 20 (February 1989): 49–51; Ross Evans Paulson, *Radicalism & Reform; The Vrooman Family and American Social Thought, 1837–1937* (Lexington: University of Kentucky Press, 1968); Jeremy P. Felt, "Review: *Radicalism & Reform: The Vrooman Family and American Social Thought, 1837–1937* by Ross E. Paulson," *The Journal of American History* 55, no. 3 (Dcember 1968): 646.

46. Frank, "The Leviathan with Tentacles of Steel," 51; Vrooman, "A Kansas Populist Abroad," *Taming the Trusts* (Topeka, KS: Advocate Publishers, 1900).

47. Marion Todd, *Railways of Europe and America, or Government Ownership, with Notes from Official Reports* (Boston, MA: The Arena Publishing Company, 1893). Flower, *Progressive Men*, 110.

48. Postel, *The Populist Vision*, 72–73.

49. Advertisement for Marion Todd's *Railways of Europe and America* in *The Arena* 11 (December 1894), back matter, unnumbered page.

50. "Davis, John William." *Biographical Directory of the Unites States Congress,* June 10, 2011 http://bioguide.congress.gov/scripts/biodisplay.pl?index=D000121.

51. "Books of the Day: Review of *Railways of Europe and America*," *The Arena* 8 (October 1893): xvi–xxi and 10 (June 1894): xxi.

52. Daniel Rodgers, "In Search of Progressivism," *Reviews in American History* 10, no. 4, The Promise of American History: Progress and Prospects (December 1982): 124. Daniel Rodgers, *Contested Truths : Keywords in American Politics since Independence* (Cambridge, MA: Harvard University Press, 1998), 183.

53. This sub-heading uses the title of a book by the reformer William McCracken. See William McCracken, *Swiss Solutions of American Problems* (Boston, MA: Arena Publishing Company, 1894)

54. Flower, "The Difference Between a Real and a Pseudo Republic," 29 (April 1903): 421.
55. William Denison McCrackan, *An American Abroad and At Home, Recollections of W.D. McCrackan, M.A.* (New York: M.E. Starr, 1924), 161.
56. Hamlin Garland, "In Memoriam William Denison McCrackan," 217, Mary Baker Eddy Papers, Subject Files entries for McCrackan, Box 158, Mary Baker Eddy Library, Boston, MA.
57. Flower, "Notes and Announcements," 6 (June 1892): liv–lv; *Progressive Men*, 62–63. Eltweed Pomeroy, "The Direct Legislation Movement and Its Leaders," *The Arena* 16 (June 1896): 29–43. Charles Borgeaud, "Practical Results which Have Attended the Introduction of the Referendum in Switzerland," *The Arena* 33 (May 190): 486. Thomas Goebel, "'A Case of Democratic Contagion': Direct Democracy in the American West, 1890–1920," *Pacific Historical Review*, 66 no. 2 (May 1997): 219.
58. See C. B. Galbreath, "Provisions for State-Wide Initiative and Referendum," *The Annals of the American Academy of Political and Social Science*, 43 (September 1912); 83–84. Flower himself wrote extensively about the benefits of direct democracy. In addition to the articles mentioned in this paper, see for example: *Progressive Men*, 61–70; "Topic of the Times. The Imperative Need of the Referendum Emphasized by Recent Attempted Legislation," 26 (October 1900): 425–30; "In The Mirror of the Present. Direct Legislation in Oregon and the Misrepresentation of the Reactionary Press," 38 (July 1907): 80–85; "In the Mirror of the Present. "Professor Frank Parsons on the Success of Direct Legislation in Switzerland," 39 (May 1908): 618–19; "The Direct-Legislation Campaign in the Empire State," 39 (June 1908): 650–61; "Editorials. The Australian Referendum: Its Significance and Its Lessons," *The Twentieth-Century Magazine*, 4 (September 1911): 553–54.
59. W. D. McCrackan, "The Swiss Referendum," *The Arena* 3 (March 1891); "The Swiss and American Constitutions," 4 (July 1891); "Books of the Day: Review by W.D. McCrackan of *Direct Legislation by the Citizenship through the Initiative and Referendum* by J.W. Sullivan," 5 (May 1892).
60. Flower, "The Difference Between a Real and a Pseudo Republic," 424.
61. "A Conversation with Eltweed Pomeroy on Direct Legislation and Social Progress," 25 (March 1901): 317.
62. McCrackan, "Review by W.D. McCrackan of *Direct Legislation*," xxxiii.
63. Pomeroy, "The Direct Legislation Movement and Its Leaders," 30; "Direct Legislation: A Symposium II. Objections Answered," *The Arena* 22 (July 1899): 109. O. K. Hewes, "Switzerland and Her Ideal Government; or, Direct Legislation in the Alpine Republic," *The Arena* 33 (April 1905): 373.

64. McCrackan, "The Swiss Referendum," 464. Pomeroy, "Practical Measures for Preserving Democracy: Two Argument Against Direct Legislation," *The Arena* 30 (February 1904): 156.
65. Flower, "Direct Legislation and Popular Government," 39 (May 1908): 611.
66. Rodgers, *Contested Truths,* 35.
67. McCrackan, "The Swiss Referendum," 463.
68. William James, "The Social Value of the College-Bred," *in The Works of William James. Essays, Comments and Reviews. Volume 15* (Cambridge, MA: Harvard University Press, 1987), 106.
69. Rodgers, *Atlantic Crossings,* 26.
70. Flower, "Authoritative Statements as to the Practical Working of Direct-Legislation in Switzerland and America," 38 (August 1907): 322.
71. Flower, "Democracy and Municipal Government; or, How the Richest Town in the World Is Ruled by the Referendum," 32 (October 1904): 380.
72. I would like to thank Berkeley Professor Richard Candida Smith for his luminous analysis of common-sense philosophy in American culture. Common sense implied that citizens, expert of not, could see the facts plainly and take decisions and come to an unbiased conclusion by sharing their perspectives.
73. Flower, "Review of *The Rise of The Swiss Republic* by W.D. McCrackan," 6 (September 1892), xliv.
74. Flower, "Democracy and Municipal Government," 388; "An American Municipality for Two Hundred Years Under Direct-Legislation," 35 (January 1906): 70.
75. Flower, "Pensioning Public Servants: Brookline Leads the Way," 33 (June 1905): 656.
76. "A Primer of Direct-Legislation.—Chapter II.—The Initiative" by Leading New-World Authorities on Direct Legislation, *The Arena* 35 (June 1906): 602.
77. Pomeroy, "Objections answered," 101. Pomeroy, "Practical Measures for Preserving Democracy: Two Argument Against Direct Legislation," *The Arena* 30 (February 1904): 156.
78. Dr Ellis P. Oberholtzer, "Direct Legislation in America," *The Arena* 24 (November 1900): 497–505.
79. "Organic progress consists in a change from the homogeneous to the heterogeneous." Herbert Spencer, "Progress: Its Law and Causes," *The Westminster Review,* 67 (April 1857): 446.
80. "A Primer of Direct-Legislation.—Chapter I.—The Referendum, by Leading New-World Authorities on Direct Legislation," *The Arena* 35 (May 1906): 507. "A Primer of Direct-Legislation.—Chapter II.—The Initiative," 600–603.
81. William Dwight Porter Bliss, ed., *The New Encyclopaedia of Social Reform, Including All Social-Reform Movements and Activities, and*

the Economic, Industrial, and Sociological Facts and Statistics of All Countries and All Social Subjects (New York: Funk and Wagnalls Company, 1908), 915.

82. Pomeroy, "The Direct Legislation Movement and Its Leaders, 29–43.

83. Ibid., 35–36.

84. John R. Commons, "Direct Legislation in Switzerland and America," *The Arena* 22 (December 1899): 725. Edwin Maxey, "The Referendum in America," *The Arena* 24 (July 1900): 47.

85. William S. U'Ren, "The Operation of the Initiative and Referendum in Oregon," *The Arena* 32 (August 1904): 122. George H. Shibley, "Initiative and Referendum in Practical Operation," *The Arena* 40 (August–September 1908): 142.

86. Rodgers, *Contested Truths*, 110.

87. Parsons, "Public Ownership," *The Arena* 29 (February 1903): 123. E. W. Bemis & F. F. Ingram, "How the People Should Acquire Public Utilities: A Criticism of Mr. Brown's Paper," *The Arena* 34 (July 1905): 47. To give another example, Carl Vrooman used the Swiss model to praise the symbiosis of Populism, direct legislation, and public ownership: In "A Kansas Populist Abroad," Vrooman claimed that "the Populists are in control of Switzerland," in the sense that the Swiss government operates all natural monopolies and public utilities. In that most politically mature of nations, Vrooman wrote that, "the people run the government and the government runs the monopolies and corporations." Frank, "The Leviathan with Tentacles of Steel," 51. Vrooman, "A Kansas Populist Abroad," 41, 57.

88. Frank Parsons, *Our Country's Need, or, The Development of a Scientific Industrialism* (Boston: Arena Publishing Company, 1894); "The Philosophy of Mutualism," in *Present-Day Problems*, vol. 1 no.9 (April 1894), pamphlet offprint from *The Arena*.

89. For biographical details: Bliss, *The New Encyclopedia of Social Reform*, 871.

90. Rodgers, *Atlantic Crossings*, 149.

91. National Civic Federation, Commission on Public Ownership and Operation, *Municipal and Private Operation of Public Utilities. Report to the National Civic Federation Commission on Public Ownership and Operation. In Three Volumes* (New York: National Civic Federation, 1907). John W. Sullivan was another member of the commission. He advocated both direct legislation and public ownership—another example of the eclecticism of reformers. Parsons, "The National Civic Federation and Its New Report on Public-Ownership," *The Arena* 38 (October 1907): 401–408.

92. Parsons, "The National Civic Federation and Its New Report on Public-Ownership," 401. Flower, "The National Civic Federation's Fairy-Tale in the Interests of Private-Ownership of Public Utilities,

and Facts which Prove Its Münchausen-Like Character," 38 (August 1907): 327–28.

93. Bliss, *The New Encyclopaedia of Social Reform*, 871.

94. Olivier Zunz, *Why the American Century?* (Chicago, IL: University of Chicago Press, 2000), xi.

95. Parsons, "Glasgow's Great Record: A Complete History of the Pioneer Experiment in Municipal-Ownership of Street-Car Service in Great Britain," 32 (November 1904): 461.

96. Carl Vrooman concurred. Appendix 4 to his *Taming the Trusts* describes the success of municipalization in Birmingham, in particular praising the leadership of Joseph Chamberlain.

97. For editorials, see for instance: "Another Victorious Year for Glasgow's Municipal Street-Railways" 36 (October 1906); "Another Splendid Record Made by the Glasgow Municipal Street Railway," 40 (October 1908). Flower also praised public ownership in his other magazines: "The Passing Day. II— An Object Lesson in Municipal Ownership from across the Ocean," *The Coming Age*, 2 (October 1899): 440–41; "Editorials. Liverpool's Street Railways: Another Illustration of the Benefits of Municipal Ownership," *The Twentieth-Century Magazine*, 2 (May 1910): 174; "Editorials. The Past Year's Record of Glasgow's Municipally Owned Street Railways," *The Twentieth-Century Magazine*, 2 (September 1910): 555–56; "Editorials. Last Year's Record of the State-Owned Railways of New Zealand," *The Twentieth-Century Magazine*, 3 (November 1910): 168–69; "Editorials. The Recent Report of the Glasgow Municipal Railways," *The Twentieth-Century Magazine*, 4 (August 1911): 455–56.

98. Parsons, "The National Civic Federation and Its New Report on Public-Ownership," 408.

99. Flower, "Municipal Advance. Growth of Sentiment in Favor of Municipal-Ownership," 34 (December 1905): 644; "Municipal-Ownership of Street-Railways in Germany: A Conservative Educator's Report," 35 (January 1906): 81.

100. Flower, "Review: *The British City*: A Study of the Beginnings of Democracy," 200–208; "Public-Ownership in Great Britain," 37 (April 1907): 410.

101. Parsons, "The National Civic Federation and Its New Report on Public-Ownership," 407.

102. Parsons, "The People's Highways," *The Arena* 12 (May 1895): 222–23.

103. Flower, "Five Reasons Why We Favor Municipal-Ownership," 35 (May 1906): 526–29.

104. Parsons, "Glasgow's Great Record," 470.

105. *The City for the People* was a book by Parsons that expounded his views on public ownership and direct legislation. Frank Parsons, *The City for the People; or, The Municipalization of the City Government and of Local Franchises* (Philadelphia, PA: C.F. Taylor, 1900).

106. Clara Bewick Colby, "What the Second City of Great Britain Is Doing for Her People: or, Where Municipal-Ownership Is in Full Flower," *The Arena* 33 (April 1905): 361–69. Flower, *Progressive Men*, 139.

107. Parsons, "Glasgow's Great Record," 469.

108. Parsons, "The Taxation Fallacy," 37 (January 1907): 89–90.

109. Parsons, "The Telegraph Monopoly. XIV," 18 (November 1897): 628.

110. "The Municipal Ownership Convention," 481–83. Flower, "The London *Times* as a Tool for Public Service Corporations," 29 (June 1903): 657; "Public-Ownership in Great Britain," 408.

111. Parsons, "Glasgow's Great Record," 466.

112. For example: Flower, "The Inheritance Tax in England," 24 (December 1900): 656.

113. Flower, "The Rising Tide of Popular Interest in Favor of Public-Ownership," 32 (December 1904): 651.

114. For one example among many: Richard T. Ely, "Symposium: Why the Government Should Own the Telegraph," *The Arena* 15 (December 1895): 52.

115. On the idea of the "Atlantic community" as an extension of Western Christendom: Bailyn, "The Idea of Atlantic History," 22.

116. Parsons, "The Telegraph Monopoly," 251.

117. Ibid., 255.

118. Parsons, "Chicago's Message to Uncle Sam," 10 (September 1894): 496.

119. Vrooman, *Taming the Trusts*, 102–104.

120. William L. Wilson, "Why I Oppose Governmental Control of The Telegraph," *The Arena* 15 (January 1896): 248.

121. Parsons, "The Telegraph Monopoly," 254.

122. Parsons, "Nationalization of Railways in Switzerland," 36 (December 1906): 582; "Glasgow's Great Record," 470; "The Telegraph Monopoly. IX," 16 (June 1896): 652.

123. Parsons, "On the Stoa of the Twentieth Century: City Ownership and Operation of Street Railways," 25 (February 1901): 207.

124. Flower, "Mutualism vs. Commercial Feudalism," 25 (March 1901): 327.

125. Flower, *Progressive Men*, 141.

126. Parsons, "The President and the Trusts," *The Arena* 28 (November 1902): 352.

127. Flower, "Mutualism vs. Commercial Feudalism," 327.

128. Rodgers, *Contested Truths*, 181.

129. Flower, "The Latest and Ablest Work on the Railroad-Rate Question," 35 (June 1906): 658–59. Parsons, "The Railway Experience of Germany." Part I and II, 37 (February and March 1907).

130. Carl S. Vrooman, "The Ultimate Issue Involved in Railroad Accidents," 39 (January 1908): 14–18; "Railway Nationalization in

France," 40 (August–September 1908): 156–63; "A 'Square Deal' for the Railroads," 40 (October 1908): 273–82; "Our Railroad Riddle," 40 (December 1908): 553–60.

131. Parsons, "Nationalization of Railways in Switzerland," 584.

132. Edward Tregear, "How New Zealand is Solving the Problem of Popular Government," *The Arena* 32 (December 1904): 574; "Recent Humanistic Legislation in New Zealand," 37 (April 1907): 371.

133. Flower, "Book Studies. II. Professor Parsons' *Story of New Zealand*," 30 (May 1904): 430; "New Zealand's Present Prosperity," 34 (October 1905): 423.

134. Flower, "Notes and Comments," 30 (May 1904): 555; "A Successful Experiment for the Maintenance of Self-respecting Manhood," 15 (March 1896): 544–54.

135. Edward Tregear, "How New Zealand Is Solving the Problem of Popular Government," 574.

136. Flower, "Opposing Views on Municipal-Ownership: A Notable Symposium by Leading Specialists," 37 (February 1907): 185.

137. Flower, "How the Standard Oil Greed Has Recently Been Manifested in the Robbing of the Toilers of New Zealand," 35 (February 1906): 215.

138. Robert Brown, "Progress of the Garden City Movement in England," *The Arena* 40 (November 1908): 460. Flower, "The Struggle between Life and Death in the Economic World. The Warfare of Three World-Wide Social Theories," 27 (March 1902), 321.

139. Flower, "'The People's Trust: A Promising Co-operative Movement,'" 28 (October 1902): 434. Rodgers, "In Search of Progressivism", 123.

140. Flower, "A Conversation with George F. Washburn, General Manager of the People's Trust of America, on How To Meet the Trust Problem Through Co-Operation," 28 (October 1902): 406; Parsons, "The Rise and Progress of Co-Operation in Europe," 30 (July 1903): 29.

141. J. C. Gray, "The Present Status of Coöperation in Great Britain," *The Arena* 33 (March 1905): 262. Pomeroy, "The English Friendly Societies," 27 (January 1902): 14. Flower, "Co-Operation in England, or The New Industrial Democracy," *The Coming Age*, 1 (February 1899): 187–93; "A Conversation with George F. Washburn," 408; "The Triumphal March of Coöperation in Great Britain," 40 (December 1908): 633; "Editorials. Industrial Co-operation in Great Britain," *The Twentieth-Century Magazine*, 3 (December 1910): 268–69. Brown, "Progress of the Garden City Movement in England," 460.

142. Flower, "A Conversation with George F. Washburn," 410; "Topic of the Times. Co-Operative Conference at Lewiston," 28 (September

1902): 320–22. Hiram Vrooman, "The Co-Operative Association of America," *The Arena* 26 (November 1901): 585.

143. Thomas E. Will, "A College for the People", *The Arena* 26 (July 1901): 15–20.

144. Carl Vrooman also taught there after 1900.

145. Flower, "The People's Trust," 434.

146. Flower, "A Conversation with George F. Washburn," 412.

147. Bradford C. Peck, *The World a Department Store: A Story of Life Under a Coöperative System*, (Lewiston, ME and Boston, MA: privately printed, 1900), 189. "The Struggle between Life and Death in the Economic World," 322.

148. Flower, "A Conversation with George F. Washburn," 412–13; "The Struggle between Life and Death in the Economic World," 322; "The Keynote of the Present Revolutionary Movement," 89; "The Golden Rule in Modern Business," 37 (May 1907): 535; Parsons, "Co-Operative Undertakings in Europe and America," 30 (August 1903):165. Gray, "The Present Status of Coöperation in Great Britain," 260–61.

149. Wallace Evan Davies, "A Collectivist Experiment down East: Bradford Peck and the Coöperative Association of America," *The New England Quarterly* 20, no. 4 (December 1947): 489–90. Francine C. Cary, "The World a Department Store: Bradford Peck and the Utopian Endeavor," *American Quarterly* 29, no. 4 (October 1977): 370–84.

150. "Buying a Town Outright," *The New York Times*, April 14, 1902.

151. Davies, "A Collectivist Experiment Down East", 491.

152. Flower, "A Conversation with George F. Washburn," 408.

153. See for example: Flower, "The Menace of Plutocracy," 5 (September 1892): 516; "Extension of Public Ownership of Railways," 29 (January 1903): 91. McCrackan, "The Initiative in Switzerland," 548. Parsons, "The Telegraph Monopoly. V," 5 (May 1896): 953.

154. Flower, "Henry D. Lloyd –An Apostle of Progressive Democracy," 30 (December 1903): 654.

155. Flower, "Topics of the Times. An Earnest Word to Young Men and Women of America," 24 (November 1900): 538–541.

156. Flower, "Municipal Ownership and Coöperation," 32 (December 1904): 660.

157. Flower, "How England Averted a Revolution of Force," 378.

158. Flower, "Co-Operation in Great Britain," 25 (February 1901): 212.

159. Flower, "Taking Over the Waters," 38 (December 1907): 719.

160. A phrase he used constantly. See for example: Flower, *Progressive men*, 19,153, 260.

161. Pierre-Yves Saunier, "A Tale of Pendular Times: On Board the Spirit of St. Louis with Daniel T. Rodgers," *H-SHGAPE Discussion: Symposium on Daniel Rodgers*, November 3, 1999. June 15, 2011 <http://www.h-net.org/~shgape/disclist/rodgers.html>.

The phrase "long reform moment" is a modified version of the "long agrarian moment" used by scholars of Populism to express the continuity between the Populism of the 1890s and national Progressivism in the 1910s. Robert D. Johnston, "Peasants, Pitchforks, and the (Found) Promise of Progressivism," review of *Roots of Reform: Farmers, Workers, and the American State, 1877–1917* (Chicago: Chicago University Press, 1999) by Elisabeth Sanders, Reviews *in American History* 28, no. 3 (2000): 394. Robert C. McMath Jr, "C. Vann Woodward and the Burden of Southern Populism," *The Journal of Southern History* 67, no. 4 (November 2001): 744. See also: Walter Nugent, *Progressivism: A Very Short Introduction* (New York: Oxford University Press, 2009).

162. J. Heniker Heaton, "The Cable Telegraph Systems of the World," *The Arena* 38 (September 1907): 225–36.

163. "Cooperation Means Union in Place of Conflict, Harmony instead of Antagonism." Parsons, "The Rise and Progress of Co-Operation in Europe," 30.

164. Flower, "The Inheritance Tax in England," 656.

165. Flower, *Progressive Men*, 300.

166. Flower, "The Struggle between Life and Death in the Economic World," 320.

Chapter 4

In Search of a Populist Atlantic: The Transatlantic Travels of William Jennings Bryan and Robert M. La Follette Jr

Daniel Scroop

Daniel Rodgers's *Atlantic Crossings* spawned a wave of impressive new scholarship on transnational and transoceanic political reform. Thanks to Rodgers, as well as to other historians who work in this field, we now have a richer and deeper understanding than ever before of the complex worlds of reform that crisscrossed the Atlantic in the nineteenth and twentieth centuries. However, significant gaps in our knowledge remain. Accordingly, this essay focuses on a notable blind spot in historical writing on Atlantic reform: populism. Historians have written copiously on the subject of the intertwined relationship between populism and progressivism in US local, regional, and national politics but the transatlantic dimensions of this relationship have attracted scant attention.[1] Indeed, *Atlantic Crossings* proceeds on the assumption—deep rooted in US historiography—that populism, unlike other components of the US reform tradition, simply did not travel. This essay challenges that assumption through an examination of the transatlantic travels and connections of two leading US populist-progressives of the late-nineteenth and twentieth centuries, William Jennings Bryan (1860–1925) and Robert M. La Follette Jr (1855–1925).

Bryan and La Follette are towering figures in the US politics of reform. Bryan was a three-time presidential candidate who for a generation—from the 1890s to the 1920s—was among the two or three most powerful and popular figures in the Democratic Party. La Follette was an outstanding progressive governor of Wisconsin whose subsequent achievements as a US Senator have rarely been matched. His 1924 campaign for the presidency was one of the most successful third-party challenges in modern US history. The vital role played by these two leading reformers is not in doubt. Their marginal role in the historical scholarship on transatlantic reform owes much, I argue here, to the populist quality of their politics.

Populism infused both the style and the substance of Bryan and La Follette's politics. It was present, most obviously, in the extent to which their political influence and leverage rested on their claim to "speak for the people." In order to make this core populist claim credible they took pains to expose themselves regularly to the public, relying on face-to-face, open-air campaigning in order to rally support and energize their followers. They campaigned with passionate intensity, striving not just to communicate their formal political positions but also to personify the project of reform in the eyes of their publics. Whether speaking from the rear of a train, at revivalist campgrounds, or in university lecture theatres, they sought to embody in their mode of delivery, choice of language, and repertoire of gestures a politics predicated on the notion that they spoke authentically for "the little man" who needed to be defended and empowered in an increasingly complex and confusing world.[2] Substantively, in terms of ideology and policy orientation, their debt to populism was most evident, perhaps, in their shared distrust of concentrated economic power and in private monopoly in particular, which both men interpreted as a dire threat to the democratic traditions and prospects of the United States.[3] "[M]onopoly in private hands is indefensible from any standpoint," Bryan stated bluntly in 1899."[4] "[T]he encroachment of the powerful few on the rights of the many," La Follette insisted in his classic 1913 autobiography, was the paramount problem of US political life.[5] Bryan and La Follette belonged to opposing political parties—Bryan was a Democrat, La Follette a Republican—but on a range of key issues from workingmen's compensation to tariff reform, graduated income tax, women's suffrage, railroad nationalization and the direct election of senators, they stood shoulder to shoulder. It is true that Bryan's Christian faith was the wellspring of his politics and that this in some ways set him apart from otherwise like-minded reformers such as La Follette, for whom religious convictions were in political (and in his case also personal) terms relatively unimportant. But such contrasts should not obscure what Bryan and La Follette held in common: a deep and consistent commitment to restoring the United States to "the people" through a program of economic and social reform whose chief purpose was to mitigate and then to counter the effects of the new forms of large-scale industrial and finance capitalism that emerged in the late nineteenth and early twentieth centuries.

The world of William Jennings Bryan, 1903–1906

William Jennings Bryan is typically portrayed as a figure whose career illustrates the limits of an inward-looking mode of US agrarian populist politics that failed to adapt to the demands of the modern world.[6] The Boy Orator of the Platte, as some mocking commentators called him, was just 36 when he made his electrifying "Cross of Gold" speech at the 1896 Democratic party national convention, surely one of the most extraordinary interventions in post-Civil War US political history.[7] The speech won him the presidential nomination and presaged a remarkable campaign in which the youthful Nebraskan led a crusade for "free silver" in an effort to turn the tables on the nation's political and financial establishment.[8] Bryan's 1896 campaign has been represented as the last gasp of localized rural resistance to the rise of a new consumer-oriented political and economic order, which was in the process of making the United States a more modern, more cosmopolitan nation.[9] It is paradoxical, therefore, that this campaign had the effect of making Bryan world famous. During the campaign Bryan received letters of support from around the globe. He won the enduring admiration of the great novelist Leo Tolstoy, who kept a portrait of him on his bedroom wall.[10] In fact, contrary to his historiographical reputation, Bryan was one of the most globally connected and widely traveled party politicians of his era. His transatlantic crossings and connections, therefore, are best understood in the wider context of engagement with a patchwork of overlapping transoceanic and transnational networks of moral, political, and social reform. His concerns were global in reach and ambition, not merely transatlantic.

In total Bryan made four trips to Europe. On each occasion he combined elements of tourism with political work designed to forge alliances and to discuss public policy ideas, as well as to burnish his credentials as an international statesman.[11] The most extensive visits were in 1903–1904 and in 1905–1906 and it is these that we will look at here in some depth, beginning with the latter case.

In the autumn of 1905 Bryan went on an 11-month tour, during which he and his family circumnavigated the globe.[12] On this occasion, however, the Bryans set off not with a transatlantic journey from the eastern seaboard of the United States but with a transpacific voyage taking them from San Francisco to Hawaii.[13] From Hawaii they continued westwards through Asia and the Middle East, and so were nearing the end of their adventure when, tired and yearning for home comforts, they reached Europe in the summer of 1906. By this time they had long ago completed the most politically charged phase of the tour, their travels under military escort through the southern islands of the United States-occupied Philippines.[14] For the Bryans then, this time at least, Europe represented an opportunity to rest, to see old friends, and to recover cultural equilibrium after disorienting experiences elsewhere. When they reached Vienna they stopped for two weeks, "replenishing their wardrobes" in the process.[15] Bryan's daughter, Grace, who had lost 30 lbs of weight in East Asia, was sent to a *pension* in Hanover in order to fatten up; his lovesick son, William Jr, was sent home to the United States to be with his fiancée.[16] Meanwhile Bryan and his wife traveled first to Russia, where they saw the Duma in session, and then to Norway, where they attended the coronation of King Haakon VII, taking the chance while there to admire the fjords, mountains, and midnight sun.[17] In Britain he enjoyed an audience with King Edward VII, attended a debate in the House of Commons, and paid homage to his literary heroes by visiting Shakespeare's Stratford and the birthplace of Robert Burns in Alloway, Scotland.[18] This was hardly the earnest, social policy exchange that is the subject of *Atlantic Crossings.*

Bryan, however, was not indifferent to social politics as he toured Europe in 1906. In Finland, for instance, he waxed lyrical on the subject of Helsinki's city parks, which he considered superior to their American counterparts.[19] He praised the Swedish education system and noted, approvingly, that its legislature had recently passed child labor and accident insurance laws.[20] And in Britain he was excited by the Liberal party's recent electoral landslide, welcoming its commitment to introduce progressive income and inheritance tax legislation.[21] But during his world tour, Bryan's political business more often concerned moral reform and peace diplomacy than it did social politics. In late June 1906, for example, he participated in the fourteenth Inter-parliamentary Union conference in London. Here he spoke out in favor of disarmament and successfully pressed amendments to a model arbitration treaty in order to include questions of national sovereignty and honor.[22] Intervening forcefully in the debate, he argued that international relations conflicts might be avoided with the adoption of "cooling off" treaties under which an international commission of inquiry would be appointed to settle differences.[23] It could be argued that Bryan's involvement in this conference had a transatlantic element in that it arose from an invitation he received in the summer of 1904 when he met European representatives of the Union who were touring the Rocky Mountains.[24] His approach to reforming the arbitration process however was not that of a proto-typical transatlantic progressive: it was that of a globally aware Christian politician for whom the triumph of peace and love over war and force was the paramount issue. This interpretation is consistent with the way Bryan constructed his world tour itinerary. As he traveled through Asia, the Middle East, and Europe he spoke as frequently on religious as on political themes. His schedule featured visits to Christian mission stations, schools, and hospitals, allowing him to tap into powerful and preexisting worldwide networks of moral reform.[25] Like many other moral reformers of his era, Bryan was convinced that Christian nations and individuals had an obligation to participate in "reforming the world."[26] He saw no contradiction between his avowed antiimperialism and his determination to use transnational moral reform networks to promote the spread of Christian values in the name of peace and progress.[27]

It is clear from the above that in 1905–1906 Bryan was operating in a global and not just a transatlantic world of reform and that his political activities were inseparable from his Christian faith. Indeed these two factors were evident when, in June 1910, Bryan was a delegate to the World Missionary Conference in Edinburgh.[28] The conference, which excluded Roman Catholics and Eastern Orthodox Christians, brought together missionaries from across the world.[29] Bryan, who had recently returned from an extensive tour of Central and South America, used the conference further to promote his arbitration treaty ideas. As he explained in a letter to President William Howard Taft, he thought that if nations could be guided through agreed formal processes based on considered reflection and proper investigation overseen by an independent panel then wars might be averted.[30] Bryan's religiously inspired peace work at the Edinburgh conference suggests once again the inapplicability to Bryan of an approach to the politics of reform structured principally around transatlantic connections. The work of the missions—and of peace promotion and diplomacy—was global in scope.

The impressive geographic reach of Bryan's world of moral reform should not however obscure the importance to his politics of the kind of transatlantic exchange described in *Atlantic Crossings*. Bryan did engage in transatlantic social politics, tapping into and exploiting the reform networks described by Daniel T. Rodgers. However, the populist cast of Bryan's progressivism made his encounters with Europe and Europeans distinctive, pointing, in fact, to the existence of a populist Atlantic operating sometimes within and sometimes without the world of social politics portrayed in the voluminous historiography of transatlantic reform. The best evidence for this lies in Bryan's account of his first trip to Europe, which he took with his son William Jr in 1903–1904.[31]

After a brief stop at Cobh on the west coast of Ireland—the port from which the Titanic would set sail nine years later—Bryan began his tour of Europe in England, having disembarked from the White Star steamer, *The Majestic*, at Liverpool in mid-November 1903.[32] Immediately he threw himself into the tariff debates that were raging throughout the land, reporting on speeches he had heard on the topic given by Joseph Chamberlain, Herbert Asquith, and Lord Rosebery.[33] "An American feels at home in England just now," he noted wryly, "for he constantly reads in the newspapers and hears on the streets the tariff arguments so familiar in the United States."[34]

Bryan was a strong lifelong opponent of high tariffs, which he considered to be a form of theft orchestrated by wealthy cartels intent on swindling humble consumers, but the account he published of the British tariff debates was surprisingly detached.[35] On the related issue of currency reform, however, he proved more willing to declare his political interest in what was after all a matter peculiarly close to his populist heart. In London, for example, at the invitation of the US Ambassador to the United Kingdom Joseph Choate, Bryan was pleased to meet Moreton Frewen, a writer on monetary reform, and Prime Minister Arthur Balfour, who, Bryan noted, was also an advocate of bimetallism.[36] Bryan actively sought out bimetallists as he swung through Europe in 1903–1904, practicing as he did so a mode of transatlantic politics that mixed conventional progressive elements with nonstandard destinations and encounters marked by his populism. In Ireland, which was his next stop, Bryan's populist sympathies came out into the open. Shortly after arriving in Dublin, he attended a lavish Mansion House event at which he dined with many of Ireland's leading nationalists, among them John Redmond, John Dillon, and Michael Davitt. (Davitt had been engaged in transatlantic land reform activism for more than two decades when he met Bryan; in 1880 he had traveled to New York to meet Henry George, author of *Progress and Poverty*, who was keen at that time to influence debates in Ireland.)[37] Bryan was fascinated by the plight of Irish tenants and indeed by the entire Irish land question. It was an issue that resonated powerfully with his agrarian populism, chimed with his anti-imperialist leanings, and played to his longstanding interest in currency reform. He was cheered to the rafters when he declared his support for home rule.[38]

For Bryan, however, the highlight of the Mansion House dinner was his meeting with the Archbishop of Dublin, William J. Walsh, who in addition to being deeply involved in debates over religious education and other social and political matters, was also an ardent bimetallist.[39] In 1893 Walsh had published a widely circulated pamphlet, *Bimetallism and Monometallism*, in which he stated that the introduction of bimetallism was "an imperative necessity" to save Ireland's tenants from "inevitable ruin."[40] This made perfect sense to Bryan whose 1896 presidential campaign had been predicated on the assumption that the adoption of bimetallism would help restore the moral and economic vitality of a nation whose producing classes were, he had argued, being oppressed by hostile, parasitic forces.[41] Echoing arguments Walsh made in his 1893 pamphlet, Bryan observed in his account of the tour that Irish tenants subject to long-term fixed payments were peculiarly vulnerable to currency fluctuations and that this made them precariously dependent upon the stability of the US dollar.[42]

In fact, since 1896 Bryan had worked gradually to distance himself from the cause of free silver, but his writings on his encounters with European bimetallists show that currency reform remained a live issue on the populist wing of transatlantic progressive politics in the early years of the twentieth century. What is more, it was not only in England and in Ireland that Bryan sought out his fellow bimetallists. In his account of meeting President Loubet of France at the Élysée Palace, Bryan praises the Frenchman for his mastery of the principles of bimetallism.[43] Indeed, his comments on France contain an extended discussion of monetary policy in which he compares English, Mexican, and American bank practices while debating the proper ratio between deposits and capital stock.[44] In addition to his conversation with Loubet, Bryan also discussed bimetallism with Senator Fougeirol, a politician from the Ardèche who for over a decade had taken a lead role in the French National Bimetallic League.[45] Finally, while in Berlin, Bryan made a point of speaking with Dr Otto Arendt, a Reichstag deputy who was also the leading exponent of bimetallism in Germany and the secretary of its national bimetallic organization.[46] Bryan observed that like other European advocates of monetary reform, Arendt had been frustrated in his ambitions by "English financiers."[47]

Bryan's interest in forging links with Irish nationalists and European bimetallists sets him apart from the social policy world elaborated in *Atlantic Crossings*. It is important to be clear, however, that his two-month tour of Europe in 1903–1904 had an itinerary that would have been familiar to transatlantic progressives with no particular populist leanings. Bryan made a point, for example, of

engaging in the comparative study of municipal reform. It is surely
no coincidence that the growth of his interest in the public ownership of utilities and in railroad nationalization occurred in the first
decade of the twentieth century, precisely the period in which he was
exposed for the first time to Europe and to Europeans.[48] In Glasgow,
he learned about the city's publicly owned water, gas, electricity, and
transport provision, praising what he saw as its enlightened municipal administration.[49] He reported approvingly on its council houses,
lodging houses, and public baths.[50] In London, accompanied by fellow teetotaller John Burns, MP for Battersea, he met members of the
county council, pored over statistics, and admired a "sterilized milk
station" designed to improve the health of London's impoverished
and undernourished children.[51] He then met Sidney and Beatrice
Webb with whom he discussed both municipal ownership and industrial cooperation.[52] In Nottingham, Birmingham, and Belfast he was
further impressed by the achievements of municipal leaders in the
sphere of public ownership; his accounts of the experience—which
were published in the Hearst press as well as in his own journal, *The
Commoner*—show that he was eager to proselytize for this major progressive cause.[53] "Nothing has impressed me more in my visit to the
British Isles," Bryan wrote, "than the interest which the leading citizens of the municipalities are taking in problems of government and
sociology."[54] Here Bryan showed himself to be more forward looking and open minded than some other prominent American travelers. Not all of Bryan's fellow countrymen shared his conviction that
Americans might learn lessons from Europe. The African American
leader Booker T. Washington, for example, was also given a tour of
London by John Burns, but according to the sociologist Robert E.
Park, who accompanied him, he returned believing that "everything
in America surpassed anything in Europe."[55] Similarly, labor leader
Samuel Gompers wrote on returning from a 1909 visit to England,
where he was born, that the problems of the "Old World" were "not
linked up with America."[56]

For the remainder of his European trip, Bryan continued to be
more interested in public policy issues that in the esthetic experience
of Europe had so gripped the imaginations of well-to-do American
travelers who took the grand tour in the nineteenth century.[57] He
dutifully traipsed around Italy's galleries and monuments but the
postcards he sent home suggest that he found its culinary delights
more interesting than its art.[58] He enjoyed a private audience with
Pope Pius X and visited the Coliseum and Forum in Rome but there
is nothing in his account of these experiences to suggest that he

found them especially thrilling.[59] Questions of government and politics, however, were a different matter entirely. He was intrigued, for instance, by the German railway system, noting that the "ownership of the railroads by the various states does not in the least interfere with the operation of the lines."[60] Swiss-style direct democracy in the form of the referendum and initiative captivated him, as it did many other American progressives. "It is the most democratic government on the face of the earth," he wrote.[61] In his European writings, such observations on public policy and democratic reform are interspersed with comments that reveal his anti-imperialism and commitment to peace diplomacy. In Copenhagen, for example, he bemoaned the fact that US failure to grant full citizenship to inhabitants of the Philippines and Puerto Rico had hampered its diplomacy in relation to Denmark's colonial possessions.[62] In the Netherlands, he lauded the work of the Hague tribunal, praising it for "cultivating a public opinion which will in time coerce the nations into substituting arbitration for violence in the settlement of international disputes."[63]

Bryan found much to interest and to stimulate him, therefore, in his various engagements with European political life. There is no doubt however that from a personal point of view the real highlight of the 1903–1904 tour came in the form of a pilgrimage rather than from an exchange over public policy or governmental systems. In December 1903, following a path trodden by numerous American reformers before and after him, he journeyed through Russia to pay homage to Leo Tolstoy.[64] Their meeting was comparatively unusual because it was inspired by genuine mutual admiration.[65] Tolstoy followed Bryan's career closely, keeping track of it through the Russian papers and his correspondence. He told his American friends to vote for the Nebraskan whose antipathy toward imperialism, protectionism, and the domination of "the people" by unaccountable elites he shared.[66] Bryan, for his part, used his newspaper, *The Commoner*, to promote and disseminate Tolstoy's ideas.[67] They spent 12 companionable hours together during which Tolstoy was impressed by the "progressive" Bryan's "naturally quick perception."[68] Despite their differences—Bryan was neither an anarchist nor a pacifist—they found common ground in their shared conviction that the bases of politics were fundamentally moral and spiritual. Tolstoy, Bryan wrote, was "the moral Titan of Europe."[69]

The remarkable meeting between Bryan and Tolstoy in late 1903 highlights the multivalent character of Bryan's politics. His crusades for peace and moral reform ran alongside his campaigns for currency reform and his pursuit of social politics. To isolate any one of these various strands of his politics and raise it above the others would be to make a false analytical move. Out of a combination of political necessity, personal inclination, and ideological orientation, Bryan fought his battles for reform on several fronts simultaneously. His politics was bound together and given coherence by two things: his Christian faith and his populism. The former infused his politics entirely, giving him a powerful sense of mission and a fierce moral energy; the latter framed his style, which was based on the claim that he spoke for "the people," and underpinned his support for policies aimed at challenging concentrated private power. Although historians have written extensively on the importance of religion in a transatlantic context, they have yet fully to recognize populism's contribution to the politics of transatlantic reform.

Robert M. La Follette in Europe, 1923

Historians have been much kinder to Robert La Follette than to William Jennings Bryan.[70] It is true that the scope and significance of La Follette's achievements have been questioned by scholars who argue that he was distinguished more by his quality of personal courage than by his record as a reformer.[71] Nevertheless, his status as one of the great progressives of his age remains largely intact. Bryan's religiosity, the emotional element of his popular appeal, and his majoritarian understanding of democracy all contributed to making him an inviting target for intellectuals who shared neither his particular Christian worldview nor his faith in "the people." In contrast, La Follette's open embrace of social scientific expertise, combined with his strong civil liberties record, have shielded him from both scholarly barbs and reputational harm.

Despite Bryan's reputation for parochialism, La Follette had much less direct experience of the world beyond the borders of United States than did his Nebraskan counterpart. In fact La Follette did not leave the North American continent until he was 68 years old. When, on August 1, 1923, he boarded the steamship *George Washington* in New York, accompanied by his wife, his son Bob Jr, and his friends Basil and Mollie Manly, he was—much to his regret—about to visit Europe for the first time. "It was wrong that Belle and I did not go to Europe thirty years earlier," he told his daughter Mary. "Everyone should go to Europe and go in youth."[72] Lack of overseas travel experience does not, of course, necessarily preclude a cosmopolitan awareness of cultural difference. La Follette's early career in Wisconsin state politics routinely exposed him to vexed questions of ethnic, linguistic, and religious identity as he strove to win the trust and support of first- and second-generation immigrants from Germany and Scandinavia who at that time were seeking to secure a firmer foothold in the mainstream of US politics.[73] Furthermore, La Follette's interest in such matters extended well beyond the minimum required to climb through the ranks of the Badger state's Republican Party—he was genuinely fascinated by alternative governmental systems and by comparative public policy. Throughout his career, for example, he made extensive use of the comparative studies produced by students of his friend, the labor economist John Commons, who taught at the University of Wisconsin in Madison. More than most politicians of his era, therefore, he was willing to engage with and learn from foreign experiments in policymaking, even if he did not go to Europe himself. La Follette did not travel as widely as Bryan but his connection with the world of European social and political reform was, if anything, deeper and more sustained.

The timing of Bryan and La Follette's travels is also worth noting. The Europe Bryan encountered in the first decade of the twentieth century was relatively prosperous and stable. When La Follette crossed the Atlantic in 1923, however, Europe was reeling from the twin shocks of the Russian Revolution and the First World War. Its economies were broken, its political systems were in flux, and its social hierarchies were unstable. The political, social, and ideological upheaval brought about by these tumultuous events had the effect of placing US progressive politics under tremendous strain. Divisions among progressives as to how to respond to the war were bitter. Some progressives were impressed that war might be used to expand the state's capacity and to bring discipline, efficiency, and patriotic unity to the reform agenda at home, but others despaired at its human cost, militarism, and state repression.[74] La Follette, as it happens, sat squarely in the latter camp. He had opposed US entry into the war, had very nearly been thrown out of the Senate for taking this stand, and considered that the Versailles Treaty was a sham, which would prove a breeding ground for future conflicts.[75] He went to Europe, he wrote, because he feared the United States would soon be dragged into another war and wanted to "see for myself as far as possible just what the situation is...."[76]

If the historiographical contexts and chronological settings of Bryan and La Follette's travels were different, it is important to note that they went to Europe for broadly the same reasons, following similar itineraries, meeting the same kinds of people, and in the process illuminating for us the salience in the early decades of the twentieth century of a populist mode of transatlantic politics that, arguably, has rarely been given the attention it deserves. La Follette practiced social politics in the course of his 1923 Atlantic crossings but, like Bryan, he simultaneously pursued other modes of politics, and he did so in ways wholly consistent with his broader populist-inflected political commitments.

Bryan's travels in 1903–1904 and in 1905–1906 were part of a strategy designed to boost his presidential prospects. He aimed to demonstrate that he was a global statesman with wide experience of diplomatic affairs and an understanding of the world's peoples and cultures. In 1923 La Follette, too, was readying himself for a run at the presidency. As his autobiography amply demonstrates, losing the 1912 Republican Party nomination to Theodore Roosevelt had been a bitter blow.[77] Now, with Roosevelt dead and Woodrow Wilson dying, La Follette had one last chance to show that he was the authentic representative of the US progressive movement. Time spent in Europe would give the Wisconsin senator the opportunity to refresh his contacts with likeminded reformers on the other side of the Atlantic, and it might also lend greater weight and authority to his foreign policy pronouncements. Funded by a wealthy benefactor, William T. Rawleigh, La Follette (unlike Bryan) could afford to turn down lucrative offers from press baron William Randolph Hearst to publish his travel impressions and political observations.[78] The only major cause for concern was the senator's failing health, which deteriorated during the trip, causing his family constant worry.[79] As a matter of fact, their anxiety was warranted: had he won the presidency in 1924 La Follette would have spent just three months in the White House; his running mate, Montana Democrat Burton K. Wheeler would have served the bulk of his term.

La Follette spent 11 weeks of his life in Europe, arriving in Plymouth, in the southwest of England, on August 9 and departing from Cherbourg on the north coast of France in late October. His itinerary was affected by his heart condition, which dictated that at the end of his trip he was unable to accept an invitation to speak at the Albert Hall in London on the subject of the French occupation of the Ruhr, and that he was forced to cancel planned meetings with, among others, Britain's first Labour Prime Minister, Ramsay MacDonald, the South African military leader and statesman Jan Smuts, and the Anglo-Irish agricultural reformer, Horace Plunkett.[80] Even so, he devoted a considerable portion of his tour to discussing political affairs with leading public figures. In England at the beginning of his trip, for example, he met the economist John Maynard Keynes, the editor of the *Manchester Guardian* C. P. Snow, the Labour MP and journalist Norman Angell, and the architect and planner Raymond Unwin.[81] In Germany, which he reached in mid-August, he met the new Chancellor, Gustav Stresemann, as well as a number of members of the Reichstag, and assorted newspaper editors, businessmen, and labor representatives.[82] In Berlin, aided by his son, Robert M. La Follette, Jr, he collected data on the food supply crisis unfolding in the French-occupied Ruhr.[83] In the Soviet Union, where he reached at the end of August, he was introduced to numerous leading Soviet politicians, among them Georgy Chicherin, Alexei Rykov, Anatoly Lunacharsky, and Leonid Krasin.[84] (La Follette's friends, muckraking journalist Lincoln Steffens and the sculptor Jo Davidson, joined him for the Russian leg of his tour. His guides in the Soviet Union were the pro-Soviet journalists Anna Louise Strong and Santeri Nuorteva.)[85] On leaving the USSR, he traveled through Poland, Austria, and then Italy, where he met Mussolini, quizzing him persistently on the wisdom of restricting freedom of speech and freedom of the press.[86] Leaving Rome on September 23, La Follette and his party made their way back to Germany, seeing Munich, Nuremburg, Frankfurt, Wiesbaden, Cologne, and Essen.[87] In the Ruhr, traveling in a Ford provided by the American banker James Causey, La Follette visited hospitals and children's feeding stations, an experience that intensified his hostility toward both the French government led by Raymond Poincaré, and the architects of the Versailles Treaty.[88] On October 5 they returned to Berlin, headed straight for Copenhagen and then, a few days later, for Paris, which they reached late on the evening of October 10, staying for the remainder of their tour at the luxurious Hôtel de Crillon on the Place de la Concorde.[89]

In addition to these meetings with political allies, statesmen, and opinion formers, La Follette engaged in tourism. In England he followed in Bryan's footsteps by visiting the castles at Windsor, Kenilworth, and Warwick, and in sampling Shakespeare's Stratford-upon-Avon. In Manchester's Albert Square he stopped to admire the statue of the mid-nineteenth-century Quaker radical John Bright, whose oratorical skills, attacks on slavery and aristocratic privilege, and criticisms of Palmerston's foreign policy La Follette identified with.[90] Later, in Austria, accompanied by his cousin Suzanne, who lived in Vienna, the senator and his party spent three days sightseeing, taking in the city's art museums, its palaces, and the State Opera House, where they saw the great Moravian soprano, Maria Jeritza, sing the lead in *Carmen*.[91] In Italy they motored along the Appian Way and savored Rome's wonders, ancient and modern. The La Follette family's tastes were more high-cultural than Bryan's: in Germany they enjoyed Nuremburg's medieval churches and sought out the homes of Albrecht Dürer, Hans Sachs, and Goethe; in Denmark—which Bob Jr described as being like "the anteroom to Paradise" compared to the terrible scenes they had witnessed in the Ruhr—they went to Helsingør (Elsinore) so that Bob Sr could see Kronborg castle, where Shakespeare's *Hamlet* was set.[92]

The notes, letters, and articles La Follette wrote during and after his visit to Europe illuminate his populist conviction that concentrated power in monopoly form was the overriding problem faced by modern society. His intense interest in the cooperative movement was a function of his antimonopoly perspective as it was predicated on the view that cooperation might resolve issues of scale and complexity, which, to his mind, imperilled democratic life on both sides of the Atlantic. Visits to cooperative factories and discussions with leading cooperators in England and Denmark were highlights of his tour. Indeed the opportunity to "study the great cooperatives of producers and consumers" in Europe was, he wrote, one of his main reasons for wanting to see Europe in the first place.[93] Following a tour of the Cooperative Wholesale Society in Manchester he noted that the CWS was "a truly big business, but it belongs to the people."[94] His notes supply a barrage of statistics designed to show that the movement was both profitable and efficient as well as being an instrument of economic justice.[95] Cooperative federations such as the CWS in Manchester were, he believed, a means of "escaping from the operation of the monopolies and combinations which are slowly but surely throttling the economic life of America."[96] He was inspired by the way in which "millions of humble folk in Europe have applied the principles of self-government to the conduct of a large part of their economic relations.[97] He found the Danish cooperative system to be no less impressive.[98] In terms of agricultural science, he argued, the Danes were no more knowledgeable than their American counterparts, but their cooperatives were superior in their methods of marketing and credit, and it was this, he judged, that delivered higher standards of living.[99] Leaders of US farm states, he concluded, should "make a thorough study of the European cooperative situation on the ground" and at the same time press for legal privileges and immunities on a par with those enjoyed by corporations.[100] In this way the playing field of US economic and political life would be leveled.

La Follette's antipathy to concentrated power was not confined to the economic sphere. It informed his approach to governance, diplomacy, and the role of the state. Some of La Follette's progressive friends, including his traveling companion Lincoln Steffens, were powerfully drawn to the radical ambition of the Soviet Union's experiments in planning and large-scale social reform. But although it is true that the senator from Wisconsin was fascinated by the work of Russian cooperatives, and commented approvingly on the fact that farm workers owned land, Lewis S. Feuer's argument that for La Follette the Soviet Union was "in large measure Midwestern Populist Progressivism realized" is unconvincing. La Follette took a much dimmer view of the Soviet Union than either Steffens or his wife Belle Case La Follette, on whose accounts the Soviet Union Feuer leans rather heavily.[101] La Follette was utterly opposed to political dictatorship. What is more, the form of antimonopoly progressivism he practiced was wholly inconsistent with large-scale economic planning and collectivization. His experiences in the USSR helped to persuade him that he should not work with communists during his 1924 presidential campaign.[102] The articles he wrote on his return from the USSR show that he well understood the devastation and violence caused by the Russian Revolution, and that although he admired "the character of the people," he did not think highly of the Soviet regime.[103] As one might expect of a populist-progressive from a rural state, he praised the Soviet government's policy of giving farm workers free rail tickets to attend the Moscow exposition, and applauded it for acknowledging the fundamental importance of food production to the economy, but he also made clear that in the absence of freedom of speech and assembly, and given the ongoing nefarious activities of the secret police, the Russian people were, fundamentally, not free.[104] "I bitterly detest the suppression of civil liberties, the control of elections, the exile and outrageous treatment of political opponents and the many other examples of anti-democratic government that I found in Russia," he wrote.[105] These were not the words of a man seduced by his pro-Soviet guides. He had "grave doubts," he continued, concerning "the complete government monopoly of industry."[106] The Soviet Union had been "crushed by the Communist oligarchy" just as Italy had been "destroyed by Mussolini and his Fascism."[107] Democratic principles, he concluded, were being "ground to dust" between "the upper and nether millstones of imperialistic and communistic dictatorships—between the fascists and bolshevists of the different countries."[108] La Follette returned from his tour convinced that the cure for these ills, both in Europe and in the United States, lay in "the application of genuine republican principles."[109]

    La Follette's antimonopoly brand of populist-progressivism was also reflected in his approach to the diplomatic crises that enveloped

Europe before, during, and after the First World War. He was at pains in his writings on Europe to emphasize that ordinary people in the countries he visited were not consumed by hatred, except when "inflamed by propaganda."[110] Instead they were "longing for peace."[111] La Follette's belief that "the people" were essentially virtuous but were threatened by unseen and unaccountable forces is a classic populist trope, and one that pervades his discussions of the Great War and its aftermath. Europe's people were tired of war, he wrote, making them "easy prey to the forces of reaction and tyranny."[112] He argued that in the debates about whether the United States should enter the war, the American people were sold a false prospectus— the conflict was never really about making a world "safe for democracy," it was essentially an "imperialistic enterprise."[113] The existence of "secret treaties," he thought, belied the lofty pronouncements of military and political leaders.[114] In his view the rise of dictatorships across Europe was a symptom of people's loss of faith in their capacity for self-government. This was regrettable but given the strength of monopoly power it was also understandable: in France the Comité des Forges operated as a "steel trust"; in Germany the industrialist Hugo Stinnes was more powerful than Chancellor Stresemann.[115] The "machinations of the industrialists and militarists of both France and Germany," he wrote, obstructed the work of representative institutions and exacerbated popular tensions in those countries.[116]

Senator La Follette summed up his visit to Europe by declaring himself grateful that the United States was separated from Europe by 3,000 miles of ocean.[117] His 11 weeks in Europe had enabled him to refresh his transatlantic networks, and to forge new connections. He especially enjoyed learning more about the cooperative movement. But his appreciation of European social politics was tempered by a deep antipathy to the concentration of political and economic power, which delimited his commitment to collectivist policies and made him wary of big-state solutions. The populist antimonopoly element of his progressive politics made it impossible for him to profess enthusiasm for the Soviet Union in the way that some of his fellow progressives did. The stands he had made for civil liberties and for free speech in opposition to the Red Scare at home dictated that he could not overlook the suppression of freedoms abroad. He returned to the United States with his faith in what he termed the "American tradition of democracy" renewed.[118] Accordingly, his 1924 presidential campaign was notable less for its embrace of European-style social reforms than for its message that concentrated power was the preeminent threat to the democratic future of the United States.[119]

It was the last time in US history that a major candidate for the presidency made antimonopoly the centrepiece of a bid for the White House. Running against two conservatives—the Democrat John W. Davis and the Republican Calvin Coolidge—he won the support of 4.8 million voters, which, at that time, was the most ever won by a third party candidate.[120] He secured 16.6 percent of the popular vote, a proportion bettered only twice in the post-Civil War era by a third party candidate: Theodore Roosevelt (Progressive) won 27.4 percent in 1912; Ross Perot (Independent) won 18.9 percent in 1992.

Populism, antimonopoly, and transatlantic reform

In the first quarter of the twentieth century, William Jennings Bryan and Robert M. La Follette—the two leading US populist-progressives of their generation—participated actively in the world of transatlantic reform. As this chapter has shown, they did so in ways that complicate our general understanding of the US historiography of reform, and of these two important figures in particular. Bryan's networks were more global and extensive than historians typically recognize—he traveled widely, mixing social politics with moral reform work and peace advocacy. La Follette, in contrast, was not an experienced traveler—he only visited Europe once—but he showed in his wider political life an unusual degree of openness toward European public policy ideas. It is ironic therefore that overseas travel ultimately persuaded him of the virtues of geographical separation as much as they impressed upon him the advantages of dense networks of transatlantic contact and exchange. In these ways this essay aims to shift perceptions of Bryan and La Follette in the context of the rather rigidly exceptionalist US historiography of reform.

Furthermore, this chapter makes a case for more serious consideration of populism's contribution to the world of reform that traversed the Atlantic in the first decades of the twentieth century. It has shown that not only Bryan and Follette practiced social politics in the mold of Daniel T. Rodgers's *Atlantic Crossings*, but also that they engaged in alternative modes of politics, in this way revealing the multivalent character of early-twentieth-century transatlantic reform. Bryan's populism manifested itself in his hostility to imperialism, his affinity for the land reform policies of Irish nationalists, and in the connections he forged with fellow bimetallists across Europe. La Follette's populism manifested itself in his determination to interpret European political, social, and diplomatic affairs through the lens of antimonopoly language and thought, and in his insistence that the virtuous peoples of Europe were being manipulated by unaccountable elites.

Finally, this chapter invites further investigation of the significance of populism's exclusion from the extant literature on transatlantic reform. The transnational turn has not weakened the exceptionalist bias of the historiography of reform as much as one might expect. In fact it may be that exceptionalism exerts such a powerful pull on how historians of the United States write about the politics of reform that, on occasion, even its critics are prone to indulge it. A closer look at Rodgers's own writings on progressivism and the politics of reform over the entire span of his career secures this point. In a 1982 essay entitled "In Search of Progressivism" Rodgers identified antimonopoly as one of three distinct yet malleable "social languages" progressives used to give voice to their "discontents and social visions."[121] It was "the oldest," the "most peculiarly American" and, in the period 1900–1910 at least, the most powerful of these languages, he wrote.[122] The other two languages he singled out—those of social bonds and of social efficiency—were more cosmopolitan, he claimed, drawing as they did on numerous international influences such as German mutualism in the former case, and on the proposals for bureaucratic reform that emerged from the complex traffic of ideas between European and American social scientists in the latter. In contrast, the lineage of antimonopoly could be traced, Rodgers stated, "through the Populists, through Henry George, and on at least to Andrew Jackson."[123] In this way populism is figured in Rodgers's schema as an exclusively national political tradition that, as such, was not susceptible to transnational currents, influence, and exchange.

Rodgers has been a notable critic of nation-centered and inward-looking scholarship on the history of US reform.[124] His work can be understood as a rebuke to the notion that US social, intellectual, and political development should be studied as if it were more or less immune from external influence. In his treatment of antimonopoly, however, Rodgers defers to exceptionalism, assuming it would appear, that the international reach of this key language of reform was negligible. The languages of social bonds and of social efficiency are examined and analyzed in detail in *Atlantic Crossings*, but the antimonopoly strand, with its populist roots, is almost entirely overlooked.

Reflecting on this omission, it is hard to avoid the conclusion that antimonopoly—one of the pillars of late-nineteenth- and early-twentieth-century US progressivism—was a necessary victim of Rodgers's mid-career shift in scholarly focus from national to transnational history. For some scholars steeped in the lore of US exceptionalism, the idea that populism was a mobile, and sometimes outward-looking, mode of politics remains a bridge too far. By failing to acknowledge the existence of an antimonopoly Atlantic, Rodgers unwittingly reveals the enduring power of exceptionalism in US historical writing, a tradition sometimes disavowed by historians who nevertheless continue to pay it obeisance.

Notes

1. On Populism's contribution to US progressivism and state building see especially Elisabeth Sanders, *Roots of Reform: Farmers, Workers, and the American State, 1877–1917* (Chicago: University of Chicago Press, 1999). On populism as a persistent nonprogrammatic mode of political articulation in US political culture see Michael Kazin, *The Populist Persuasion: An American History* (New York: Basic Books, 1995). For agrarian radicalism in transatlantic perspective, see Thomas Summerhill and James C. Scott, eds, *Transatlantic Rebels: Agrarian Radicalism in Comparative Context* (East Lansing, MI: Michigan State University Press, 2004).

2. Michael Kazin, *A Godly Hero: The Life of William Jennings Bryan* (New York: A. A. Knopf, 2006), 121–41; Daniel Scroop, "A Life in Progress: Motion and Emotion in the Autobiography of Robert M. La Follette," *American Nineteenth Century History* 13, no. 1 (June 2012), 45–64.

3. This is best traced by reading Bryan and La Follette's own words. See for example William Jennings Bryan, "The Trust Problem," in *William Jennings Bryan: Selections* ed. Ray Ginger, 99–112 (Indianapolis, IN: Bobbs-Merrill Company, 1967) and Robert M. La Follette, *La Follette's Autobiography: A Personal Narrative of Political Experiences* (Madison, WI: Robert La Follette Company, 1913).

4. Bryan, "Trust Problem," 100.

5. La Follette, *Autobiography*, 321.

6. The classic statement of this position is Richard Hofstadter, "William Jennings Bryan: The Democrat as Revivalist," in Richard Hofstadter, *The American Political Tradition: And the Men Who Made It* (New York: A. A. Knopf, 1948), 239–64.

7. On the political timing and emotional power of the speech see Richard Bensel, *Passion and Preferences: William Jennings Bryan and the 1896 Democratic Convention* (Cambridge: Cambridge University Press, 2008).

8. Kazin, *Godly Hero*, 45–79.

9. Hofstadter, "Democrat as Revivalist," 239–64 passim.

10. Kazin, *Godly Hero*, 170.

11. Bryan wrote extensively as he traveled. See Bryan, *Under Other Flags: Travels, Lectures, Speeches* (Lincoln, NE: 1904) and Bryan, *The Old World and Its Ways* (Lincoln, NE: 1907).

12. Bryan, *The Old World*. The reminiscences of Bryan's daughter, Grace, are in numerous respects more interesting than her father's hurried despatches. Grace Bryan, "William Jennings Bryan," unpublished manuscript, vol. 1, "Notes on Foreign Travel," p. 456, Box 57, William Jennings Bryan papers, Manuscript Division, Library of Congress.

13. Grace Bryan, "Notes on Foreign Travel," 5.

14. Scroop, "World Tour," 15–20.

15. Grace Bryan, "Notes on Foreign Travel," 456.

16. Ibid.

17. Ibid. See also Bryan, *The Old World*, 403–34.

18. Bryan, *The Old World*, 435–55.

19. Ibid., 419–20.

20. Ibid., 423–24.

21. Ibid., 437–38.

22. Paulo Coletta, *William Jennings Bryan, Political Evangelist* (Lincoln: University of Nebraska Press), 1:371.

23. Ibid. See also Merle Curti, *Bryan and World Peace* (Northampton, MA: Smith College Studies in History, 1931).

24. Colletta, *Political Evangelist*, 1:371.

25. See Tyrell, *Reforming the World*.

26. William Jennings Bryan, *The Commoner*, July 6, 1906,13.

27. Scroop, "World Tour", 15–21.

28. Louis W. Koenig, *Bryan: A Political Biography of William Jennings Bryan* (New York: G. P. Putnam's Sons, 1971), 463.

29. For an account of the conference, see Brian Stanley, *The World Missionary Conference, Edinburgh 1910* (Grand Rapids, MI: William B. Eerdmans Publishing, 2009).

30. Koenig, *Bryan: A Political Biography*, 463.

31. Bryan's account of this tour can be found in his *Under Other Flags*, 9–124 and in *The Old World*, 492–575.

32. Bryan, *Under Other Flags*, 7, 10.

33. Ibid., 15–21.

34. Ibid., 13.

35. Ibid., 13–21.

36. Coletta, *Political Evangelist*, 1:316–17; Bryan, *Under Other Flags*, 112–13.

37. On Davitt, George and the Irish land question see Anna George De Mille, "Henry George: The Fight for Irish Freedom," *American Journal of Economics and Sociology* 3, no. 2 (January 1944): 251–72, 251 and Michael Silagi and Susan N. Faulkner, "Henry George and Europe: Ireland, the First Target of His Efforts to Spread His

Doctrines Internationally, Disappointed Him," *American Journal of Economics and Sociology* 46, no. 4 (October 1987): 495–501.
38. Ibid., 317.
39. Thomas J. Morrissey, *William J. Walsh, Archbishop of Dublin, 1841–1921: No Uncertain Voice* (Dublin: Four Courts, 2000).
40. The Most Reverend Dr Walsh, *Bimetallism and Monometallism: What They Are and How They Bear Upon the Irish Land Question* (Dublin: Browne and Nolan, 1893).
41. William Jennings Bryan, "The Cross of Gold Speech," in *William Jennings Bryan: Selections*, ed. Ray Ginger, 37–46 (New York: Bobbs-Merrill, 1967).
42. Walsh, *Bimetallism and Monometallism*, 2–4. Bryan, *Under Other Flags*, 23–24.
43. Bryan, *Under Other Flags*, 40.
44. Ibid., 44–46.
45. See "French Hopes For Silver," *New York Times*, May 29, 1897, http://nytimes.com/.
46. Bryan, *Under Other Flags*, 70.
47. Ibid.
48. Coletta, *Political Evangelist*, 1:317.
49. Bryan, *Under Other Flags*, 29–30.
50. Ibid., 31.
51. Ibid., 32–33.
52. Ibid., 114.
53. Ibid., 33–37.
54. Ibid., 34.
55. Rodgers, *Atlantic Crossings*, 39.
56. Ibid.
57. Ibid., 38.
58. Postcard, December 14, 1903, Box 27, William Jennings Bryan papers. "We are at Bologna, the home of the sausage, (I will not try to spell it)," he wrote.
59. Bryan, *Under Other Flags*, 86–95.
60. Ibid., 121.
61. Ibid., 52.
62. Ibid., 60.
63. Ibid., 65.
64. Ibid., 96–108.
65. Compare Bryan's experience to that of Jane Addams, whom Tolstoy criticized for her fancy clothes: Jane Addams, *Twenty Years at Hull-House* (New York: MacMillan, 1911), 267–73. The fullest historical account of the meeting is Kenneth C. Wenzer, "Tolstoy and Bryan," *Nebraska History* 77 (Fall/Winter 1996): 140–48.
66. Kazin, *Godly Hero*, 126.
67. *The Commoner*, April 7, 1905, 2.

68. To compare Bryan and Tolstoy's accounts of their philosophical differences see Bryan, *Under Other Flags*, 96–108 and Leo Tolstoy, "Introduction to a Short Biography of William Lloyd Garrison," *The Kingdom of God and Peace Essays* (London: Oxford University Press for the Tolstoy Society, 1935), 579.

69. Ibid., 96.

70. The family biography is an important historical document despite it hagiographical nature: Belle Case La Follette and Fola La Follette, *Robert M. La Follette, June 14, 1855—June 18, 1925*, 2 vols (New York: MacMillan, 1953). Other major works sympathetic to La Follette include Edward N. Doan, *The La Follettes and the Wisconsin Idea* (New York: Rinehart & Co., 1947); Bernard A. Weisberger, *The La Follettes of Wisconsin: Love and Politics in Progressive America* (Madison: University of Wisconsin Press, 1994); Nancy C. Unger, *Fighting Bob La Follette: The Righteous Reformer* (Madison: Wisconsin Historical Society Press, 2000).

71. For critical perspectives see Robert S. Maxwell, *La Follette and the Rise of the Progressives in Wisconsin, 1896–1928* (Madison: State Historical Society of Wisconsin, 1956); Herbert F. Margulies, *The Decline of the Progressive Movement in Wisconsin* (Madison: State Historical Society of Wisconsin, 1968); David Thelen, *The New Citizenship: Origins of Progressivism in Wisconsin, 1885–1900* (Columbia: University of Missouri Press, 1972); and David P. Thelen, *Robert M. La Follette and the Insurgent Spirit* (New York: Little, Brown, 1976).

72. Belle Case La Follette and Fola La Follette, *Robert M. La Follette*, 2:1086.

73. On this subject see Jørn Brøndal, *Ethnic Leadership and Midwestern Politics: Scandinavian Americans and the Progressive Movement in Wisconsin, 1890–1914* (Northfield, MN: The Norwegian-American Historical Association, 2004).

74. On the First World War and US progressivism see Rodgers, *Atlantic Crossings*, 267–317; Alan Dawley, *Changing the World: American Progressives in War and Revolution* (Princeton, NJ: Princeton University Press, 2003); and Robert Westbrook, *John Dewey and American Democracy* (Ithaca, NY: Cornell University Press, 1993).

75. For a general account of La Follette's position on the First World War and of the attempt to have him expelled from the Senate, see Unger, *Fighting Bob*, 239–62.

76. Robert La Follette, "Articles on Europe," I, p. 1, Box 227, Speeches & Writings File, La Follette Family Papers, Library of Congress.

77. La Follette, *Autobiography*. See especially chapters XI–XIII.

78. Belle Case La Follette, postcard sent October 4, 1923, Folder: Belle Case La Follette, August–December 1923, Box 29, Series A, La Follette Family Collection.

79. Ibid. See also Belle Case La Follette to Fola La Follette, October 11, 1923, Belle Case La Follette, August–December 1923, Box

29, Series A, La Follette Family Collection; Robert La Follette, Jr
letters to "Dear Ones," November 12, 1923, November 17, 1923,
November 23, 1923 and December 4, 1923, Folder: Robert M.
La Follette Jr, August–December 1923, Box 30, Series A, La Follette
Family Collection.

80. Belle Case La Follette and Fola La Follette, *Robert M. La Follette*,
    2:1086.
81. Ibid., 1076, 1077.
82. Ibid., 1078.
83. Ibid.
84. Ibid., 1081.
85. Ibid., 1079. The La Follettes' visit to the Soviet Union is discussed in
    Lewis S. Feuer, "American Travelers to the Soviet Union 1917–32:
    The Formation of a Component of New Deal Ideology," *American
    Quarterly* 14, no. 2 (Summer 1962): 119–49; Belle Case La Follette,
    "With Senator La Follette in Russia," *La Follette's Magazine* XV
    (1923), 185–86; and Jo Davidson, *Between Sittings: An Informal
    Autobiography* (New York: Dial Press, 1951), 178–81.
86. Ibid., 1083–84.
87. Ibid., 1084.
88. Ibid., 1078–79, 1084.
89. Ibid., 1085–86.
90. Ibid., 1076–77.
91. Ibid., 1083.
92. Ibid., 1084–85.
93. Robert La Follette, "Articles on Europe," I, 1.
94. Ibid., V, 4.
95. Ibid., 1–10.
96. Belle Case La Follette and Fola La Follette, *Robert M. La Follette*, 1078.
97. Robert La Follette, "Articles on Europe," V, 1.
98. Ibid., 5.
99. Ibid., 6–8.
100. Ibid., 10.
101. Belle Case La Follette to Mary La Follette, October 4, 1923, Belle
     Case La Follette, August–December 1923, Box 29, Series A, La
     Follette Family Collection.
102. Bernard A. Weisberger, *The La Follettes of Wisconsin*, 266.
103. Robert La Follette, "Articles on Europe," IV, 5.
104. Ibid., 6–7.
105. Ibid., 8.
106. Ibid.
107. Belle Case La Follette and Fola La Follette, *Robert M. La Follette*,
     2:1087.
108. La Follette, "Articles on Europe," I, 4.
109. Belle Case La Follette and Fola La Follette, *Robert M. La Follette*,
     2:1087.

110. La Follette, "Articles on Europe," I, 3.
111. Ibid.
112. Ibid.
113. La Follette, "Articles on Europe," VII, 5.
114. La Follette, "Articles on Europe," I, 4.
115. La Follette, "Articles on Europe," I, 5
116. Ibid., 5–6.
117. Ibid., 8.
118. Ibid., 7–8.
119. For La Follette's 1924 campaign see Unger, *Fighting Bob*, 281–303; Belle Case La Follette and Fola La Follette, *Robert M. La Follette*, 2:1107–47; and David L. Waterhouse, *The Progressive Movement of 1924 and the Development of Interest Group Liberalism* (New York: Garland Publishing, 1991).
120. La Follette's achievement was surpassed in 1968 by George Wallace who won 9.9 million votes running as an American Independent.
121. Daniel T. Rodgers, "In Search of Progressivism," *Reviews in American History*, 10, no. 4 "The Promise of American History: Progress and Prospects" (December 1982): 123.
122. Ibid.
123. Ibid., 123, 124–27.
124. See Daniel T. Rodgers, "Exceptionalism," in *Imagined Histories: American Historian Interpret the Past*, Anthony S. Molho and Gordon S. Wood, eds (Princeton, NJ: Princeton University Press, 1998) and Daniel T. Rodgers, "American Exceptionalism Revisited," *Raritan* 24, no. 2 (Fall 2004): 21–47.

Chapter 5

Beyond Uplift and Efficiency: Isaac M. Rubinow, Immigration, and Transatlantic Health Care Reform, 1900–1935

Axel Schäfer

The question of how to reconcile broad-based public support for comprehensive systems of social provision with high levels of immigration has confounded generations of social reformers and academic observers. Welfare states, the late British historian Tony Judt has noted, have usually only worked in small, homogenous countries. In places "where immigration and visible minorities have altered the demography," however, mistrust and suspicion have often led to a loss of identification with the social welfare institutions of the liberal state.[1]

Few pivotal figures in the creation of modern Western welfare states were more aware of this dilemma than Isaac Max Rubinow (1875–1936). Often referred to as the "greatest American expert of his generation" on social insurance and the father of Social Security, Rubinow embodied the cosmopolitan breadth and intellectual vitality of American reform from the late nineteenth century to the New Deal.[2] As a German-speaking Lithuanian Jew, his roots were both in the Old World and in the immigrant cultures of New York City; as a Socialist, he participated in the raucous urban politics of the Progressive era and repeatedly ran for Congress on a socialist ticket; as a physician, he witnessed first-hand the ravages of urban poverty and frequently refused to charge his poverty-stricken immigrant patients; as a teacher and writer, he taught night classes for immigrants and wrote articles for Russian and Jewish periodicals in Russia; and as a professional actuary, he worked for the furtherance of progressive legislation. In the words of his biographer, Rubinow "could have created the appearance of a social movement single-handedly."[3]

This chapter argues that Rubinow's concern with the relationship between migration and social policy formed the basis of a distinctive transnational and civic vision of social insurance that sought to reconcile ethnic diversity, participatory politics, distributive justice, and cultural modernity. In Rubinow's eyes, creating a modern social insurance system out of traditions of immigrant mutualism was a means of democratizing the social order and integrating immigrants into the body politic. He linked the welfare state to the expansion of a public sphere of control that enabled individuals of all ethnic backgrounds to participate in non-commercial and democratic organizations. Rubinow recognized the close connection between economic fear and ethnic and racial hostility, arguing that effective and universal social insurance eased social conflict. The new avenues of social interaction and democratic participation provided by self-governed insurance funds, he maintained, would enable individuals to recognize that their freedom was intrinsically tied to their social being. In other words, insurance reform would facilitate the intersubjective development across ethnic divides of social norms more commensurate with the realities of industrial interdependence than the proprietarian individualism and moral precepts of traditional republican and agrarian ideology.[4]

Rubinow's concept of social citizenship, however, was sidelined in the aftermath of the First World War. The war, though legitimizing expanded state social provision, discredited the transatlantic and immigrant roots of the social insurance campaign. Indeed, the war-generated growth of the interventionist and bureaucratic capacities of government, hailed by many progressives, was fundamentally at odds with Rubinow's ethnic, social-relational, and redistributive dimension of progressivism. Public policy in the wake of the war, including immigration restrictions, gradually replaced the prewar effort to expand opportunities for meaningful public participation. Instead of promoting a welfare state actively engaged in creating public spheres of control, it focused on repressive or rehabilitative intervention; a functionalism centered on cost–benefit calculations; and a vision of government as a handmaiden to private business. While broadening the scope for government, wartime social reform in effect circumscribed its ability to address fundamental issues of socioeconomic injustice and the maldistribution of wealth.

Revisiting Rubinow's understanding of social reform enables us to recover a tradition of "cultural social politics" that can be distinguished from both conventional prewar progressivism and the reform agendas of the 1920s. Rubinow and others challenged the focus of many native-born progressives on either "moral uplift" or "industrial efficiency." At the same time, his concept pointed beyond a "third way" that simply sought to merge aspects of market provision and state planning. Instead, it reflected an effort to mold a pluralistic society into a community of democratic norms and values without either subordinating policy to the utilitarian calculations of liberal capitalism or reproducing entrenched racial, ethnic, and gender hierarchies via government intervention. Based on these findings, the essay argues for further research into the transatlantic networks of professionals and social activists that shaped the semantic and institutional webs linking immigration and social policy in the interwar years.

Rubinow and Transatlantic Progressivism

In recent decades the renewed scholarly focus on the transatlantic dimension of social politics has shown that European reform was constitutive of American progressivism and vice versa in ways that have previously been neglected. In the late nineteenth and early twentieth centuries, intricate networks of personal friendships, organized exchanges, institutional ties, and professional publications linked American progressives to European social reform. Mass circulation periodicals such as *Outlook, Arena, Scribner's* and *Review of Reviews* were filled with articles such as "The Municipal Spirit in England," "How Germany Cares for Her Working People," and "Public Ownership in France." Professional journals and mouthpieces of social reform, such as *Survey, National Municipal Review*, and *City Plan*, alerted their readers to British garden cities, German social insurance, or French syndicalism. European models were scrutinized by Americans who embraced causes ranging from public playgrounds to public housing; from protective laws for women workers to unemployment insurance; and from prison reform to municipally owned utilities. As the ubiquitous reformer Henry Demarest Lloyd exclaimed, Americans should "have the wit to make a salad of all the good ideas of Europe and Australasia."[5] Likewise, progressive journalist Walter Weyl asserted in 1912 that "Europe does not learn at our feet the facile lessons of democracy, but has in some respects become our teacher."[6]

The cultural, political, and intellectual transfer these ties facilitated meant that American social politics "was of a part with movements of politics and ideas throughout the north Atlantic world that trade and capitalism had tied together."[7] Foreign reforms, which emerged as images, projections, or icons whose meanings were produced in the discourses of the borrowing culture, profoundly shaped the progressive agenda. The close interaction between American and European social thought, James Kloppenberg has argued, helped construct a radical body of ideas cut loose from "atomistic empiricism, psychological hedonism, and utilitarian ethics."[8] Likewise, Daniel Rodgers, the foremost historian of transatlantic social politics, has maintained that the progressives' transatlantic gaze "exploded the syllogisms of classical economic liberalism."[9]

The scholarly efforts to reconstruct the "progressive international" and trace its role in the intellectual sea changes during the Progressive era, however, has primarily focused on the complexities of cross-cultural representation and on the way social problems were culturally named and framed in the transfer process. Meanwhile, the role of immigrants and immigration in social reform has received remarkably little attention.[10] Moreover, although immigration has been the subject of much analysis of domestic progressivism, the focus tended to be on working-class protest, rather than on immigrant intellectuals. A closer examination of Isaac M. Rubinow and the campaign for compulsory health insurance can help address this gap in three ways. First, it sheds light on ethnic, social, and intellectual sources of progressive reform that historians have frequently overlooked. Second, it shows how immigration legislation and perceptions of immigrants shaped social policy. And finally, it suggests that the intellectual engagement with issues of migration is at the core of the transformation of transatlantic social thought during the first part of the twentieth century.[11]

Isaac Max Rubinow was the son of an affluent and assimilated textile merchant in Russian Lithuania. In 1893, aged 17, he moved with his family to New York in the wake of restrictions and pogroms under Czar Alexander III. In the autumn of the same year, he entered Columbia University, and later went on to New York University Medical School, where he received his degree in 1898. While working as a physician in the ghettoes of New York City, Rubinow once again enrolled at Columbia to study economics, statistics, sociology, and political philosophy. In 1903, having given up medical practice, he began to pursue a career as researcher, actuary, and statistical expert. Working for the US Department of

Commerce and Labor in 1908, Rubinow joined a group of investigators compiling a comprehensive reference work on systems of workmen's insurance. The polyglot and cosmopolitan Rubinow was at an advantage, as US Commissioner of Labor Carroll D. Wright "obliged its researchers to become familiar with European experiments with social insurance."[12]

This massive report, which became a standard reference book for Progressive-era reform, showed just how much Rubinow had become immersed in the social insurance campaign. After leaving government service for a career as a statistician in the private insurance business, he established himself as a leading campaigner for public insurance. By 1912, the Progressive Party used his work for a platform that called for the introduction of social insurance. And in 1913, Rubinow published *Social Insurance with Special Reference to American Conditions*, a book that attracted favorable attention in American and European academic and reform circles and became the standard text on the subject at American universities.[13]

Rubinow moved easily between his identity as socialist Jewish immigrant and as an urban, educated, middle-class, and morally driven progressive. Indeed, it was his transnational background and concern about immigrants that enabled him to formulate a vision of progressive reform that went beyond the focus of many native-born progressives on either "uplift" or "efficiency." He advocated a communitarian, social-democratic concept in which health insurance was conceived of as a means of furthering political participation, civic engagement, industrial democracy, and redistributive justice.[14] His distinctive strand of progressivism merged the social-relational theory of democracy pioneered by John Dewey, the revisionism of Eduard Bernstein, and European traditions of mutualism. In addition, it reflected Randolph Bourne's vision of a "trans-national America," spelled out in his famous July 1916 essay in *Atlantic Monthly* that viewed the United States as a "no-place" where multiple ethnic, national, and racial "citizenships" were constantly formed and defined through processes of social and cultural interaction.[15]

The campaign for compulsory health insurance, which Rubinow spearheaded by the early twentieth century, was not only among the most passionate efforts of prewar American progressives, but was also intimately tied to the issue of immigration. This link is best illustrated by the way in which the health insurance movement fits into the "social bonds," "efficiency," and "antimonopoly" discourses Daniel Rodgers has identified as the intellectual core of Progressivism.[16]

First, culturally constructed ideas of race and ethnicity shaped the social health and sanitation narratives of the Progressive era. This found expression in two primary "social bonds" discourses. On the one hand, many reformers, in keeping with traditional notions of social control and moral uplift, constructed immigrants and their "diseases" as a cultural threat to normative and societal cohesion. Images of unsanitary conditions among immigrants often formed the conceptual core of their "poverty knowledge" that associated disease with behavioral deviance, moral deficiencies, and cultural pathology. Stories of Italian mothers giving wine to their babies, Irish juveniles terrorizing neighborhoods, swarthy and bearded immigrants clad in strange dress living in the "alien enclaves" of the urban slums and practicing "popery and superstition" reflected middle-class fears associated with urban life, industrial capitalism, poverty, crime, and overcrowding. Interventionist social policies were thus frequently couched in a language that denounced the morality and cultural practices of the "queer conglomerate mass of heterogeneous elements…with a taint of whiskey."[17]

On the other hand, however, breakthroughs in understanding illness and diseases stressed the interdependence of culturally diverse populations in modern urban and industrial society. To view sickness as purely a matter of personal responsibility was "in glaring contradiction to the teachings of modern medicine and hygiene," the physician Rubinow declared: "By what theory of justice or right can a man be blamed for inhaling bacteria of diphtheria from his neighbor's mouth in an overcrowded factory?"[18] Or, as his fellow insurance reformer Charles Henderson pointed out, society was "discovering that neglected disease or wounds involve public loss and danger," and that "no man can be sick unto himself."[19] In short, immigration highlighted the need for the development of a new ethic of interdependence adapted to the social realities of urban and industrial life.[20]

Second, health insurance reform reflected the emphasis on efficiency and labor force consolidation that pervaded progressivism. This became particularly apparent when the First World War catapulted health issues to the forefront of public debates. The most effective publicity for the need for improvements in public health was the embarrassing fact that 33 percent of the men examined for the National Army were rejected on grounds of physical unfitness. "Such conditions place a serious handicap upon the social well-being and productive efficiency of the nation," the National Industrial Conference Board, a research organization established by major industrial trade organizations, warned in 1918.[21] In turn, many reformers expected that energies mobilized to fight the Germans could also be channeled into fighting poverty and disease. They placed their hopes in what John Dewey famously called the "social potentialities of war," namely that wartime regulation, standardization, and social planning would result in social harmony, rationalized production, and economic efficiency. At the same time, they saw health insurance as a way of cementing "the labor element to the government" across ethnic divides.[22]

Finally, progressives used compulsory health insurance to attack the "monopolies" within American public and private social provision linked to the spoils system, corrupt party machines, and the "malefactors of great wealth." The central features of insurance reform based on immigrant mutualism, such as self-government, equal representation, equal payment to men and women, and entitlement to benefits, challenged the "state" by providing an alternative to the corrupt and inefficient Civil War pension system. Marred by a legacy of exclusions, arbitrariness, and an overbearing bureaucracy, this "first costly and extensive national social benefits effort" for many progressives embodied the deficiencies of centralized government schemes. In the same vein, they resented the control of urban government by political machines, which, while offering jobs and a measure of social security to a working-class clientele, created dependencies, relied on patronage, and were marred by fraud.[23] Finally, compulsory health insurance provided an alternative to the "market." It undermined the stranglehold of paternalistic social policies pursued by big business, which often made benefits dependent on worker behavior and threatened the loss of payments in case of job changes. Likewise, it challenged the private insurance behemoths that paid out very little while gobbling up high premiums for administrative outlays.[24]

The Health Insurance Campaign before the First World War

The organization that instigated and sustained the organized social insurance movement in the years before and during the First World War was the American Association for Labor Legislation (AALL). Founded in 1906, the AALL went from a clearinghouse for information to an active body of social reform advocacy. Among its most active members were Chicago sociologist Charles R. Henderson, labor advocate John Graham Brooks, social worker Florence Kelley—and,

of course, Rubinow himself.[25] In 1909, the AALL made an arrangement with Paul Kellogg's social work magazine *Survey* to publish
"from month to month a few typical examples of advanced social
legislation from European experience."[26] As the *Survey* and the
American Labor Legislation Review became the main vehicles for
spreading the gospel of social insurance, Rubinow, who had became
contributing editor in 1911, moved to the forefront of the campaign. In 1913, he also became a member of the newly organized
Social Insurance Committee of the AALL, chaired by social worker
Edward T. Devine. The committee also included Henry Rogers
Seager, Rubinow's erstwhile professor at Columbia University;
Charles Henderson, then secretary of the Illinois Commission on
Industrial Diseases; AALL secretary John B. Andrews; lawyer and
actuary Miles Dawson; Rubinow's former Department of Labor col-
league Henry J. Harris; and his subsequent nemesis, Frederick L.
Hoffman.[27]

By this time, Rubinow's Socialist Party activities, which so far
had been the focus of his political activism, were waning, although
his efforts on behalf of social legislation within the AALL were
growing. In particular, he masterminded the organization's campaign for compulsory health insurance, which the AALL had by
1911 decided to focus its main energies on. The British National
Insurance Act of that year, which implemented health and unemployment insurance, had added urgency to calls for commensurate American legislation. Equally important in generating a push
toward prioritizing health issues were the 1911 reforms in Germany
to compulsory sickness insurance. Dating back to 1883, Germany
had created a system of decentralized, mainly worker-controlled
local mutual funds, integrating existing communal and local associations, factory funds, union benefit societies, friendly societies,
and guild associations.[28]

Whereas the *Review* published papers on social insurance, the state
branches of the AALL drafted bills and lobbied state legislatures.
In 1916, the organization published a model health insurance bill
that became the centerpiece of its campaign. The proposal mainly
reflected Rubinow's conception of health insurance. It required
compulsory coverage through a state insurance fund, and granted
benefits as an entitlement, without means tests or questions of fault.
Following the German precedent, it called for local, self-governed
funds, jointly managed by employers and employees under public
supervision with regular membership elections, to deliver medical
care and decide upon services. In a departure from the German

model, however, the model bill suggested that contributions should also come from the state.[29]

A follower of Eduard Bernstein, Rubinow regarded social insurance as part and parcel of modern democracy that challenged the established concentration of power and economic resources. He saw in it an effort "to readjust the distribution of the national product more equitably."[30] For him, social insurance was a means of infusing modern society with more justice and rationality—a way of redistributing wealth while simultaneously addressing the threat of pauperism in a system of industrial capitalism, where workers were unable to accumulate sufficient individual savings to pay for health-related contingencies. Health care reform, he argued, would reduce costs for laborers by eliminating the profit motive, shifting administrative expenditures to the state, and making the better off pay for it. By the same token, self-governing insurance funds would strengthen the working classes' moral backbone, political education, and intellectual abilities in preparation for the broader socialist emancipation.[31]

At the same time, the social democrat Rubinow was leery of revolution. Although reform meant that control of the sickness funds "will not rest with a group of business men eager to cut down benefits," Rubinow also reasoned that the administration of self-governed mutual funds "means that the organization will not be dominated by a small coterie of radical workers who may not be guided by sound business principles."[32] Indeed, he was convinced that both Malthus, who thought poverty an inevitable law, and Marx, who believed in progressive impoverishment as a prerequisite for revolution, were mistaken. Following Bernstein, he argued that "class struggle does not necessarily mean class war," and that "conflicts, born out of despair, are more bloodthirsty, more destructive, and less productive of positive results than intelligent collective action for the common weal."[33]

Crucial for Rubinow was that insurance should be extended to the whole class of wage earners as a matter of right, not charity or reward. He vigorously denounced the distinction between worthy and unworthy poor, and between productive and nonproductive workers, which underlay the injustice, degradation, and insufficiency of welfare. "The real issue is, not insurance versus savings, but insurance versus charity," he explained.[34] If the advantages of labor insurance were granted only to a limited group, he explained, competitive pressure would result in lower wages.[35] Likewise, he rejected the paternalism of company plans where benefits were received "not as

a matter of right, but a favor given only for continuous 'good behavior.'"[36] Rubinow reasoned that compulsion was necessary; otherwise
the financial burden would be shifted to the workers, even if employers were required to pay for insurance coverage.[37] He also called for a
hefty employers' contribution to the care of the sick, "just as business
is supposed to cover the expenses of fire insurance and wear and tear
of the inanimate machine."[38]

Indeed, Rubinow saw health insurance as an important step in
overcoming established ethnic, racial, and gender-based divisions
within American society. He rarely missed an opportunity to trumpet
the immigrant roots of health care reform. In his view, immigrant self-
help organizations had pioneered mutualistic forms of health insurance in the United States. In particular, he cited immigrant German
Krankenkassen (sickness funds), English fraternal orders, Italian societies, and Jewish lodges as having "laid the foundations of both the
main features of sick-insurance, medical aid and financial sick-bene-
fits."[39] What is more, Rubinow, together with Florence Kelley, was
one of the most scathing critics of the discrimination of immigrants
in existing American laws and one of the most outspoken advocates
of social insurance as a means of furthering ethnic and racial integration. Locating ethnic and racial stereotypes in economic conditions,
rather than genetic traits, he regarded self-governed health funds as
means of generating a sense of common bonds beyond racial and ethnic exclusiveness.[40] Keenly aware of the pitfalls of the dual labor force
in the United States, where divisions along ethnic, race, and skills
lines formed the bedrock of the cheap labor economy and prevented
a unified trade union movement, he insisted that insurance coverage
had to be universal and compulsory. As Kelley had put it, "I do not
see why, if it is possible to look out for the shifting mass of unskilled
workers who surge into the great German cities, it should be impossible for us to do the same thing in this country."[41]

Moreover, displaying a rare trait among progressives, Rubinow
criticized private pension plans and the federal Civil War pension program for excluding not only immigrants but also African Americans.
Indeed, he wrote the "first extended Marxian analysis of black history
in America," which linked the emancipation of blacks to the emancipation of workers.[42] His position resembled that of W. E. B. Du
Bois, with whom he corresponded. By the same token, he maintained
that social insurance would help undermine gender-based discrimination that regarded only men as rights-bearing entities while depict-
ing women as dependent subjects of their care. Hence, following the
German precedent, the 1916 AALL plan was not restricted to males,

but was extended to female workers. It also included maternity benefits that did not differentiate between illegitimate and legitimate children, thus avoiding the moralism that haunted the American debate.
Nonetheless, health insurance was mainly geared toward restoring
health and productivity to male workers. It did not address the problem of women facing discrimination because of pregnancy, left the
care of invalids to charity, and excluded casual, farm, and domestic
workers.[43]

However compelling Rubinow's vision was, it nonetheless differed
markedly from that of many of his native-born progressive wayfarers
in the AALL. Brooks and Henderson, for example, promoted compulsory health insurance primarily as a means of reasserting traditional social hierarchies and moral control. They were enamored of
the conservative and organicist foundations of the German system. As
Henderson put it, the German insurance system retained the features
of "personal moral bonds," which diminished the "temptation to
malingering."[44] Insisting on the clear distinction between industrious
and socially useful workers and the *Lumpenproletariat*, Henderson
declared that social insurance was neither for the wealthy, nor for the
"dependents, defectives, and delinquents," but rather for the "vast
majority of those who live on small wages or salaries."[45] For him,
social insurance was not designed to expand the service functions of
the state or to redistribute wealth, but rather to restore opportunities
for advancement to independent producers in an industrial setting.
Focusing on "uplift," Henderson bemoaned that the hope of rising
into the "diminishing capitalist–manager class has been definitely
abandoned by workingmen and people on salaries."[46]

Rubinow's approach also clashed with another school of thought
in the AALL, represented by Henry Rogers Seager and political scientist William Franklin Willoughby. They viewed compulsory health
insurance primarily as a utilitarian tool that addressed a social need in
a more cost-effective way by taking the matter "out from the domain
of litigation and the courts." Neither social ethics nor civic participation, but "efficiency" formed the core of their thinking. Their aim
was to ease the burden of poor relief and to provide "a more simple,
economical, expeditious and certain machinery."[47] They considered
compulsory insurance as first and foremost a problem-solving device
"the adoption of which should depend upon the manner in which it
performs its functions."[48]

For the immigrant socialist Rubinow, however, the health insurance campaign had little to do with either asserting a traditional
order, restoring market relations, discharging with a function more

efficiently, or strengthening centralized government. He was critical of the many progressive reformers who were more concerned with the cultural deviancy of immigrants than with their poverty; more focused on corrupt business practices than on the economic system that sanctioned them; and more obsessed with morals testing than with socioeconomic inequality. By the same token, Rubinow was acutely aware that the emphasis on efficiency—modeled on work-men's compensation systems rather than the democratic mutualism of health insurance—left business in control and denied decision-making power to workers.[49] He charged that it meant "straight out-and-out state insurance" at odds with both European precedent and the civic aspirations of the reform campaign.[50] Workmen's compensation, he argued, had benefited employers more than workers by replacing cheaper compensation coverage for more expensive liability insurance, and by allowing for low settlements while taking away workers' recourse to the courts.

War and Transatlantic Social Reform

Initially, the future seemed bright for Rubinow's plans for health insurance. In 1916, the AALL succeeded in introducing its model bill in three industrial Eastern states: New York, Massachusetts, and New Jersey. In 15 other states bills were introduced in 1917. By 1920, 20 states had considered the model health bill. Commissions or legislative committees had been appointed in 9 states, and the majority reported in favor of compulsory insurance. In California and New York, health care legislation was almost passed.

Nonetheless, the movement for compulsory health insurance, hailed in the early teens as the next step in social progress, was utterly defeated by the early 1920s. Opponents of the movement, Rubinow later bemoaned, were "strong enough to kill even the agitation, the very thought of it, for many years to come."[51] One of the main culprits was the hyper-patriotism, xenophobia, and anti-German hysteria of the war years. The First World War undermined the transnational and immigrant foundations of the campaign. In the prewar years, progressives had framed reform in terms of social and cultural development achieved through transatlantic exchange and immigrant experiences. As the war unfolded, however, the semantic web progressives had spun began to unravel. This proved particularly fateful for causes that had promoted an idealized image of Germany as a means of legitimizing reform in the United States—as was the case with the health insurance campaign.

As older patterns of nativism merged with the new rabid nationalism and 100-percent Americanism of the war years, opponents depicted the scheme as a Hun-inspired master plan of the Kaiser to turn Americans into slaves of an autocratic government. George Creel's powerful Committee on Public Information commissioned a series of articles exposing German insurance as a fraud against workers. Frederick L. Hoffman, an AALL member who subsequently emerged as a key lobbyist against compulsory health insurance, charged that the "German cause of world conquest was largely conditioned by the German conception of so-called social or compulsory insurance."[52] John O'Reilly of the Kings County (New York) Medical Society exclaimed that the insurance bill and the AALL were "MADE IN GERMANY as part of the Infamous Kultur and imported to this Country by a Russian disciple of Bolshevism and I WON'T WORKISM."[53] During the climax of the postwar Red Scare, health insurance advocates were dubbed crypto-Bolshevists, Marxists, and Jewish conspirators. In turn, public opinion blamed compulsory health insurance for everything from anarchism to the common cold.[54]

The war-related change in the popular perception of Germany from a well-governed civil service state to a militaristic, barbaric nation, however, was not the only reason the campaign began to flounder. Another cause was that the reformers had underestimated the organizational weaknesses of the movement and the effectiveness of organized opposition. Their Progressive-era faith in enlightened public opinion exaggerated the political support the campaign could muster. Enthusiasm for health insurance reform, however, was largely confined to academic and professional supporters. In California, for example, progressive Governor Hiram Johnson, who had asked Rubinow to help the state's Social Insurance Commission prepare a pioneering report on the scheme, was worried about the 2 million dollar share that insurance would impose on the state. He subsequently withheld his support from the AALL plan and proposed a referendum on the issue to be held in 1918. When Californians went to the polls in November, they soundly defeated the initiative for compulsory health insurance.[55]

Meanwhile, powerful insurance interests took up the fight against the proposal. In particular, they objected to the funeral and maternity benefits included in the AALL bill, which threatened the profitable life insurance business.[56] In California, the insurance companies mustered a considerable force against compulsory insurance by setting up the California Research Society of Social Economics, which, according to its employees, neither conducted research nor studied economics. Instead, it busied itself with distributing pamphlets that showed a picture of the Kaiser over the words "Made in Germany. Do you want it in California?"[57]

Business groups forged alliances not only with the National Association of Manufacturers (NMA) and the National Civic Federation (NCF), but also the American Federation of Labor (AFL). The divided stance of organized labor, in particular, weakened the prospects for insurance reform. Rubinow and the AALL had hoped that organized labor would lend its support to the campaign. They were encouraged by the fact that during the war years many labor organizations endorsed the bill. Influential labor leaders, such as John Mitchell of the United Mine Workers, and William Green of the AFL, supported the plan. Although this tally of supporters sounded impressive, overall enthusiasm for the plan remained low.[58] Moreover, the powerful AFL president Samuel Gompers emerged as one of the most vocal critics of compulsory health insurance. Gompers, who had committed the AFL to the war effort, reasoned that fighting the proposal would show labor's patriotism and simultaneously undermine his nemesis, the socialists, who had come out in support of compulsory health insurance.[59]

Another nail in the coffin of the campaign was that a crucial ally abandoned the cause midway. Initially, the reformers of the AALL and the physicians organized in the American Medical Association (AMA) had formed a united front. Indeed, in May of 1916 the association had hired Isaac Rubinow as secretary of its Social Insurance Commission. This cooperation, however, was sustained for the most part by doctors and administrators affiliated with institutions, governmental bodies, or large organizations.[60] As Rubinow later analyzed, supporters of the bill within the medical profession were "either very successful men who were far above any fear for their own economic future or professional standing, or they were specialists in the field of public health." Meanwhile, to private practitioners, compulsory insurance "appeared as a sinister influence upon their entire life."[61] By 1920, the AMA had changed course and declared that it was opposed to "the institution of any plan embodying the system of compulsory contributory insurance against illness."[62]

There is no doubt that wartime hysteria, political miscalculations, business lobbying, and trade union opposition played an important role in stopping health insurance reform in its tracks. However, the high emotional drama of the war years tends to overshadow the fact that the AALL had actually succeeded in making significant progress in its campaign. Indeed, wartime health needs and the public outcry over the devastating effects of venereal diseases, tuberculosis, typhus, and alcohol meant that the US government significantly expanded its role in the area of social insurance provision. "The government of the United States has become the largest single life insurance organization, as well as the safest and cheapest, in the world," Samuel McCune Lindsay, president of the AALL in 1919, hyperbolically declared. In his view, wartime insurance, which proved its value during the 1919 influenza epidemic, constituted "so striking a forward step in social insurance that it may almost be said to atone for our previous backwardness and to place the United States abreast of modern European countries."[63]

The main piece of wartime insurance legislation, the War Risk Insurance Act of 1917, was a case in point. Drawn up by progressives, including judge Julian Mack, social worker Julia Lathrop, and actuary Lee K. Frankel, it constituted the most liberal and comprehensive provision for the protection of servicemen. The Act mirrored the extension of state insurance benefits in European countries during the war, offering life insurance, medical care, vocational education, and disability benefits for war-related injuries or death. It also forced enlisted men to send home a family allowance, which was subsidized by the government. It eventually insured 4 million American soldiers and sailors, offering life insurance, medical care, vocational education, and disability benefits for war-related injuries or death.[64]

Many progressives hoped that this war-related expansion of public health benefits would be the first step toward universal insurance coverage. As Samuel McCune Lindsay predicted, "a new concept of governmental duty and opportunity growing out of our recent experiences in preparing the nation for...the war" will result in generalized health insurance.[65] In their enthusiasm, however, many reformers either consciously or unconsciously ignored a crucial flaw in the wartime government scheme: it was fundamentally at odds with Rubinow's civic, social-relational ideal embedded in the model of decentralized, self-governed insurance funds. Indeed, wartime health insurance was characterized by the very features Rubinow had warned about all along: it was based on selective benefits, centralized government provision, social control, efforts to increase worker productivity, and enhanced government–business cooperation.

First, wartime insurance remained limited to servicemen and government workers and never developed into a system of broad-based insurance coverage. Likewise, the extension of insurance programs to government workers in the 1920s introduced health benefits for targeted recipient group that created privileges for a limited range of beneficiaries. Both effectively thwarted the progressives' hope that insurance would be extended to all workers. Wartime and postwar reform thus created a segmented and fragmented system of provision on the basis of exclusionary coverage for "deserving" groups. They cemented the selective and reward-based foundation of American social insurance, following the precedent set by the Civil War pension system.[66] "Are we ready to admit that a life full of toil is of less social value than a life full of play and parade, with a few occasional battles thrown in?" Rubinow had asked in 1904.[67] The war revealed that the question had been answered in the affirmative: Workers and soldiers would continue to be treated according to different standards.

Second, the war primarily provided government with broader leverage in the area of regulation and police power, rather than legitimizing the use of the state as an instrument of social justice. As Ronald Schaffer has pointed out in his study of the treatment of shell-shock cases, subtle manipulation, behavior modification, language control, and peer pressure were "the style of management often used by the United States Government to fight the Great War."[68] In turn, measures such as Prohibition, initiatives against public smoking, preventive safety measures, and compulsory physical examinations were the basis for expanding public health benefits. In 1919, for example, the majority of the Illinois Health Insurance Commission decided against pushing for a broad-based system of social security or attempts to establish decentralized and self-governed mutual funds. Instead, it recommended that the "authority and powers of the state Department of Public Health be enlarged."[69]

Likewise, mothers' pensions and the amendment of existing workmen's compensation acts in the 1920s forestalled any reform in the direction of universal coverage and democratic participation, as neither system was based on the principle of effective worker representation and control. Although often touted as the success stories of interwar reform—by 1920, 43 states had enacted compensation legislation and 39 states had passed widows' and orphans' pension laws—they effectively undercut the more radical elements of the health insurance campaign.[70] Pointing out the irony of it all, Rubinow noted, that "the 'un-American' institution of state insurance in the field of compensation has become more extensive in the United States than it has ever been in Europe."[71] Although opponents of compulsory insurance incessantly called German-inspired compulsory insurance "despotic" and "paternalistic," the only manifestations of the paternalistic model were genuinely American.

Third, although wartime rhetoric invoked an image of social cohesion and harmony that appealed to progressive sensitivities, government intervention was designed to enforce social order, cultural exclusion, and political repression. The goal of wartime insurance reform, AALL president Irving Fisher suggested in 1918, was the "cementing of the labor element to the government," not the expansion of political participation.[72] In general, the only agencies that broadened their power base were traditional repressive agencies, such as justice and interior. The war legitimized in the public mind the use of the state as a restrictive police power. As Uriel Rosenthal concluded, this revealed that the traditional repressive element in the American state was better institutionalized than the welfare complex.[73]

Fourth, the war linked insurance with national efficiency, productivity, and economic supremacy, rather than with the extension of democratic participation. In 1918, for example, AALL president Fisher encouraged his fellow progressives to use reform to awaken the dormant higher motives that had made workers good soldiers. Inspired by Thorstein Veblen, he suggested that labor unrest could be averted if the modern workplace satisfied the instinct of workmanship and addressed the desire for self-sacrifice, love, loyalty, and worship.[74] Industrial psychology in particular became a new arena for reformist fervor in the interwar years. This helped channel reformist energies away from an effective critique of socioeconomic structures into promoting rehabilitative measures and therapeutic intervention.

Finally, the war focused energies on cooperation with business, helping to restore the tarnished prewar image of the corporate sector and accelerating the rationalization of industry. The government machinery put together to organize war production was predominantly staffed by men drawn from industry. Despite Woodrow Wilson's misgiving that "war means autocracy...we shall be dependent on the steel, oil and financial magnates," Wall Street's Bernard Baruch, the Burlington & Ohio Railroad's Daniel Willard, and International Harvester's Alexander Legge became wartime icons as enlightened captains of industry.[75] The close wartime ties between business and government came to determine the nature of federal regulation in the future. In the 1920s, government remained active in establishing partnerships with private enterprise by promoting voluntary agreements in business, supporting government-sponsored planning and research, and providing public aid for American business ventures abroad. The foundations had been laid by the Underwood–Simmons tariff and the Merchant Marine Act. Postwar legislation built upon this with the Webb–Pomerene Act of 1918, which suspended anti-trust laws for private combinations in foreign trade. The Esch–Cummins Act of 1921 returned the railroads to their previous owners, but imposed price controls, set profit margins, encouraged consolidation, and mediated labor conflicts. And prewar regulatory agencies, such as the Federal Trade Commission, the Food and Drug Administration, and the Interstate Commerce Commission, remained powerful, but steered a decidedly business-friendly course in the 1920s.[76] "Progressivism may have laid the egg of the regulatory state, and hatched it," historian Otis Graham concluded, "but the formative war-time years were spent with foster parents from Wall Street."[77]

In summation, the war and the postwar years, while undermining the broader aspirations of universal mutualistic health insurance for greater socioeconomic equality and industrial democracy, laid the foundations for some of the basic structures of the modern US welfare state.[78] Its features, however, were rather ambivalent. On the one hand, enlarging the scope of government during the war failed to create an effective bureaucratic and administrative legacy in the public sector. Most wartime agencies, such as the War Industries Board, the Food and Fuel Administrations, and the Public Health Service, were dismantled in the months and years after Armistice Day. Postwar America retained the dispersed and competing political power of state governments, courts, legislatures, parties, and interest groups, lacking an "organizationally autonomous national administrative core," and thus limiting the possibilities of social welfare development.[79] On the other hand, the war legitimized the expansion of the state as a centralized service provider for selected beneficiaries, restrictive police power, regulatory body, subsidizing agency of private business, and instrument for the promotion of economic growth. In short, what historians consider the "end" of progressivism in the 1920s is not the failure to establish a legacy of government intervention. Rather, it is the demise of a particular conception of government to help create new spheres of democratic public control. As Norman Furniss and Timothy Tilton have noted, the United States developed into a corporate-oriented positive state, rather than a social security state that emphasized minimum standards, or a social welfare state that operated on radically democratic and egalitarian principles. This also explains in part the contemporary paradox of the growth of the state being accompanied by widening insecurity, wealth gaps, and socioeconomic deprivation.[80]

Progressivism, State Building, and Immigration in the 1920s and 1930s

"And where, in these glittering twenties, were the hopes which I and my kind had held so high in the first two decades of the new century?" journalist William Allen White lamented in the postwar period, "looking around me in the gathering roar of prosperity, the only rising political force seemed to be the dark bigotry of the Ku Klux Klan."[81] White was giving voice to an overarching sense in reform circles that the 1920s had brought about the demise of Progressivism, including stopping the campaign for compulsory universal health insurance in its tracks. However, it can also be argued that the war's legacy of interventionism mainly produced a shift in the reform discourse toward a vision that had been present within Progressive reform all along. As federal agencies established a precedent for the postwar extension of government regulatory and police powers, centralized bureaucratic control, and subsidies to private business, many reformers equally changed their tune. In their interwar reform efforts, they frequently embraced selective social provision, regulation, therapeutic efforts to increase worker efficiency, enhanced government–business cooperation, and progressive models of welfare capitalism. What is more, the social expertise developed during the war continued to inform federal and state efforts to address social welfare needs in the 1920s. Indeed, the 1920s opened up new opportunities for experts and professionals from the social sciences and social work to enter government and shape public policy.[82]

The AALL was a case in point. Reeling from the defeat of health insurance, those who now dominated the organization decided to cut loose from "the traditions of Rubinow and the German basis" by focusing on workmen's compensation and unemployment insurance.[83] Spearheaded by mainstream, native-born progressives, such as John R. Commons and John Andrews, and assisted by younger experts such as Paul and Elizabeth Brandeis Raushenbush, they pursued the "Wisconsin Plan" that promoted the establishment of company-based reserve funds paying out unemployment benefits in times of economic downturns. Commons' brainchild, the Wisconsin State Industrial Commission, regulated unemployment reserve funds based on a scheme of reward and punishment for companies, according to their record of employing or laying off workers. In contrast to Rubinow's call for effective measures against the inevitable pitfalls of industrial employment in a capitalist society, the plan was indebted to accident prevention ideas, rather than the insurance principle. It sought to create company-based reserves funds that paid out capped amounts whenever workers were laid off.[84] Designed primarily to encourage employment stabilization, it lacked actuarial soundness by basing payments on the amount available in individual company funds; limited the liability employers might face by capping the funds; and failed to provide for worker participation in decision-making. Crucially, the plan institutionalized what Rubinow had feared all along: the fragmentation and segmentation of social provision. As he complained in 1930, progressives now talked of "workmen's *compensation*, mother's *pensions*, sick *benefits*, medical *organization*, wage fund *reserves*, and what not," but no one talked of social *insurance*.[85]

In the same vein, many progressives came to the conclusion that business hostility, rather than a lack of unity among reform groups, had ushered in the failure of the health insurance movement. In contrast, the success of workmen's compensation had come about mainly as a result of business support. This postwar transition toward business collaboration ushered in a crucial intellectual shift toward business progressivism within the movement. This encompassed not only John R. Commons's emphasis on employer cooperation in Wisconsin, but also William C. Redfield and Herbert Hoover's efforts to build the "associative state" by promoting trade associations and cooperative trade practices.[86] In addition, the War Finance Corporation was revived in 1921 to deal with the farm crisis, and the Bureau of War Risk Insurance was turned into the Veteran's Bureau. Neither, however, entertained ideas about effective industrial democracy and worker participation in management. Instead, they promoted policies more akin to the modern regulatory and corporate welfare state. In the words of social worker Edward T. Devine, the state was obligated to "fix the levels below which the exploitation of workers and consumers would not be tolerated," and above which "the principles of free competition might safely and advantageously be left free to operate."[87]

Industrial psychology and therapeutic intervention—equally significant markers in the division between pre- and postwar reform—also moved up the agenda of the AALL. Brighter colors, cafeterias, and company-sponsored outings, rather than democratic participation and economic redistribution, came to be seen as the solution to labor unrest and a staple of welfare capitalism. Rubinow deeply disliked the therapeutic and psychological orientation of social work in the 1920s, deriding its focus on individual adjustment. The therapeutic mindset viewed complaints such as "wages are too low" as reflections of personal discontent, rather than structural inequalities, and judged interventions on the basis of their effectiveness in adjusting the individual to the dominant social order. Instead, he continued to emphasize that poverty and deprivation were the result of exploitation and the workings of market capitalism.[88]

The AALL's shift from health insurance toward more innocuous campaigns for accident prevention, employment stabilization, state regulation, industrial psychology, and welfare capitalism cannot be seen in isolation from either the delegitimization of the transatlantic sources of prewar progressivism or its images of immigrant self-help. Whereas Rubinow's experience "highlights Progressivism's intellectual as well as its ethnic inclusiveness," in the 1920s, "Americans ignored the foreign-born, socialist, Jewish statistical expert who asked them to learn from Europe."[89] As the close ties of progressives to Europe, their cosmopolitan outlook, and their attempts to forge an international movement for reform were discredited in the wake of the war, the reformers increasingly renounced foreign influences. They learned the lesson that "the less identification with Europe, the better the prospects of social insurance."[90] This parting of the ways reflected as much a cultural as a political split. Wartime hysteria had caused the disruption of the tenuous ties between progressivism and socialism. In turn, the political confluence of progressivism and evolutionary socialism embodied by Rubinow, which had become a "legitimate part of political discourse" in the prewar years, began to disappear.[91]

In the same vein, the immigrant roots of mutuality in health insurance that Rubinow had placed at the center of the campaign now proved a burden in promoting reform. The war and the postwar period altered the ways in which the "immigrant problem" was defined in public debates. In contrast to Rubinow's cultural social politics, which sought to use health insurance reform as means to create non-discriminatory civic and structural foundations for the integration of immigrants on the basis of recognizing their own cultural institutions, many postwar progressives broadly subscribed to limited state-building along regulatory, therapeutic, efficiency, and business lines. In the same way as the AFL turned restrictionism into social policy, progressives in the 1920s formulated social policies that, although on the surface less clearly nativist, largely neglected the immigrant experiences Rubinow had placed at the center. Workmen's compensation and mothers pensions, for example, not only ignored the mutualistic and democratic dimensions of the health insurance camping. They also tended to reaffirm, rather than challenge, established race, class, and gender hierarchies. In offering benefits to limited groups based on a variety of coded ethnic, class, and gender criteria, they shifted attention away from issues of structural inequality, while sanctioning morals testing, gender discrimination, and racialized welfare provision. In the end, policies along these lines often amounted less to an effort to solve social problems than an attempt to reaffirm social hierarchies.[92]

Moreover, the war established restrictive immigration policy as a growth area of government interventionism, opening up new opportunities for progressive expertise while circumscribing its transatlantic and cosmopolitan legacy. The First World War and the 1920s were a formative period for modern immigration policy and bureaucracy, a time when the transatlantic "liberal moment," which imposed few limits on either exit or entry, came to an end.[93] As the 1920s became a crucial historical moment when state-building was negotiated in the context of revived academic and popular debates about immigration, "the campaigns to formulate a national immigrant policy are particularly important instances of the experts' efforts to realize the promise the war seemed to hold." Indeed, organizations such as Frances Kellor's National Americanization Committee achieved quasi-governmental status "that most interest groups would only dream of."[94] They also reduced progressivism's civic dimension to the issue of "Americanization."

Throughout the 1920s, progressive expertise continued to inform immigration policy, and supported the efforts of the nation-state's bureaucratic apparatus to classify immigrants according to a set of ascribed ethnic and racial characteristics.[95] Renewed debates about scientific racism and eugenics in the 1920s categorized immigrants on the basis of shifting clusters of discreet bio-cultural groups into which traditional cultural, regional, and religious identities were collapsed. Within this identity, "whiteness" became the normative core that allowed for the diminution of differences between European immigrants while sustaining racial discriminations.[96]

This was not the end of the story, however. Despite the "tribal twenties" and the disillusionment with foreign models, the war also revived interest in transnational solutions to social problems. A moment of Europe's social, economic, and political breakdown, it paradoxically paved the way towards an expansion of internationalism and cooperation. Indeed, the interwar years, despite the rise of racially and ethnically based nationalisms, were a particularly fertile period in academia and public life for new transnational discourses. The creation of new international bodies, such as the League of

Nations, and the International Labor Organization (ILO) and the International Federation of Settlements (IFS), promoted transcultural cooperation and exchange. A range of foundations and institutions, including the Rockefeller Foundation, the Milbank Memorial Fund, the Oberlaender Trust, and the Guggenheim Foundation, furthered the institutionalization and professionalization of international cooperation.[97]

The volatile and fluid postwar setting also saw new networks of social scientists, civic reformers, trade unionists, and immigrant activists reject "efficiency" and "uplift" in favor of a transnational cultural social politics that can be distinguished from the conventional progressivism of the prewar years. Shaped by the trauma of the First World War, and keenly aware of the period's reactionary nativism, xenophobia, and paranoia, a new generation of social thinkers was skeptical toward the prewar faith in reason and enlightened public opinion. Repelled by the autocratic tendencies and business-oriented corporatism of wartime government, they promoted a concept of social citizenship centered on an expanded public sphere. In areas such as public housing, social work, and the cooperative movement, the interwar years became an incubus for a lively institutional and political subculture that transcended both "states" and "markets".[98] Indeed, Rubinow was very much part of this new transnational orientation. After the health insurance debacle, he left the United States for Palestine in 1919. As head of the American Zionist Medical Unit, he pursued medical and social work by setting up hospitals, infant care stations, and rural medical programs. Returning to the United States in 1923 from a very different life than that of a statistician, actuary, and insurance campaigner, he worked, among other things, for the Jewish Welfare Society of Philadelphia and then, in 1929, became secretary of the Independent Order of B'nai B'rith in Cincinnatti.[99]

The interwar years may have been characterized by a new emphasis on scientific racism, eugenics, and ethnic assimilation, but they also witnessed the intellectual maturation of concepts of cultural relativism. Sociologists Robert Park and W. I. Thomas, public intellectuals W. E. B. Du Bois and Randolph Bourne, social reformers Grace Abbott and Frederick Howe, and journalists Walter Weyl and Herbert Croly, for example, formulated a vision of the welfare state that sought to revive a progressive tradition of civic engagement, democratic participation, and redistributive justice. Building upon the cultural relativism of Franz Boas, Max Weber's haunting images of dehumanizing modernity, and intellectual breakthroughs in psychology (Sigmund Freud, Victor Adler), they sought a "revival of creative experience at the forefront of a new democratic politics" in new social and civic institutions.[100]

Finally, the "quiet, structural, behind-the-scenes institutionalization of European-acquired social insurance knowledge in the key university business departments and policy centers" in the 1920s meant that the issue would return to the public arena when the time was ripe.[101] This moment came with the New Deal and the Social Security Act of 1935. This also seemed to be the moment of the return to the political limelight of Isaac Rubinow, who had upon his return to the United States renewed his efforts on behalf of social insurance. Though he did not pursue them with the same vigor as in the heady years before and during the First World War, they culminated in his landmark publication on the issue: his book *Quest for Social Security*, which was published on the day Franklin D. Roosevelt announced his commitment to national social insurance.[102]

Although widely recognized as a leading authority in the field of social insurance, however, Rubinow was largely sidelined in the actual preparation and formulation of the Social Security Act. Secretary of Labor Frances Perkins, who chaired the cabinet Committee on Economic Security that had the job of drafting the bill, rarely sought his advice, turning instead to the Wisconsin school. Eager to avoid any association with immigrant socialism, she selected Edwin Witte, a student of Commons, to direct the committee's work. As Rubinow put it, the "Brandeis–Commons–Raushenbush–Andrews–Perkins combination is pretty hard to break."[103]

That Rubinow's advice was only sought at the margins, however, was not just the result of Perkins's wariness. It also reflected the split within the social insurance movement in the 1920s. As mentioned earlier, the AALL's prevention-focused program clashed with Rubinow's emphasis on immigrant traditions and cultural social politics. When the AALL launched a nationwide campaign for Commons bill in winter of 1930–1931, it paved the way for Rubinow's break with the organization. Instead, he became vice president of the American Association for Old-Age Insurance (later renamed American Association for Social Security), founded in 1927 by his friend Abraham Epstein, a Russian-born economist.

In the end, Rubinow and Epstein's communitarian, social-democratic, and cultural vision remained sidelined, and the Social Security Act of 1935 put in place a rather different system than the one Rubinow had advocated. It provided less comprehensive coverage, dropped health insurance for political reasons, was riddled with exclusions, offered only inadequate provision for mothers with dependent children, and lacked a government financial commitment to the contributory insurance funds. At the same time, however, the Social Security Act was the clearest illustration of the revival of transatlantic social politics. It grew out of the accrued social policy expertise that became politically achievable after the failure of Republican efforts to address the economic disaster of the Great Depression with conventional means. As Rodgers put it, it was the eruption of the progressive past into the present, the "great gathering in from the progressive political wings of a generation of proposals and ideas."[104] By the same token, the legislation, passed a year before Rubinow's death, symbolized his position as leading insurance reformer. Roosevelt himself acknowledged this in a very personal way when he sent a copy of *Quest for Security* signed by himself to Rubinow. Indeed, Roosevelt was keen to implement social insurance as a universal package, not just the unemployment insurance pushed for by Perkins and AALL. And there is another, rather neglected reason Rubinow could be hopeful. Although many of the ambitious brain trusters lacked his foreign experience, the policy cauldron of the New Deal contained more Jews, Catholics, and experts with immigrant backgrounds than any previous administration.[105]

In conclusion, progressivism in the 1920s, insofar as it embraced the wartime patterns of state building, sanctioned segmented provision, restrictive moralism, industrial efficiency, and business control. It forestalled reform in the direction of broadening the public sphere of control and democratic participation. Crucially, this cannot be seen in isolation from 1920s nativism and immigration restrictions, because they helped direct progressive energies away from an ethnic, civic, democratic, and redistributive model of the welfare state rooted in a transatlantic gaze and immigrant experiences. As wartime and postwar legislation provided the structural foundations for administrative state building in the decades to come, it constructed social welfare either as an issue of punitive or rehabilitative intervention, or as a matter of macroeconomic policy aimed at generating economic growth. Although the New Deal ushered in a revival of both the transformative and the transatlantic dimensions of prewar progressivism, it also retained important elements of state building pioneered during First World War and the 1920s at the expense of the mutualistic models advocated by Rubinow.

As Tony Judt has suggested, however, this effectively meant abandoning the "web of reciprocal services and obligations that bind citizens to one another via the public space" in favor of the "invocation of economics in all discussions of public affairs." By the same token,

Richard Sennett has recently suggested that an excessive focus on the politics of (ethnic) solidarity, rather than on the more mutualistic concept of cooperation, is at the root of the contemporary political disaffection with welfare states.[106] Exploring the historical nexus between immigration and the welfare state from the Progressive era to the New Deal, therefore, can contribute to a growing literature that is seeking to disentangle the ways in which immigration debates, the codification of restrictionist policies, and the rise of an immigration bureaucracy circumscribed the modern welfare state while promoting nation-state building. At the same time, revisiting Rubinow's transatlanticism and cultural social politics adds to other efforts to recover alternative progressive conceptions of civic culture and deliberation, such as, for example, the international dimension of the agrarian, antimonolopy impulses that Daniel Scroop and Charles Postel have delineated.[107]

Notes

1. Tony Judt, "What Is Living and What Is Dead in Social Democracy?" *The New York Review of Books*, December 17, 2009, 86–97.
2. J. Lee Kreader, "America's Prophet for Social Security: A Biography of Isaac M. Rubinow" (Ph.D. diss., University of Chicago, 1988), 1, 36–37. Kreader's thesis is the only (unpublished) biography of Rubinow.
3. J. Lee Kreader, "Isaac Max Rubinow: Pioneering Specialist in Social Insurance," in *Compassion and Responsibility: Readings in the History of Social Welfare Policy in the United States*, Frank R. Breul and Steven J. Diner, eds (Chicago: University of Chicago Press, 1980), 289.
4. Isaac M. Rubinow, "Health Insurance through Local Mutual Funds," *American Labor Legislation Review* 7 (1917): 69–78; Isaac M. Rubinow, "Social Security and Intergroup Relations," unpublished paper, August 1935, Rubinow Papers, Catherwood Library Kheel Center for Labor-Management Documentation & Archives, Cornell University (herafter cited as Rubinow Papers, Catherwood Library), box 25, folder 1; Isaac M. Rubinow, *Social Insurance. With Special Reference to American Conditions* (New York: Henry Holt and Co., 1913), 283. See also J. Joseph Huthmacher, "Urban Liberalism in the Age of Reform," *Mississippi Valley Historical Review* 49 (September 1962): 231–41.
5. Quoted in Arthur Mann, "British Social Thought and American Reformers of the Progressive Era," *Mississippi Valley Historical Review* 42 (March 1956), 675.
6. Walter Weyl, *The New Democracy: An Essay on Certain Political and Economic Tendencies in the United States* (New York: Macmillan, 1912), 2.

7. Daniel T. Rodgers, *Atlantic Crossings. Social Politics in a Progressive Age* (Cambridge, MA: The Belknap Press of Harvard University Press, 1998), 3.

8. James Kloppenberg, *Uncertain Victory. Social Democracy and Progressivism in European and American Thought, 1870–1920* (New York: Oxford University Press, 1986), 298–99.

9. Daniel T. Rodgers, "An Age of Social Politics," in *Rethinking American History in a Global Age*, Thomas Bender, ed. (Berkeley: University of California Press, 2002), 256. I have explored the transatlantic transfer of ideas and reforms in Axel R. Schäfer, *American Progressives and German Social Reform: Social Ethics, Moral Control, and the Regulatory State in a Transatlantic Context* (Stuttgart: Franz Steiner Verlag, 2000); Axel R. Schäfer "W. E. B. Du Bois, German Social Thought, and the Racial Divide in American Progressivism, 1892–1909," *Journal of American History* 88 (December 2001): 925–49; Axel R. Schäfer, "Britain, Europe and the Critique of Capitalism in American Reform, 1880–1920," in *Critiques of Capitalism in Modern Britain and America*, Mark Bevir and Frank Trentmann, eds (London: Palgrave, 2002), 98–126; and Axel R. Schäfer, "German Historicism, Progressive Social Thought, and the Interventionist State in the US Since the 1880s," in *Markets in Historical Contexts*, Mark Bevir and Frank Trentmann, eds (Cambridge: Cambridge University Press, 2004), 145–69.

10. Among notable recent exceptions to this are Alan Lessoff and Christof Mauch, eds, *Adolf Cluess, Architect: From Germany to America* (New York: Berghahn Books, 2005).

11. A synthesis of social policy and migration studies is still missing in the scholarly literature, as most publications are either single-nation studies, provide comparative analyses, or treat welfare states and immigration policies as independent variables. See, for example, Cybelle Fox, *Three Worlds of Relief: Race, Immigration and the American Welfare State, from the Progressive Era to the New Deal* (Princeton: Princeton University Press, 2012); Christian Joppke, *Immigration and the Nation-State: The United States, Germany, and Great Britain* (Oxford: Oxford University Press, 1999).

12. Kreader, "Prophet for Social Security," 62. See also United States Bureau of Labor, *Workmen's Insurance and Compensation Systems in Europe.* Twenty-Fourth Annual Report of the Commissioner of Labor, vol. 1 (Washington, D.C.: Government Printing Office, 1911), 978.

13. Kreader, "Prophet for Social Security," 190. Although Rubinow left no formal papers, significant records of his insurance reform activism in the American Association of Labor Legislation are in the Catherwood Library.

14. Kreader, "Prophet for Social Security," 3, 124–25.

15. Randolph Bourne, "Trans-National America," *Atlantic Monthly* 118 (July 1916): 86–97.
16. Daniel T. Rodgers, "In Search of Progressivism," *Reviews in American History* 10 (1982): 113–32.
17. Jacob Riis, *How the Other Half Lives: Studies among the Tenements of New York* (New York: Charles Scribner's Sons), 22. Complex federal laws excluded people on a variety of grounds. In 1891, Congress excluded from admission people likely to become public charges, people with certain contagious diseases, "convicts, lunatics, idiots," and polygamists. Prohibitions for anarchists and subversives were added in 1903, and laws passed in 1907 excluded people with "mental defects" and those who had committed crimes of "moral turpitude." A key impetus for restrictive legislation were the findings of the Dillingham Commission set up by Congress in 1907 to investigate immigration. Chaired by Senator William Dillingham, the Immigration Commission maintained that many of the new immigrants could not be assimilated and were the cause of many of the country's economic ills.
18. Isaac M. Rubinow, "Labor Insurance," *Journal of Political Economy* 12 (June 1904): 369.
19. Charles R. Henderson, "The Logic of Social Insurance," *Annals* 33 (March 1909): 272.
20. Other examples that reflect this view in progressive thought and reform include Florence Kelley, *Modern Industry in Relation to the Family, Health, Education, Morality* (New York: Longmans, Green, 1914); Frederic C. Howe, *The City: The Hope of Democracy* (New York: Charles Scribner's Sons, 1905); Leo S. Rowe, *Problems of City Government* (New York: D. Appleton and Co., 1908); and Albion W. Small, *Between Eras from Capitalism to Democracy* (Kansas City: Inter-Collegiate Press, 1913).
21. National Industrial Conference Board, "Sickness Insurance or Sickness Prevention," *Research Report* 6 (May 1918): 3.
22. Irving Fisher, "Health and War," *American Labor Legislation Review* 8 (1918): 13, 16–17. For detailed discussions of wartime reform and the efficiency discourse, see, for example, Allen F. Davis, "Welfare, Reform, and World War I," *American Quarterly* 19 (Fall 1967): 516–33; Burl Noggle, *Into the Twenties: The United States from Armistice to Normalcy* (Urbana: University of Illinois Press, 1974). See also Edward T. Devine, "Social Forces in Wartime," *Survey* 38 (July 7, 1917): 316.
23. Theda Skocpol, *Protecting Soldiers and Mothers: The Political Origins of Social Policy in the United States* (Cambridge, MA: Harvard University Press, 1992), 7, 96–101, 261ff.; Theda Skocpol and John Ikenberry, "The Political Formation of the American Welfare State in Historical and Comparative Perspective," in *The Welfare State, 1883–*

1983, Comparative Social Research, no. 6, Richard F. Tomasson, ed. (Greenwich, CT.: JAI Press, 1983), 91.

24. For a closer discussion, see Edward Berkowitz and Kim McQuaid, *Creating the Welfare State: The Political Economy of Twentieth-Century Reform* (Lawrence: University Press of Kansas, 1992).

25. On the AALL, see Roy Lubove, *The Struggle for Social Security, 1900–1935* (Cambridge, MA: Harvard University Press, 1968), 29, 67; and Skocpol and Ikenberry, "Political Formation of the Welfare State," 100.

26. John B. Andrews, "Report of Work," 1909, n.p., Henry W. Farnam Papers, Manuscripts and Archives, Sterling Memorial Library, Yale University, Princeton, NJ.

27. "New Committee on Social Insurance," *Survey* 29, March 15, 1913, 827. See also Isaac M. Rubinow, "Social Insurance: What the New Phrase Means and Why," *Survey* 31, December 6, 1913, 268–69, 278–83; Rubinow, "Health Insurance: The Spread of the Movement," *Survey* 36, July 15, 1916, 407–409; and Rubinow, "Sickness Insurance," *American Labor Legislation Review* 3 (June 1913): 162–71.

28. Kreader, "Prophet for Social Security," 138, 153.

29. Committee on Social Insurance, "Health Insurance. Tentative Draft for an Act," *American Labor Legislation Review* 6 (June 1916): 250ff. The bill mirrored the 1911 revisions in German insurance legislation, which reduced the original two-thirds majority of workers in the insurance funds, established in the 1883 laws, to equal representation. In turn, workers' contributions were limited to 50 percent.

30. Rubinow, *Social Insurance*, 491.

31. Isaac M. Rubinow, "Compulsory State Insurance of Workingmen," *Annals* 24 (September 1904): 336; "Brief for Health Insurance," *American Labor Legislation Review* 6 (June 1916): 229. See also Isaac M. Rubinow, "Edward Bernstein and Industrial Concentration," *International Socialist Review* 3 (February 1903): 486–89.

32. "Brief for Health Insurance," *American Labor Legislation Review* 6 (June 1916): 229.

33. Rubinow, *Social Insurance*, 480–82, 500–501.

34. Rubinow, "Labor Insurance," 362.

35. Rubinow, "Compulsory State Insurance," 335.

36. Rubinow, "Labor Insurance," 379.

37. Rubinow, "Compulsory State Insurance," 335.

38. Isaac M. Rubinow, "Civic Lessons from Europe. Compulsory Insurance," *Chautauquan* 41 (March 1905): 49.

39. Rubinow, *Social Insurance*, 283.

40. See, for example, Rubinow, "The Economic Conditions of the Russian Jews in New York City," in *The Russian Jew in the United States: Studies of Social Conditions in New York, Philadelphia, and*

    Chicago, Charles S. Bernheimer, ed. (Philadelphia: J. C. Winston
    Co., 1905), 116–17.
41. Florence Kelley, minutes and discussions, *Proceedings of the National
    Conference of Charities and Correction* (1905): 578. For an insightful
    discussion of the link between race and the welfare state, see Gwendolyn
    Mink, "The Lady and the Tramp: Gender, Race, and the Origins of
    the American Welfare State," in *Women, Welfare, and the State*, Linda
    Gordon, ed. (Madison: University of Wisconsin Press, 1990), 92–122.
42. Kreader, "Prophet for Social Security," 79; see also 81–82 and 183.
    See also I. M. Robbins [Isaac M. Rubinow], "The Economic Aspects
    of the Negro Problem," in 16 installments, *International Socialist
    Review* 8–10 (February 1908–June 1910), passim.
43. Rubinow, "Compulsory State Insurance," 338; Rubinow, "Civic
    Lessons from Europe," 50; Linda Gordon, *Pitied But Not Entitled.
    Single Mothers and the History of the Welfare State* (Cambridge, MA:
    Harvard University Press, 1994), 145–81.
44. Henderson, "Logic of Social Insurance," 268.
45. Charles R. Henderson, *Industrial Insurance in the United States*
    (Chicago: University of Chicago Press, 1909), 43.
46. Henderson, "Logic of Social Insurance," 269.
47. William Franklin Willoughby, "Problem of Social Insurance: An
    Analysis," *American Labor Legislation Review* 2 (June 1913): 157,
    160–61.
48. William Franklin Willoughby, *Workingmen's Insurance* (New York:
    Thomas Y. Crowell, 1898), 2–3. See also John B. Andrews, "Social
    Insurance," *Annals* 69 (January 1917): 47.
49. Rubinow, "Health Insurance through Local Mutual Funds," 74–75.
    Seager and Willoughby modeled their approach on the AALL's other
    main campaign—the pursuit of workmen's compensation—which
    reflected more clearly the economic and administrative wishes of the
    private sector. See Berkowitz and McQuaid, *Creating the Welfare
    State*, 43. See also Kreader, "Isaac Max Rubinow," 296.
50. Rubinow, "Civic Lessons from Europe," 49.
51. Isaac M. Rubinow, *The Quest for Security* (New York: Henry Holt,
    1934), 209.
52. Frederick L. Hoffman, "Some Lessons of the German Failure in
    Compulsory Health Insurance," in *Facts and Fallacies of Compulsory
    Health Insurance*, 2nd ed. ([Newark, NJ: Prudential Press], 1920),
    186.
53. Form letter to AALL members, c. 1918, AALL Papers, Catherwood
    Library, quoted in Ronald L. Numbers, *Almost Persuaded: American
    Physicians and Compulsory Health Insurance, 1912–1920*, The Henry
    E. Sigerist Supplements to the Bulletin of the History of Medicine,
    n.s., no. 1 (Baltimore: Johns Hopkins University Press, 1978), 87.
54. For examples of opponents of health insurance labeling Rubinow
    and the campaign pro-German, see Lubove, *Struggle for Security*,

chapter 4; Numbers, *Almost Persuaded*, 88; Clarke Chambers, *Seedtime of Reform: American Social Service and Social Action, 1918–1933* (Minneapolis: University of Minnesota Press, 1963), 25.

55. Numbers, *Almost Persuaded*, 81. For a discussion of the California campaign, see also Arthur J. Viseltear, "Compulsory Health Insurance in California, 1915–1918," *Journal of the History of Medicine* 24 (April 1969): 151–82.

56. For details on the significance of the funeral benefit, see Paul Starr, "Transformation in Defeat: The Changing Objective of National Health Insurance, 1915–1980," in *Compulsory Health Insurance: The Continuing American Debate.* Contributions in Medical History, no. 11, ed. Ronald L. Numbers (Westport, CT: Greenwood Press, 1982), 123. For business opposition, see, for example, a discussion of the National Civic Federation in Hace Sorel Tishler, *Self-Reliance and Social Security, 1870–1917* (Fort Washington: Kennikat Press, 1971). See also Rubinow, *Quest for Security*, 213.

57. Numbers, *Almost Persuaded*, 81.

58. Eighteen state federations supported compulsory insurance by 1918, in addition to 21 Internationals and a range of leading reform organizations, such as the National Consumers' League, the Women's Trade Union League, and various state federations of women. See "Prominent Labor Organizations Already on Record for Health Insurance," *American Labor Legislation Review* 8 (1918): 319; "Prominent Endorsements of Health Insurance," *American Labor Legislation Review* 9 (1919): 177–78.

59. Samuel Gompers, "Labor versus Its Barnacles," *American Federationist* 23 (April 1916): 270. "Attitude of Labor Organizations," *American Labor Legislation Review* 8 (1918): 173. Moreover, the AFL had profited under war conditions from higher wages, shorter hours, federal mediation, and union recognition at the expense of more radical labor organizations. In turn, many AFL unions expressed fear that social insurance would cement low wages, because competitive pressure would force employers to deduct their contribution from wages.

60. "Statements of Prominent Persons in Favor of Health Insurance—Physicians and Nurses," *American Labor Legislation Review* 8 (1918): 324–27; Numbers, *Almost Persuaded*, 36.

61. Rubinow, *Quest for Security*, 213.

62. "Minutes of the House of Delegates," *Journal of the American Medical Association* 74 (1920): 1256, quoted in Numbers, *Almost Persuaded*, 105.

63. Samuel McCune Lindsay, "Next Steps in Social Insurance in the United States," *American Labor Legislation Review* 9 (March 1919): 111.

64. "War Time Extension of Social Insurance," *American Labor Legislation Review* 8 (1918): 188. See also Frank J. Bruno, *Trends*

in *Social Work, 1874–1956: A History Based on the Proceedings of the National Conference of Social Work* (New York: Columbia University Press, 1957; repr., Westport, CT: Greenwood Press, 1980), 231.

65. Lindsay, "Next Steps in Social Insurance," 110.

66. Chambers, *Seedtime of Reform*, 156; Hugh Heclo, "Toward A New Welfare State?" in *The Development of Welfare States in Europe and America, 1850–1950*, Peter Flora and Arnold J. Heidenheimer, eds (New Brunswick: Transaction Books, 1981), 285.

67. Rubinow, "Labor Insurance," 372.

68. Ronald Schaffer, *America in the Great War: The Rise of the War Welfare State* (New York: Oxford University Press, 1991), 212.

69. *Report of the Health Insurance Commission of the State of Illinois* (Springfield: Illinois State Journal Co., 1919), 167.

70. National Industrial Conference Board, "Sickness Insurance," 22; Kreader, "Isaac Max Rubinow," 288. Workmen's compensation laws became a fundamental element of the rudimentary welfare state created during the early twentieth century. They enjoyed widespread support in business circles because they averted the threat of litigation. See, for example, Berkowitz and McQuaid, *Creating the Welfare State*, 43; Gaston Rimlinger, *Welfare Policy and Industrialization in Europe, America, and Russia* (New York: Wiley, 1971), 120; see also Lubove, *Struggle for Social Security*, 57.

71. Rubinow, "Health Insurance through Mutual Funds," 74–75.

72. Fisher, "Health and War," 13.

73. Uriel Rosenthal, "Welfare State or State of Welfare? Repression and Welfare in the Modern State," in *The Welfare State, 1883–1983*, ed. Tomasson, 295.

74. Fisher, "Health and War," 13–17; see also Frederic C. Howe, *Socialized Germany*, (New York: Charles Scribner's Sons, 1914), 171.

75. Woodrow Wilson to Josephus Daniels, in *Woodrow Wilson. Life and Letters*, vol. 6, *Facing War, 1918*, Ray S. Baker, ed. (Garden City, NY: Doubleday & Page, 1927–39), 506. See also Otis L. Graham, *The Great Campaigns: Reform and War in America, 1900–1928* (Huntington, NY: Robert E. Krieger, 1980), 103, 105, 107; Robert D. Cuff, *The War Industries Board: Business–Government Relations during World War I* (Baltimore: Johns Hopkins University Press, 1973); Berkowitz and McQuaid. *Creating the Welfare State*, 57.

76. For a detailed discussion, see Robert H. Ferrell, *Woodrow Wilson and World War I, 1917–1921* (New York: Harper & Row, 1985); Noggle, *Into the Twenties*; Graham, *Great Campaigns*, 106.

77. Graham, *Great Campaigns*, 107.

78. For a good discussion of the development and legacy of public policy during the First World War, see Schaffer, *America in the Great War*.

79. Skocpol and Ikenberry, "Political Formation of the Welfare State," 91.

80. Norman Furniss and Timothy Tilton, *The Case for the Welfare State: From Social Security to Social Equality* (Bloomington: Indiana University Press, 1977), x. On government social provision serving different social groups based on separate administrative mechanisms, see Michael K. Brown, "The Segmented Welfare System: Distributive Conflict and Retrenchment in the United States, 1968–1984," in *Remaking the Welfare State: Retrenchment and Social Policy in America and Europe*, Michael K. Brown, ed. (Philadelphia: Temple University Press, 1988), 188ff. On moral considerations in welfare policies, see Handler and Hasenfeld, *Moral Construction of Poverty*. On growth politics sidelining a civic and redistributionist agenda, see Robert M. Collins, *More: The Politics of Economic Growth in Postwar America* (New York: Oxford University Press, 2000); and Alan Wolfe, *America's Impasse: The Rise and Fall of the Politics of Growth* (New York: Pantheon Books, 1981).
81. William Allen White, *The Autobiography of William Allen White* (New York: Macmillan, 1946), 627.
82. According to John F. McClymer, the war had a decisive effect upon the development of social expertise. It opened up new opportunities for experts to enter government and influence social planning in areas of Americanization, wartime mobilization, postwar reconstruction, and antiradicalism. McClymer, *War and Welfare: Social Engineering in America, 1890–1925* (Westport, CT: Greenwood Press, 1980), 74.
83. Alexander Lambert to John B. Andrews, May 3, 1920, AALL Papers, Catherwood Library, quoted in Numbers, *Almost Persuaded*, 105.
84. John R. Commons and John B. Andrews, *Principles of Labor Legislation* (New York: Harper & Brothers, 1920); Kreader, "Isaac Max Rubinow," 298, 303.
85. Quoted in Rodgers, *Atlantic Crossings*, 433.
86. Ellis W. Hawley, "Herbert Hoover, the Commerce Secretariat, and the Vision of an 'Associative State,' 1921–1928," *Journal of American History* 61 (June 1974): 116–40.
87. Edward T. Devine, *When Social Work Was Young* (New York: Macmillan, 1939), 4.
88. Isaac M. Rubinow, "Needed: A Social Insurance Revival," *Survey Midmonthly*, May 15, 1926, 233–34, 283; Kreader, "Isaac Max Rubinow," 303. As Jeffrey Sklansky has argued, the "social self" of progressive theory, by tying value formation to social interaction and declaring the poor deficient in the development of their social norms, defined poverty as a problem of insufficient socialization, rather than as a problem of the maldistribution of income. Jeffrey Sklansky, *The Soul's Economy: Market Society and Selfhood in American Thought, 1820–1920* (Chapel Hill: University of North Carolina Press, 2002).
89. Kreader, "Isaac Max Rubinow," 306–307.

90. Lubove, *Struggle for Social Security*, 115, see also 168–70; Rubinow, *Quest for Security*, 213.
91. On wartime hysteria disrupting the tenuous ties between progressivism and socialism, see David Shannon, *The Socialist Party of America: A History* (New York: Macmillan, 1955), 100; John Higham, *Strangers in the Land: Patterns of American Nativism 1860–1925* (New York: Atheneum, 1966), 219; Kreader, "Prophet for Social Security," 286.
92. See, for example, Gordon, *Pitied But Not Entitled. Single Mothers and the History of Welfare* (Cambridge, MA: Harvard University Press, 1995); Mimi Abramowitz, *Regulating the Lives of Women: Social Welfare Policy from Colonial Times to the Present* (Boston, MA: South End Press, 1988); Robert Lieberman, *Shifting the Color Line: Race and the American Welfare State* (Cambridge, MA: Harvard University Press, 1998); and Elizabeth Lasch-Quinn, *Black Neighbors: Race and the Limits of Reform in the American Settlement House Movement, 1890–1945* (Chapel Hill: University of North Carolina Press, 1993).
93. Aristide Zolberg, "Labour Migration and International Economic Regimes: Bretton Woods and After," in *International Migration Systems: A Global Approach*, Mary M. Kritz et al., eds (Oxford: Clarenden Press, 1992), 322.
94. McClymer, *War and Welfare*, 74, 83, 112, 116.
95. See, for example, Paul Schor, *Compter et classer. Histoire des Catégories de la Population dans le Recensement Américain, 1790–1940* (Paris: Editions de l'EHESS, 2009).
96. Axel R. Schäfer, "Immigration," in *Introduction to American Studies*, Chris Bigsby and Howard Temperley, eds (London: Longman/Pearson, 2006), 164.
97. Daniel Laqua (ed.), *Internationalism Reconfigured. Transnational Ideas and Movements between the World Wars* (London: I. B. Tauris, 2011); Paul Weindling, ed., *International Health Organisations and Movements, 1918–1939* (Cambridge: Cambridge University Press, 1995).
98. See, for example, Rodgers, *Atlantic Crossings*, 381–408.
99. Kreader, "Isaac Max Rubinow," 302–303.
100. Casey Blake, *Beloved Community: The Cultural Criticism of Randolph Bourne, Van Wyck Brook, Waldo Frank, and Lewis Mumford* (Chapel Hill: University of North Carolina Press, 1990), 2, 9; Christopher McKnight Nichols, "Rethinking Randolph Bourne's Trans-National America," *Journal of the Gilded Age and the Progressive Era* 8 (April 2009): 217–57; Kenneth E. Miller, *From Progressive to New Dealer: Frederic C. Howe and American Liberalism* (University Park: Penn State University Press, 2010).
101. Rodgers, *Atlantic Crossings*, 438. On the transatlantic setting of social insurance in the 1930s, see pp. 428–43.

102. Kreader, "Isaac Max Rubinow," 305.
103. Rubinow to Raymond Rubinow, January 11, 1935, Rubinow Papers, Catherwood Library, box 28, folder 17, quoted in Kreader, "Isaac Max Rubinow," 305; Rodgers, *Atlantic Crossings*, 441.
104. Rodgers, *Atlantic Crossings*, 413–14, quote on p. 415.
105. Ibid., 438, 422. The New Deal drew conceptually more on wartime planning and collectivism than on the progressive legacy. This applies in particular to the NRA, which was stocked with former administrators of the war economy, included no labor representatives, and functioned largely as a price-and-production-fixing cartel. See Rodgers, 424–25.
106. Judt, "What Is Living?"; Richard Sennett, *Together: The Rituals, Pleasures and Politics of Co-operation* (London: Allen Lane, 2012).
107. Charles Postel, *The Populist Vision* (New York: Oxford University Press, 2007); Daniel Scroop, "The Anti-Chain Store Movement and the Politics of Consumption," *American Quarterly* 60 (December 2008): 925–50.

Chapter 6

Social Politics in a Transoceanic World in the Early Cold War Years

Jonathan Bell

There can be few historians who have done more in recent years to enhance our understanding of the international dimension of social policymaking than Daniel Rodgers. Yet the story in Atlantic Crossings (1998) of dialogue among reform movements, social planners, economists, and politicians on both sides of the Atlantic comes to an abrupt end during the Second World War. The dominant narrative in much American historiography of reform politics suggests that the war demonstrated the might of the private American economy, and gave rise to what Henry Luce termed the "American Century" dominated by private sector solutions to economic and social problems in which the federal government would play a secondary role. The search for international solutions to particular problems of social organization in the progressive and New Deal era died out, it is argued, in the wake of the United States' rise as an economic superpower at the same time as other industrialized states were left war-ravaged and dependent on American aid. The revitalization of the capitalist economy during the war coincided with the reassertion of a conservative direction in American politics, rendering a free flow of ideas between policy elites in the United States and more social democratic-leaning democracies in the United Kingdom, Scandinavia, and the Antipodes less fruitful than during the depression years.[1] Historians have also shown how progressive politicians in the United States turned away from state-led solutions to the country's problems in favor of Keynesian policies that regulated demand and consolidated social welfare policies instead of following the example of other industrialized nations in dramatically expanding the scope of the welfare state. In a climate of Cold War in which the notion of individual "freedom" was held up in binary opposition to the totalitarianism of the Soviet Union, the burden-some problem of securing civil rights for all Americans apparently loomed larger in the political consciousness of American liberals than the question of the redistribution of economic resources current in European and Antipodean circles.[2] If American politicians looked to the wider world at all for examples of how other states were managing their social welfare systems after the war, historians have tended to find that it was to discover ammunition with which to discredit those systems in the United States.[3]

This article argues that the war and its immediate aftermath helped to widen the parameters of American liberalism, rendering overseas models of social democracy potentially more important to the heirs of the New Deal than at the height of the depression. Admittedly, the perceived threat of totalitarianism in the United States in the late 1940s allowed business and other anti-statist interest groups to use foreign case studies to portray policies such as state health insurance as akin to communism. At the same time, however, the end of the depression and victory over the Axis forces left the future direction of New Deal liberalism uncertain, and American liberals found themselves looking outward for inspiration as the pace of political reform quickened in Britain under a Labour government, in Sweden under a social demo-cratic administration, and in New Zealand and Australia under left-wing governments. As American liberals struggled to establish new organs of political representation—the Americans for Democratic Action (ADA) organization, or a Democratic party freed from south-ern conservative dominance, or a political alliance between liberal activists and organized labor—left-of-center Americans attempted to forge new links with allies across both the Atlantic and Pacific oceans. Ultimately, however, liberals in the United States lacked the ideological language with which to interpret lessons of the Labour governments of the United Kingdom and New Zealand, whereas the Cold War furnished their conservative rivals with a perfect vehicle through which to manipulate foreign case studies to their own advan-tage. It was not simply that the American political system was insti-tutionally or constitutionally unsuited to European and Antipodean political agendas, though that was partly the case, nor that American social reformers did not want to learn from the example of others.[4] This chapter argues that those we term "liberals" in the United States had the opportunity in the late 1940s to use overseas case studies to reshape the ramshackle political agenda of the New Deal along more specifically social democratic lines, but that they found it impossible to match interest in the wider world with a concrete program that would overcome tension between left-wing politics and the emerging anti-totalitarianism of the Cold War.[5] By contrast, the American right conducted a highly organized publicity drive to provide new meaning for their anti-statist ideology in a post-New Deal, post-isolationist United States by using perceived failures of welfare states overseas as domestic propaganda. Both the examples of Labour Britain after 1945 and Labour New Zealand provided important case studies for American liberals and conservatives, but in the Cold War it was the American right who would gain political capital from their sustained attack upon the postwar social compact taking shape across the Atlantic and Pacific oceans.

Although the war had, in many ways, rehabilitated the political might of the private business community and other conservative forces opposed to the development of left-wing politics in the United States, it had also thrown into relief new problems of industrial economy and social policy that strengthened the hand of liberal political actors and pressure groups. An examination of battles within and outside Congress over full employment, the future of the wartime Office of Price Administration (OPA), and the International Labor Organization (ILO), as well as the rise of a new generation of liberal and anti-statist politicians shows that what Alan Brinkley has called the "end of reform" was not preordained in 1946. Although it is certainly the case that the 1946 election results and the subsequent right turn in American politics heralded a shift of political power away from the original sponsors of the full employment bill and other social welfare measures, the elections did not mark the end of attempts to inject left-of-centre ideology into Democratic politics. In 1945, the Truman administration and its supporters formed part of an international social democratic experiment, taking place from the United Kingdom to New Zealand. Although the Labour government in Britain was much more entrenched in power than liberals in the variegated political structure in Washington, the development of a political program for the left in both countries was proceeding along similar lines.[6]

The coalition of Democracy and labor had been cemented in 1943–1944 with the founding of the Congress of Industrial Organizations' Political Action Committee (CIO-PAC) to act as an electoral campaign group for liberal electoral candidates, as well as the participation of key Roosevelt administration figures, Arthur Altmeyer, Wilbur Cohen, and Isidore Falk of the Social Security Administration and Federal Security Administration, in the declaration of postwar principles of the ILO. At the planning meeting in Ottawa in late

1943, these individuals had approved a comprehensive plan for social security, including free health care, public works, and a cradle-to-grave social safety net that the CIO incorporated into its wish-list for a postwar order. This comprehensive welfare state would "appropriately be financed out of general revenue," and the program was adopted at the 1944 General Conference of the ILO in Philadelphia.[7] In addition, the 1943 report of the National Resources Planning Board set out the post-New Deal agenda of Democratic liberalism as an economic "Bill of Rights" that postulated a similar socioeconomic program to that of the Beveridge Plan in Great Britain.[8] A tripartite alliance of federal bureaucrats and politicians, organized labor, and liberal pressure groups like the Union for Democratic Action (UDA) seemed to herald at least the potential of a reinvigorated American social democratic impulse, albeit tempered by the realities of a prosperous society eager to shrug off the shackles of wartime austerity.

Certainly the agenda of social democracy, a process of reshaping market capitalism to allow the state to provide equality of opportunity for all regardless of economic status, lay at the heart of the program of the UDA, a wartime organization of liberals searching for ways to retain the political initiative for the New Deal at a time of heightened prosperity and preoccupations of war. "It is time for a standard to be raised that goes beyond the slogans and programs of the Roosevelt period," argued Joseph Lash to the New York chapter of the UDA in September 1946. The depression years had, he argued, vindicated those advocating "the development of democratic techniques for achieving collectivist objectives," including "full employment, economic efficiency, and a structure of economic democracy...Wartime developments have not invalidated this thesis."[9] Questions of how to provide jobs for thousands of returning servicemen; how to control inflationary pressures and regulate demand in the reconversion period; and how to prevent the collapse of the wartime boom after the cessation of hostilities, all captured the imagination of a network of liberal political activists inside and outside Congress. "My contacts with workers over recent months indicate to me that they will not remain quiescent under another depression, and I hesitate to think by what means they would vent their anger at such a reconversion," argued Washington UDA director Paul Sifton in February 1945. "They feel that they have a right to job security, to the opportunity to work and earn a decent living."[10] The passage in 1944 of the GI Bill of Rights had convinced UDA members and their allies in Congress that the initiative still lay with them in the developing battle over who would dominate American politics.

There had been a significant increase in the number of liberals in the Democratic party as a whole as a result of the New Deal and the war, and it would be the extent of their commitment to the expansion of social democratic reform that would decide the future of American politics just as much as the vitality of southern conservatives in the party. Equally important as the continued existence of an anti-statist strain in American politics to a discussion of the fate of the reform impulse in these years is the development of a social democratic network of activists inside and outside Congress whose ideological frame of reference was not simply, or even primarily, the New Deal, but also a politics of equality of opportunity and social welfare that transcended national boundaries. The union of Democratic, Liberal, and American Labor party forces in New York at the end of the war, the dominance of the CIO-PAC in the Ohio Democratic party, and the growing self-confidence of leftist activists who would come to form the California Democratic Council in the 1950s all formed part of a mosaic of social democratic expression in postwar America. The mosaic may have been fractured and bereft of a national coherence that helped identify the ideological focus of the British Labour party or the Swedish Social Democrats. Nevertheless, Roosevelt's Economic Bill of Rights in his 1944 State of the Union address symbolized a new start for American liberals in a political landscape dramatically altered by war. When Senators Claude Pepper of Florida and Harley Kilgore of West Virginia assembled a liberal Democratic caucus to discuss a postwar left-of-center program in 1945, they could count on over half the party's Senate contingent, and about 120 congressmen, without counting the tractable contingent of liberal Republicans and southerners.[11] More important perhaps were liberals outside Congress in groups like the UDA or the CIO-PAC, who could potentially use their growing political confidence to push the political balance further to the left in future elections. The UDA led a spirited fight to implement the Full Employment Act in 1945–1946 and to defend the OPA from being dismantled by congressional conservatives.

The way in which the war had forced the state to engage in widespread economic and social planning created momentum for further left-of-center initiatives, mirroring developments in other nations. The full employment bill mobilized a coalition of administration officials in bureaus like the Office of War Mobilization and Conversion, labor leaders, congressmen, and UDA activists. High levels of employment had been achieved in wartime "through the creation of an unlimited market by the government," argued Fred Vinson, director of the Office of War Management and Reconversion in a letter to Senator

Robert Wagner of New York. Vinson found ready allies in Congress in the form of Wagner, Senator James Murray of Montana, congressmen Wright Patman of Texas and George Outland of California, who began pushing the bill on Capitol Hill. The bill would commit the US government to "the responsibility to do everything possible to attain full employment in this country," if necessary through public works and capital projects, and not simply through fiscal policy.[12] In his statement to the Senate Banking and Currency Committee on the bill in June 1945, George Outland argued that Americans had a right to gainful employment that had to be enshrined in government policy, a right already embedded in the constitutions of several other countries, including Brazil, the USSR, and Argentina. "The prevention of unemployment is everybody's business and consequently the business of government. The responsibility for maintaining employment is too large for business alone or for any one economic group to assume."[13] The full employment bill formed part of a wider program that shifted the focus of American liberalism away from contingent responses to emergencies of depression and war and toward long-range social democratic planning that had emerged hesitantly during the second New Deal of 1935. At a meeting of leading progressive thinkers in Washington in October 1946 to map out the future of the UDA "as a Fabian society type of organization," UDA leader James Loeb "felt the central problem of our times was what were the overall controls needed to guarantee full employment... He thought the problem of the 'mixed economy' was the central one." So central was this question in 1946 that there was a consensus that "foreign policy should be considered subsequent to the investigation of a progressive position on economic policy."[14]

Battles over American membership in the ILO, and the development of a social democratic vision on the left through projects like full employment and an American Beveridge plan, brought representatives of the labor movement into the reform coalition. The UDA was vocal in supporting the United Auto Workers (UAW)-led strike at General Motors (GM) in late 1945, which caused UAW leader, Walter Reuther, to note that his union "intends to work with all progressives for an economy of abundance and security." Reuther argued that the GM strike not only represented concern over wage rates, but also prices and the attainment of "mass purchasing power for full employment" as "a serious and permanent concern." At a dinner supporting Henry Wallace's nomination to be Roosevelt's new secretary of commerce, Reuther urged that the administration create "a single, overall agency, with full authority to plan, organize and direct the conversion of our war economy to peace production so as to achieve full and continuous employment." Alongside this corporate statist vision of an alliance among bureaucrats, labor leaders, and business representatives went plans "for a far-flung public works program . . . not as an emergency glorified WPA project, but as a permanent part of a healthy, expanding national economy." This program, together with a comprehensive cradle-to-grave welfare state, formed a comprehensive blueprint for an American social democracy. Emil Rieve of the Textile Workers Union argued that union members needed to support the retention of progressives like Henry Wallace in government with his promise of 60 million jobs at the end of the war, "for there can be no lasting peace unless there are jobs for everyone—60,000,000 jobs for the 60,000,000 Americans who need them."[15]

This liberal political dialog over the future of reform after the New Deal gained an international dimension when the UDA looked to London for material with which to promote a domestic agenda. In May 1946, James Loeb organized a luncheon for UDA activists in Washington "on the general subject of American Progressives and the British Labor Government." The invitation, sent to prominent liberal activists like Congressman Jerry Voorhis of California and theologian Reinhold Niebuhr, stated that "American progressives must seek to understand the problems confronting this British government and the steps it has taken to meet them." Voorhis was urged to speak at the meeting, and to address "some of the steps that the British Government has taken internally to meet the needs of post-war Britain, including the health program, the beginnings of nationalization, etc." Former OPA head, Leon Henderson, informed a town hall meeting that he had "just returned from England and France . . . They know that they must both make certain choices to insure employment, that they must not risk the fabric of future freedom to vague laws or to Adam Smith or automaticity."[16] The UDA set up an office in London to send reports to members back in the United States. The July 1946 issue of the "UDA London Letter" commented on the first year of the Labour government in glowing terms: "This English experiment—to secure basic social change by democratic, rather than totalitarian, means—is unprecedented in world history." A month later, the focus was on nationalization of industries, the logic behind which was explained in terms of a desire "to mold the policies of employment and investment so that everyone willing to work may have a job." The National Health Service (NHS) was described as attempting to ensure access for all "to the best medical treatment that science and the nation can provide."[17] American liberal activists formed part of an international discourse on social democratic means for meeting the challenges of an uncertain peacetime economy.[18]

This transnational conversation about social democracy revealed, however, significant cracks in the commitment of American liberals to a politics of the left that would only intensify in the emerging Cold War. For one thing, a comparison of the American and British political climates revealed the limitations of the social democratic vision in the United States. In addition, the emergence of deep divisions within American liberalism over the question of relations with the Soviet Union increasingly defined the context of the international conversation among those on the left. A UDA memo written shortly after the 1946 midterm elections argued that the rationale behind the economic integration of Germany into a European economic federation was the threat of "Russian domination of Europe." The memorandum's author noted "differences in political outlook between the US and the principal countries of Europe," but stated that "our differences with governments which, broadly speaking, are social democratic, are differences in degree of public ownership and central planning. They are not comparable to the fundamental cleavage between totalitarian and democratic systems."[19] The memorandum demonstrated not only awareness on the part of liberal activists of the need to adapt the language of reform to the demands of the American political scene, but also an increasing desire by UDA liberals to shift American liberalism away from associations with any sort of popular front on the left in order to emphasize this "fundamental cleavage" between freedom and totalitarianism. British Labour politician, Jennie Lee, would note in April 1947 that American liberals had changed since the concerted drive to confirm Henry Wallace as secretary of commerce and to pass the Full Employment Act in 1945. The depth of the divisions that had given rise to the formation of the rival liberal organizations in the form of the Progressive Citizens of America (PCA) and ADA, divisions that manifested themselves far less severely in Europe, demonstrated to Lee that progressive groups "in Britain and America are dangerously out of touch with one another."[20]

The shift in political outlook and strategy of the liberal-left movement as a whole can be summarized by analysis of the changing attitudes of the newly formed ADA toward both labor and social democratic ideas. The founding of ADA in January 1947 in Washington was, in the words of founder member, Reinhold Niebuhr, "to create a climate of liberal opinion which is explicitly and uncompromisingly democratic in purpose," a clear reference to the perceived fellow traveler character of Henry Wallace's PCA. The preliminary statement of the new group rejected some sort of "simple, inexorable choice between imperialist and fascist reaction and communist totalitarianism." Instead, the group's architects asserted that the "power of government must be adequate to subordinate the exercise of private power to the general welfare, but we must also guard against undue concentration of governmental authority." The "central issue" of contemporary politics was "not between capitalism or socialism, but between those who believe in the inalienable rights of the individual and those who do not." In appropriating the term "liberalism" for an ADA brand of New Deal political action, founder members James Loeb, Niebuhr, Leon Henderson, Chester Bowles, and others were careful to avoid direct engagement with left-wing ideology when their primary purpose was to rescue the New Deal coalition from damaging associations with the extreme left. "Liberalism is a demanding faith," they argued in a statement produced in advance of the January conference. "Its basis is neither a set of dogmas nor a prescription of specific measures. Liberalism is based on a deep concern for all men, a profound faith in human reason, and an attitude of inquiry." This was a far cry from the popular front spirit that had mobilized the left behind Henry Wallace's appointment to the Department of Commerce in 1945, or the promotion of the original Full Employment Act. The principal ideological leitmotif of early ADA publicity and correspondence in 1947 was the need "to combat totalitarianism by striking boldly at the conditions of hunger, want, and insecurity which breed desperate political situations."[21]

ADA remained committed to theories of social welfare and state activity that had taken shape in the United States in the Roosevelt years. Its members also largely continued to believe that "the British experiment in reconciling political liberty with economic planning is of the highest significance—and that the future of democracy in Europe depends, in no small measure, on its success."[22] However, Labour MP Patrick Gordon Walker's visit to the United States in early 1947 put the emerging differences between American liberalism and the European left into sharp relief. Ostensibly Loeb and the other organizers of the informal visit saw themselves and the British Labour government as brothers-in-arms, and described Gordon Walker's speaking tour as an opportunity to discuss "the general subject of British labor's [sic] accomplishments in its first year and a half of its control of the government." A UDA memo told members that "liberals have waited and watched with keen and sympathetic interest this brave attempt to establish democratic socialism . . . It would be hard to overestimate the importance of this first effort to increase understanding of the

British Labor Government."[23] Paul Douglas and Hubert Humphrey were two figures involved in the establishment of ADA in 1947 who initially saw the new organization as reestablishing "the Democratic Party as a progressive force in American politics" along British lines, promoting a platform that included a "strong statement requesting [the] establishment of national economic planning...Extension of public health and medical services...are fundamentals to [a] liberal platform."[24] Gordon Walker received an enthusiastic reception from ADA chapters and local labor union groups in cities from Boston to Minneapolis, but his speeches described a political agenda increasingly untenable for a liberal movement engaged in a domestic struggle with the PCA and the extreme left. "The doctrine underlying the policy of the Labour Party...has been evolved as a revolt against the assumptions of laissez-faire," he argued. "Labour does not regard the State solely as an evil thing whose powers must at all costs be clipped." Nationalization, for instance, was to Prime Minister Clement Attlee's party

> not an end in itself; it fits into a bigger, general scheme...Thus the State will exercise an overriding influence over the whole economy: through its control over credit and taxation; through general directions to nationalized industries; through the conditions imposed upon Boards set up for and by private industries.[25]

ADA, by contrast, although appreciative of the Labour party's efforts to transform the landscape of British politics, saw liberalism's "essential purpose" in practical terms as "the protection of international security." According to ADA national chairman Wilson Wyatt, ADA's domestic program was predicated upon America's role as "the champion of democratic principles in the world...ADA is pledged to make America the world symbol of progressive democracy. We must be strong at home—free from unemployment and inflation—to be strong abroad."[26]

In an article in *Tribune*, Labour MP, Jennie Lee, warned American liberals that it was dangerous for what she termed, somewhat loosely, "the American Left" to place this international agenda at center stage, to the extent of promoting an irreconcilable split within the movement. Henry Wallace's recent visit to London had generated enthusiastic attention, Lee claimed, because he had been "wearing the mantle of Franklin Roosevelt, symbolizing those in America opposed to the American Century of Mr. Luce and working for the Century of the Common Man." Were ADA members like Leon Henderson and

Walter Reuther "so warped with fear and hatred of Communism and Soviet Russia that they give uncritical support to President Truman's foreign policy," even if this meant the collapse of a left-of-center coalition in American politics that had returned Roosevelt to the presidency in 1944? "Must Russia count among its implacable enemies in America not only American reactionaries, but also the bulk of American Liberals, Socialists, and trade unionists?" Lee asked. She answered her rhetorical question in the negative, while affirming her own party's determination not to make the mistake of the PCA of refusing to recognize the unpalatable truths about the Soviet Union. Implicit in Lee's article, however, was the assertion that American liberals needed to spend less time conjuring up anti-totalitarian slogans, and more time formulating social democratic responses to domestic political and socioeconomic questions.[27]

Those American liberals most interested in learning from the British domestic experiment were also those most critical of the growing alliance between the United States and Britain in foreign affairs. Senator Claude Pepper of Florida looked upon Britain's nationalization program, proposed national health system, and public housing program with envy in 1946.[28] He was critical, however, of a growing schism among the Big Three—the United States, Soviet Union, and the United Kingdom—over territory and ideology as the wartime grand alliance steadily unraveled over the course of the year. Many on the American left were opposed to the continued maintenance of the British Empire, and thought it hypocritical of the American and British governments to criticize the Soviets' territorial ambitions while pursuing their own expansionist agendas. When Congress authorized a 3 billion dollar loan to the United Kingdom in May 1946, Pepper noted in his diary that it was unfortunate that "the sentiment of Congress and government will not allow a decent Russian loan. We are still going [down] the sad road to another war."[29]

Essentially this perspective formed the overarching theme of Henry Wallace's presidential campaign of 1948, effectively drowning out his interesting, but underdeveloped, domestic critique of New Deal liberalism in which he argued that American liberalism needed to develop along more social democratic lines, nationalizing certain industries and building a universal welfare state. Under the guidance of former New Dealer, Rexford Tugwell, in 1948 a professor at the University of Chicago, Wallace's progressive platform was committed to a militant civil rights program, the nationalization of the railroad and aircraft industries, a larger price support program for farmers, and a social security system based on universalist principles. The marriage

of the principle of socioeconomic equality of opportunity to broader
issues of race and class in American society attracted large numbers of
African American professionals to the cause, and provided a specifically American bent to an international ideology of the left.[30]

Yet the Progressive party's increasing obsession with the Soviet
Union not only weakened its electoral credibility at a time of heightened Cold War tensions, but also blunted its domestic message and
compromised its ability to learn from international noncommunist
leftist examples. Dr George Cannon, chairman of the Harlem Wallace-
for-President Committee, who argued that Wallace "says the things
all Negroes want to hear, and not only talks but acts," also argued
that Wallace's role as apologist for the Soviets was "the major weak-
ness in Wallace's position." Progressive Senate candidate from Illinois,
Curtis MacDougall, later recalled that "the story of the Progressive
Party of 1948 is one of an unsuccessful attempt to impress the electorate with the prime importance of foreign affairs as they related
to world peace." Instead of clearly setting out a domestic left-wing
agenda, perhaps with reference to international examples, Wallace's
international vision was focused almost entirely on his opposition
to the Cold War battle lines as they had been drawn, allowing the
Truman administration and its supporters to campaign on the need
to continue in power "the party which had made a popular record
on the bread and butter issues."[31] In effect the anti-imperialist, anti-
Cold War liberals like Wallace and Pepper shared the same linguistic
and ideological limitations as leading figures in ADA and the Truman
administration: both factions, although mutually hostile, saw the lessons of the wider world in terms of concepts such as peace, individual
freedom, democracy, and international security that were of no assistance to the cause of domestic reform.

Left-wing intellectual, Lewis Feuer, argued that, if differences
could be put aside, "American progressives can develop a constructive, anti-imperialist policy and at the same time make it clear that
it rejects the pattern of Soviet society as the guide for our political
thinking."[32] Yet this was not the lesson American liberals were learning from their view of the international scene: one of the primary
reasons the new ADA invited Patrick Gordon Walker to the United
States was in order to sell Labour Britain to a liberal movement more
critical of its foreign policy than supportive of its domestic program.
Leading liberal, James Loeb, asked Congressman Jerry Voorhis in
April 1946 to speak at a meeting on the Attlee government in response
to the fact that in "recent months the British Government . . . has been
under attack in America not only from the right, as expected, but

also from liberal circles...I think it would be well...if you could emphasize as eloquently as I know you can the democratic nature of the Labor Party itself and of its program," and he was invited to counter Senator Pepper's attacks on British imperialism in the wake of the war.[33] Almost all liberal politicians in the United States were broadly supportive of the basic aims of Labour's program in Britain, but the debate over how to import some of the ideas into America was soon superseded by a debate over the place of Britain's foreign policy in the global struggle for supremacy between the United States and the Soviet Union.

American center-left politicians did not only have the opportunity in the late 1940s to flesh out an ideological agenda in the abstract: the heirs to the New Deal held power in the White House and, other than between January 1947 and January 1949, on Capitol Hill. Congressional liberals, like their left-of-center counterparts overseas, were keen to develop plans for a national health insurance system as a central plank of a social democratic postwar political settlement. The measure reflected a broad political impetus across the industrialized world to factor universal health care provision into the development of social democratic state regimes, and in the United States also represented unfinished business from the development and passage of the 1935 Social Security Act.[34] Much recent scholarship has emphasized the distinctive political and institutional obstacles to the enactment of a public sector response to health provision in the United States: the complex federal structure of government; the power of anti-statist interest groups in American politics; the over-reliance of the federal government on a small cadre of policymakers; the weak system of political allegiances within the two main parties. Some scholars have used international comparisons to highlight the particular problems faced by American policymakers. By the 1940s, health care providers were already developing private systems of health insurance for workers and their dependants that narrowed the political appeal of a federal system. In addition, the ideological foundations of New Deal welfare policy stood firmly on an insurance principle that excluded many of those who needed care most while alienating a medical lobby determined to retain control over the financial side of health care provision. The coalition of interests in Congress that formed the bed-rock of New Deal legislative activity rapidly unraveled when southern conservatives saw the long-term social ramifications of major health care reform. And labor unions increasingly became drawn to private health care packages as part of a collective bargaining process that guaranteed some sort of coverage for their workers at a time when the state seemed structurally incapable of meeting their needs under a centralized scheme.[35]

While not seeking to overturn these analyses of the institutional and structural obstacles to health care reform, it can be suggested that investigation of the ways in which American proponents of federal health insurance used case studies of health programs in the United Kingdom and New Zealand demonstrates that American policymakers not only faced obstacles to reform outside their control, but were themselves also unwilling to adopt the ideological language and strategies of the countries they were observing. As in the foregoing discussion of the evolution of the abstract principles of American liberalism after the Second World War, the formulators of an American health insurance program proved unable or unwilling to translate the language of social democracy into an American context. This assertion may seem uncontroversial given our understanding of the limits of the ideological ambition of the New Deal and the limits on its freedom of maneuver. Nevertheless, the fact that liberal policymakers and legislators were eager to investigate British and Antipodean systems suggests that they wanted to engender an international dialog on social policy, but could not see how to reinterpret the intrinsically redistributive and egalitarian rationale driving Labour governments in Great Britain and New Zealand for an American liberal movement increasingly preoccupied with anti-Sovietism. Furthermore, American private sector interest groups and their allies in Congress were also looking across the Atlantic and Pacific oceans for material with which to discredit federal health insurance plans, and they proved much more successful in translating their findings into a language appropriate for an era of heightened international tension.

It is illuminating to note that when the deputy prime minister and finance minister of New Zealand, Walter Nash, wrote in 1944 about the ideological underpinnings of the Labour Party in that country, he used documents composed largely in the United States during the war. One of the principal problems for the postwar world, Nash argued, was to ensure "the specific and progressive application of the long-range objectives of the Atlantic Charter and the Four Freedoms to the end that all people will be assured of fuller employment, greater security, and better social conditions than they have ever enjoyed before."[36] Both the Atlantic Charter of 1941 and the Four Freedoms of 1944 can be principally attributed to President Franklin D. Roosevelt, and it is clear that the eventual parting of the ways between American liberals and their contemporaries elsewhere was not preordained. A *Washington Post* review of Nash's book on his home country and on the changes his government had made to the fabric of society and politics since its election in 1935 noted that it was

> an up-to-date and informative description of a land which is already far advanced in social and economic reforms, which has been doing a great deal of independent and constructive thinking in recent years, and whose voice is definitely slated to be heard from now on in all discussions of world, and particularly Pacific affairs.[37]

The voice of New Zealand's Labour government was certainly making itself heard within the Social Security Administration in Washington. The head of the New Zealand legation there informed his superiors in Wellington in October 1945 that Dr Jacob Fisher, of the Bureau of Research and Statistics of the Social Security Administration, had written an article about New Zealand's universal social security and national health system in his department's Social Security Bulletin.[38] As would be the case with the United Kingdom after the enactment of its National Health Act of 1948, New Zealand, which had enacted a mammoth Social Security Act in 1938 including the world's most advanced system of state-provided health care, formed a vital case study for American policymakers struggling to work out the details of an American federal program.[39] Although the authors of a bill in Congress to provide federal health insurance followed the basic pay-as-you-go principle of the American Social Security Act of 1935, this was primarily because it was the most obvious homegrown model available. It was clear to policy experts like Fisher that international case studies could provide alternative models that might at least eliminate some of the imperfections in the existing US model, such as the lack of universality and the difficulty of accruing enough insurance funds to match the payouts to claimants.

It was with some justification that New Zealand's high commissioner in Australia claimed that the enactment of New Zealand's Social Security Act had increased "her international prestige."[40] A New Zealand emissary in London noted in 1946 that the "demand for information about the operation of the Social Security Scheme in New Zealand...continues to be very great." British plans for an NHS had "caused a resurgence of interest in the arrangements for a National Health Service operating in New Zealand under the Social Security Act. Our stocks of the Health Benefits pamphlet have been rapidly exhausted and only a few loan copies now remain."[41] Bureaucrats in the Social Security Administration in Washington were similarly interested in developments in New Zealand and in London, and the three Anglophone nations formed part of a transoceanic dialog about how to develop institutional pillars of postwar world social democracy. In November 1946 Jacob Fisher requested information on the financial aspects of New Zealand's health system from the government in Wellington, and was sent some published leaflets and documents. In January 1947 his superior, I. S. Falk, wrote again, claiming that his organization needed more detailed information on "the administrative organization of the New Zealand health benefits program, particularly with regard to personnel requirements, and I should appreciate your help in meeting our need." Information from the New Zealand government would "be of assistance to us in the development of estimates for personnel and administrative budgets for health insurance proposals for the United States."[42]

Whereas New Deal bureaucrats were interested in the technical know-how other states with existing social security systems could provide, left-of-center politicians in the United States seemed keen to learn the broader ideological lessons of overseas experiments in social democracy. Claude Pepper had met Walter Nash while the latter was New Zealand's roving plenipotentiary in London and Washington during the war, and in April 1948 he informed Nash that "I have many times had occasion to say, based largely upon my association with you and my knowledge through you of your New Zealand, that I know of no country in the world where Democracy was more vital and real than in your great country." He contrasted the impressive strides New Zealand's Labour government had made to enact a comprehensive social security program with the increasingly conservative outlook of the American political scene after the war. The world crisis had, he argued,

> given extraordinary encouragement to many who are not only anti-Communist but anti-Democratic in the sense that you and I believe in Democracy...I think the problem now is to prevent an explosion until we can eventually get people more of the Roosevelt mind back into the top places of authority in both the executive and legislative branches of the government.[43]

The fact that the British Labour government had by 1948 pushed the NHS bill through parliament gave heart to many American liberals as they attempted to find some domestic political credo for the center-left at a time of increasing Cold War tension. "In the ten months since the British act went into effect," wrote liberal Senator Hubert Humphrey in the *New York Times* magazine in May 1949, "professional medical opinion (once opposed), the Conservative Party and the British people have provided evidence of the act's tremendous acceptance... The Conservative Party virtually lost the important by-election at Hammersmith before they could reverse their policy and endorse the British Health Service Act." The Committee for the Nation's Health, a medical pressure group formed to support the principle of federal health insurance and to counterbalance the propaganda drive of the American Medical Association (AMA), spent much of its meager budget in the period purchasing British Information Service pamphlets on the British NHS for distribution to interested parties.[44]

The Republican party was quick to respond to this flurry of interest in social policy in the wider world. New Zealand's man in Washington, John Reid, observed with regret in June 1947 that a proposed visit to New Zealand by Jacob Fisher to study the operation of the national health insurance system there had been indefinitely postponed after a strongly worded attack on the floor of the House of Representatives by Indiana Republican Forrest Harness,

> one of the ultra-reactionaries who... alleged that Fisher has been documented by the House Committee on Un-American Activities for association with the "Communist front and fellow travelers."... This, of course, is the witch hunter's line on every public servant who was in office during the New Deal, and coming from Harness is the equivalent of a compliment to Fisher.

Reid tried to infer something positive about the state of American politics by noting that "Henry Wallace held his Washington rally on Monday night and a crowd of about 10,000 attended," but the notable thing about Reid's letter was its demonstration of the difference in political culture in the two countries in the early Cold War.[45] To a New Zealander, it seemed baffling that a representative of a center-left administration attempting to advance the common good could lose a political battle with a politician who simply had to throw out a few frightening words about communism. The battle in the United States over federal health insurance demonstrated, however, both that the anti-statist forces opposing a federal plan could also benefit from the use of foreign case studies, and that the proponents of the scheme could not find the political language necessary to make the most of overseas examples.

A coalition of Republicans in Congress, the AMA, and business lobbyists, continuing their ongoing campaign to discredit the New

JONATHAN BELL

Deal state, discovered in the late 1940s that the anti-totalitarian rhetoric of Cold War internationalism proved a powerful tool that could cast the ever-expanding federal bureaucracy in a negative light in the public mind. In an article for the *Reader's Digest*, Harness distilled his attack on the Fisher mission to New Zealand into an easily digestible form. As chair of a house subcommittee on "Publicity and Propaganda" he had discovered

> startling evidence of attempts by federal officials to make Big Government bigger and to extend, by another vast grant of power, the authority of the State over the lives of all of us ... Of recent legislative proposals, none has stronger, more obvious appeal to the devotees of the all-powerful, all-supervising State than national compulsory health insurance, often described as "socialized medicine" ... The FSA is already a vast social service establishment with 35,000 employees. Administration and enforcement of the health insurance law would be added to its domain.

Harness deliberately portrayed the New Deal state as akin to far left regimes elsewhere in the world, and noted that federal bureaucrats were looking to other states for examples of how to import socialism to the United States, and were sending men like Fisher, who Harness claimed was a fellow traveler, to New Zealand and the United Kingdom. He noted that Michael Davis, head of the pro-federal health insurance lobby the Committee for the Nation's Health, had a son who was "an official of the Public Health Service lately assigned, at Government expense, to the British Ministry of Health in London to observe Britain's system of 'socialized medicine.'" [46] Harness's subcommittee also stridently criticized a Social Security Administration mission to investigate improving health care provision in United States-administered Japan, claiming that "the health mission to Japan is composed entirely and exclusively of men long identified in the public record as advocates and proponents of socialized medicine not only in the United States but throughout the world."[47] The global marketplace of social policy ideas acted for the American right as a propaganda weapon with which they could assert American independence from dangerous foreign influences. The Harness campaign resonated with members of the medical profession in the United States: "The members of this mission [to Japan] are all known to be advocates of socialized medicine and Communism," wrote one doctor in Stephenville, Texas, in October 1947. "They have studied the system in England and now are trying to force it on Japan."[48]

The operation of Britain's new NHS quickly attracted the interest of opponents of state-sponsored health insurance. The Republican National Committee, with the help of the National Industrial Conference Board, a business lobbying organization, procured the services of Dr Marjorie Shearon, a disaffected former employee of the Social Security Administration who, in the late 1940s, ran her own private propaganda business against federal health insurance, the Shearon Medical Legislative Service.[49] Shearon made a visit to London in November 1949 during which she toured NHS practices and sent back material for her Republican party employers as well as for use in her lobbying organization's news bulletin, entitled "Challenge to Socialism."[50] The distance across the Atlantic between Europe and the United States rendered exaggerated and dramatic portrayals of the sociopolitical situation overseas easy to achieve. Congresswoman Frances Bolton (R-Ohio) was one of many in Congress to visit Britain and remark on the "maladministration" of its social programs that had "largely decreased the personal incentive to work, to produce, and to save."[51] Shearon noted US Federal Security Administrator Oscar Ewing's visit to London, and recounted the "hellish nature of a planned economy" and the "menacing shadow of Government" she had encountered. "The commonest things are unobtainable... Now after one week in England this lay politician [Ewing] has the effrontery to state that the 'national health insurance proposal will be good for America.'"[52]

The AMA executive board and its public relations advisers saw the NHS in the UK as a useful vehicle to unite the issue of federal health insurance with the broader theme of the development of a totalitarian state, a linkage that had been noticeably less significant in earlier political battles over health care. Dr Morris Fishbein, editor of the Journal of the American Medical Association, launched a new publicity drive against federal health insurance in December 1948, shortly after the Democrats' surprise victory in the November elections, with a bitter attack in the journal on Britain's health care system. Ostensibly his critique rested on the perceived impracticalities of funding public health out of the public purse, asserting that the "greatest mistake that England made in adopting its National Health Act was its failure to realize that even moderately good functioning of such an act depends on adequate medical personnel and medical facilities. These England did not have." But he then went on to argue that public health care provision and other social welfare schemes would develop "inevitably into a socialized state in which mines, banks, transportation and practically all public services become nationalized." Such an argument integrated the Cold War into an already well-versed anti-statist worldview, suggesting that at "the same time that many of our political leaders oppose communism they move toward communism by embracing socialism."[53] The *British Medical Journal*, hardly enthusiastic about the National Health Act in 1948 and full of correspondence from doctors hostile to the new legislation, noted in a leading article just as the new act came into operation in July that the "basic differences in American thought and speech should be borne in mind when one comes to examine their general reaction to such social measures as social health insurance." Noting the high percentage of Americans without any form of health coverage, the journal's New York correspondent argued that federal insurance would still fall foul of the fact that the

> average practitioner's chief objection to a health service is that it would be under the control of politicians, and for such he has a hearty loathing and contempt. There is little in America of that tradition of public service which inspires great men in England to a lifetime of arduous work.[54]

The transatlantic relationship worked in favor of the AMA, however, when it enlisted the help of anti-NHS British doctors to come to the United States to give lectures. One such doctor, Ralph Gampell, earned $19,000 from the AMA for his lectures to American audiences, and furnished the AMA with information that went into the propaganda cartoon strip "The sad case of waiting room Willie," which portrayed the NHS as a horror story waiting to happen in the United States.[55] The increasingly tense international situation, and the anger among business and medical lobby groups generated by the 1948 election results, invigorated the campaign to discredit the political legacy of the New Deal by investing vast amounts of money in a publicity drive to associate social democratic liberalism with totalitarianism.

Although the American right possessed a certainty of purpose that gave their increasingly hysterical campaign an air of authority, proponents of federal health insurance were unable to reconcile their support for the plan, and their broad sympathy for governments implementing state-sponsored schemes, with their own increasingly vocal support for the anti-totalitarian rhetoric of the Cold War. In addition, supporters of state programs had to explain details of their plans; their opponents had a readymade rhetorical arsenal with which to reject them. Claude Pepper took part in a radio debate in January

1950 against perennial Republican presidential hopeful, and now president of the University of Pennsylvania, Harold Stassen, entitled "Do We Want National Health Insurance in the United States?" Although Stassen was able to rely on unsubstantiated yet rhetorically powerful put-downs, arguing that a "Swede in Minnesota lives longer and is healthier than a Swede in Sweden...under the semi-socialistic system," Pepper struggled to explain policy differences between the British system, reliant on direct taxation as well as national insurance payments, and the American proposals, reliant entirely on individual social security taxes.[56]

In the final analysis, the international dimension of social policy-making in the United States in the late 1940s was predicated more on the anti-statist premises of the Cold War than on the sharing of policy ideas. The decline of the social democratic impulse in America was helped by other factors: the sheer financial muscle of business organizations and the AMA played a significant role in the eventual defeat of federal health insurance in the United States, although the state, by contrast, lacked the patronage networks necessary to mount a successful defence of its program. Equally important, however, was the fact that the international context to political reform increasingly favored anti-statist arguments, both because the right was able to manipulate foreign case studies more effectively than before the war and because the liberal movement was itself increasingly drawn toward abstract anti-totalitarian arguments and away from a politics of social democracy.

Notes

1. Daniel T. Rodgers, *Atlantic Crossings: Social Politics in a Progressive Age* (Cambridge, MA: Harvard University Press, 1998). In his concluding chapter, Rodgers argues that the enormous gap between US prosperity and European poverty in 1945 left the prewar dialog of reform between the two continents in tatters: "Europe was cramped and poor. Its socio-political needs were not those of the United States" (501). The increasing conservatism and particularism of the United States in the 1940s dominates extant historiography: Alan Brinkley, *The End of Reform: New Deal Liberalism in Recession and War* (New York: Vintage Books, 1995); Elizabeth Fones-Wolf, *Selling Free Enterprise: The Business Assault on Labor and Liberalism, 1945–1960* (Urbana: University of Illinois Press, 1994); Aaron Friedberg, *in the Shadow of the Garrison State: America's Anti-Statism and Its Cold War Grand Strategy* (Princeton, NJ: Princeton University Press, 2000); Patrick Reagan, *Designing a New America: The Origins of New Deal Planning* (Amherst, MA: University of Massachusetts Press, 2000).

2. Alonzo Hamby, "The Vital Center, the Fair Deal, and the Quest for a Liberal Political Economy," *American Historical Review*, 77 no. 3 (June 1972): 653–78; Mary Dudziak, *Cold War Civil Rights: Race and the Image of American Democracy* (Princeton, NJ: Princeton University Press, 2000); Thomas Borstelman, *The Cold War and the Color Line: American Race Relations in the Global Arena* (Cambridge, MA: Harvard University Press, 2001); Jennifer Delton, *Making Minnesota Liberal: Civil Rights and the Transformation of the Democratic Party* (Minneapolis, MN: University of Minnesota Press, 2002). See also Wendy Wall, *Inventing the American Way: The Politics of Consensus from the New Deal to the Civil Rights Movement* (New York: Oxford University Press, 2008).
3. Alan Derickson, "The House of Falk: The Paranoid Style in American Health Politics," American Journal of Public Health, 87, no. 11 (Nov. 1997): 1836–43; Colin Gordon, "Why No Health Insurance in the United States? The Limits of Social Provision in War and Peace, 1941–1948," Journal of Policy History 9, no. 3 (July 1997): 277–310.
4. A good overview of some of the political constraints on the emergence of social democracy in the United States is Ira Katznelson, "Considerations on Social Democracy in the United States," *Comparative Politics*, 11, no. 1 (October 1978): 77–99.
5. See Jonathan Bell, *The Liberal State on Trial: The Cold War and American Politics in the Truman Years* (New York: Columbia University Press, 2004) for a fuller treatment of this theme, albeit one that focuses on the United States alone.
6. So-called state-centred analyses of the development of social policies in the United States and elsewhere abound. See Theda Skocpol, "State Capacity and Economic Intervention during the Early New Deal," *Political Science Quarterly*, 97, no. 2 (Summer 1982): 255–78; see also essays in Peter Evans et al., eds, *Bringing the State Back In* (Cambridge: Cambridge University Press, 1985); Theda Skocpol and John Ikenberry, "The Political Formation of the American Welfare State in Historical and Comparative Perspective," *Comparative Social Research*, 6 (1983): 87–148. More recently, Daniel Rodgers has put American political reform into its international context, showing how reformers outside the apparatus of the state as well as inside it helped to shape an international dialogue of reform. His story ends in the Second World War; mine continues into the postwar years. See Rodgers, *Atlantic Crossings*. See also Meg Jacobs, "'How About Some Meat?' the Office of Price Administration, Consumption Politics, and State Building from the Bottom Up, 1941–1946," *Journal of American History*, 84, no. 3 (December, 1997): 910–41. Jacobs argues that it was only when the OPA failed to live up to its wartime record after the war that this large state organ lost public support.

SOCIAL POLITICS IN A TRANSOCEANIC WORLD 187

7. Official Bulletin, ILO, June 8, 1944, vol. XXVI, no. 1.
8. See Reagan, *Designing a New America*, 218–19.
9. Joseph Lash memo to UDA New York chapter board meeting, September 4, 1946, UDA/ADA papers, Cambridge University Library, reel 13, section 210.
10. Paul Sifton to Ralph Wolf, February 12, 1945, UDA/ADA papers, reel 6, section 91.
11. Claude Pepper and Hays Gorey, *Eyewitness to a Century* (San Diego, CA: Harcourt Brace Jovanovich, 1987), 149. For details of the make-up of Congress in the 79th Congress, see Congressional directory, 79th Congress, 2nd session (Washington, DC, 1946).
12. Vinson to Wagner, May 30, 1945, George Outland to James Loeb, December 1, 1945, UDA/ADA papers, reel 6, section 91.
13. Outland testimony, June 21, 1945, UDA/ADA papers, reel 13, section 233.
14. Minutes of UDA executive meeting, October 24, 1946, UDA/ADA papers, reel 13, section 210. The committee included Loeb, Saul Padover, Ethel Epstein, and Joseph Lash.
15. Walter Reuther to Bernice Kandel, May 24, 1946, UDA/ADA papers, reel 7, section 94; Reuther speech at UDA dinner for Wallace, January 29, 1945, UDA/ADA papers, reel 16, section 289; Emil Rieve speech to town hall meeting in support of Henry Wallace as secretary of commerce, February 26, 1945, UDA/ADA papers, reel 6, section 93. For an analysis of the left-wing political vision of CIO industrial unions at the end of the Second World War, see Nelson Lichtenstein, *Walter Reuther: The Most Dangerous Man in Detroit* (Urbana: University of Illinois Press, 1995), chapter 12; Kevin Boyle, *The UAW and the Heyday of American Liberalism, 1945–1968* (Ithaca, NY: Cornell University Press, 1995), especially chapter 2; Steve Fraser, *Labor Will Rule: Sidney Hillman and the Rise of American Labor* (Ithaca, NY: Cornell University Press, 1991), chapter 18.
16. James Loeb to Jerry Voorhis, April 12, 1946 and April 23, 1946, UDA/ADA papers, reel 7, section 94; Leon Henderson to town hall meeting for Wallace, February 26, 1945, UDA/ADA papers, reel 6, section 93.
17. UDA London Letter, July 26, 1946, August 15, 1946, November 15, 1946; UDA/ADA papers, reel 16, section 308.
18. Three useful analyses of social democracy in Britain and Sweden are John Campbell, *Nye Bevan and the Mirage of British Socialism* (London: Weidenfeld and Nicholson, 1987); Martin Francis, *Ideas and Policies under Labour, 1945–1951: Building a New Britain* (Manchester: Manchester University Press, 1997); Tim Tilton, *The Political Theory of Swedish Social Democracy: Through the Welfare State to Socialism* (Oxford: Oxford University Press, 1990).
19. UDA memorandum "On the German Problem in the Light of Soviet Policy," November 23, 1946, UDA/ADA papers, reel 7, section 95.

20. Jennie Lee, "Comment on Wallace," *Tribune*, April 29, 1947, ADA papers, reel 16, section 288.

21. Reinhold Niebuhr to Herbert Lehman, November 19, 1946; Preliminary and Provisional Statement of Principles, November 15, 1946; ADA statements on foreign and domestic policy, December 19, 1946; ADA foreign policy program for the national convention, March 29, 1947, Lehman MSS, ADA special file 17a.

22. ADA foreign policy program, March 29, 1947, Lehman MSS, ADA special file 17a.

23. James Loeb to Patrick Gordon Walker, November 26, 1946; UDA memorandum, November 7, 1946, ADA papers, reel 7, section 98.

24. Hubert Humphrey to James Loeb, January 4, 1947, ADA papers, reel 7, section 105.

25. Patrick Gordon Walker speech notes, ADA papers, reel 7, section 98. For letters detailing Walker's reception in liberal circles, see Eugenie Anderson of the Minnesota Democratic Farmer Labor party to Loeb, January 28, 1947; Johannes Hober of the Philadelphia ADA to Nathalie Panek, February 5, 1947, in ibid.

26. Wilson Wyatt speech, April 8, 1947, ADA papers, ibid.

27. Jennie Lee, "Comment on Wallace," *London Tribune*, April 29, 1947.

28. Claude Pepper diary, July 21, 1946, Pepper MSS, Claude Pepper Library, Tallahassee, Florida, S439/2/3.

29. Ibid., May 10, 1946.

30. See "The New Party's Future," *New Republic*, July 26, 1948, p. 15; "The Negro in Politics," ibid., October 18, 1948, pp. 9–15.

31. "The Negro in Politics," ibid.; Curtis MacDougall, *Gideon's Army* (3 vols, New York, NY, 1965), II, p. 330.

32. Lewis Feuer, "Russia and the Liberals," *New Republic*, November 8, 1948, 14–16.

33. James Loeb to Jerry Voorhis, April 23, 1946, UDA/ADA MSS, reel 7, full employment.

34. The *New Republic* remarked that all "over the world, governments based on widely differing ideologies are coming to recognize the responsibility of the state in this matter." *New Republic*, May 3, 1948, 14. See Gosta Esping-Andersen, *Three Worlds of Welfare Capitalism* (Princeton, NJ: Princeton University Press, 1990); Margaret Weir, Ann Shula Orloff, and Theda Skocpol, eds, *The Politics of Social Policy in the United States* (Princeton, NJ: Princeton University Press, 1988); Daniel Levine, *Poverty and Society: the Growth of the American Welfare State in International Comparison* (New Brunswick, NJ: Rutgers University Press, 1988); Raymond Richards, *Closing the Door to Destitution: The Shaping of the Social Security Acts of the United States and New Zealand* (University Park, PA: Pennsylvania State University Press, 1994); Jacob Hacker, *The Divided Welfare State: The Battle over Public and Private Social Benefits in the United States*

(Cambridge: Cambridge University Press, 2002). Two classic studies of the fight for federal health insurance in the United States are Daniel Hirshfield, *The Lost Reform: The Campaign for Compulsory Health Insurance in the United States, 1932–1943* (Cambridge: Cambridge University Press 1970); Monte Poen, *Harry S. Truman versus the Medical Lobby: The Genesis of Medicare* (Columbia, MO: University of Missouri Press, 1979).

35. The above represents a very brief summary of a vibrant and intricate area of historical scholarship, best summarized in the following: Colin Gordon, "Why No Health Insurance in the United States?" a condensed version of his recent monograph, *Dead on Arrival: The Politics of Health Care in Twentieth Century America* (Princeton, NJ: Princeton University Press, 2003); Alan Derickson, "Health Security for All? Social Unionism and Universal Health Insurance, 1935–1958," *Journal of American History* 80, no. 4 (March 1994): 1333–56; and *Health Security for All: Dreams of Universal Health Care in America* (Baltimore, MD: Johns Hopkins University Press, 2005); Hacker, *The Divided Welfare State*, chapters 4 and 5.

36. Walter Nash, *New Zealand: A Working Democracy* (London: Duell, Sloan and Pearce, 1944), 194.

37. *Washington Post*, December 5, 1943, Walter Nash MSS, Archives New Zealand, Wellington, 59/2/124.

38. John Reid, head of New Zealand legation in Washington D.C., to secretary of external affairs, Wellington, October 24, 1945, New Zealand External Affairs MSS, Archives New Zealand, 33/5/1.

39. There are many helpful comparative studies detailing the establishment of welfare states and health insurance programs: see Alexander Davidson, *Two Models of Welfare: The Origins and Development of the Welfare State in Sweden and New Zealand, 1888–1988* (Uppsala, Sweden: Acta Universitatis Uppsaliensis, 1989); Richards, *Closing the Door to Destitution*; Nicholas Timmins, *The Five Giants: A Biography of the Welfare State* (London: Harper Collins, 1995).

40. Summary of address by the high commissioner to the Australian Institute of International Affairs, Victoria Branch, March 26, 1947, External Affairs MSS, series 1, 33/5/1.

41. Acting official secretary, New Zealand government offices, London, to Department of External Affairs, Wellington, March 5, 1946, External Affairs MSS, 33/5/1.

42. Permanent head, Prime Minister's Department, to director-general of health, Wellington, November 1, 1946; I. S. Falk, director, Social Security Administration, Washington, to John Reid, first secretary, New Zealand Legation, Washington, January 6, 1947, External Affairs MSS, 33/5/1.

43. Claude Pepper to Walter Nash, April 5, 1948, Nash MSS, series 453, correspondence with Pepper. Nash responded cordially April 16, 1948.

44. "The Case for National Health Insurance," *New York Times* magazine, May 8, 1949; British Information Service pamphlets and bulletins of the Committee for the Nation's Health, Pepper MSS, 201/93/1.
45. John Reid to secretary of external affairs, June 20, 1947, Nash MSS, 59/3/276. The Fisher–Harness affair is discussed in Derickson, "The House of Falk."
46. Forest Harness, "Our Most Dangerous Lobby," part II, *Reader's Digest*, December 1947. The New Zealand legation in Washington sent a copy to the External Affairs Ministry in Wellington, December 10, 1947, Nash MSS, 59/3/276.
47. Harness to John Taber (R-New York), September 9, 1947, Tom Connally MSS, Library of Congress, box 183, socialized medicine in Japan file.
48. Dr J. C. Terrell to Senator Tom Connally (D-Texas), October 20, 1947, Connally MSS, ibid.
49. See Derickson, "'The House of Falk," 1841; Bell, *The Liberal State on Trial*, chs. 2 and 5.
50. See, for example, Marjorie Shearon, notes on British trip no. 11, November 4, 1949, Robert Taft MSS, Library of Congress, box 798, Social Security 1949 file 1 of 3.
51. Congressional Record reprint, October 13, 1949, Taft MSS, box 499, Britain file 1.
52. "American Medicine and the Political Scene," December 15, 1949, Taft MSS, box 499, ibid. The title of Shearon's newsletter was changed to "Challenge to Socialism" in March 1950.
53. Morris Fishbein, "Health and Social Security," *Journal of the American Medical Association*, December 25, 1948, 1254–56. For a more scholarly analysis of the workings of the NHS in Great Britain, see Timmins, *The Five Giants*.
54. "American Reaction to Health Insurance," *British Medical Journal*, July 3, 1948, 39–40. An example of British correspondence on the National Health Act can be found in ibid., January 3, 1948, 24–26.
55. Bulletin of the Committee for the Nation's Health, May 21, 1951, Pepper MSS, 201/93/1.
56. American Forum of the Air, January 29, 1950, Pepper MSS, 203B/1/21.

Chapter 7

Technocracy, Modernization, and Reform: The Transatlantic Politics of the Spanish Right in the 1960s

Manuel Álvarez Tardío

During the Franco dictatorship, in the decade between 1959 and 1969, a group known as "the technocrats" (*tecnócratas*) implemented a broad program of economic and administrative reform with the aim of modernizing and centralizing the government and economy of Spain. Inspired not by democracy but by the international debate about the end of ideologies and the rise of the technocratic state, they drew extensively upon ideas best summarized in (but not restricted to) Daniel Bell's classic work of political sociology *The End of Ideology*.[1] The technocrats' core assumption was that social and economic modernization, coupled with improvements in the distribution of wealth, would lead to the disappearance of the old ideologies—chiefly socialism and liberalism—that had marked political struggles between the wars.

This chapter focuses on the work of two leading Spanish technocrats: Laureano López Rodó, a conservative Catholic who opposed liberal democracy and believed modernization was possible without it; and Gonzalo Fernández de la Mora, author of *El Crepúsculo de las Ideologías* (The Twilight of Ideologies), which was one of the most influential political essays of the Spanish 1960s. It does so in order to address a neglected field in the histories of both modern Spain and transatlantic politics: the role played by the international debate about the end of ideologies in shaping an authoritarian and yet *desarrollista* (modernizing) perspective on the new Spanish right in the 1960s.

A bloody civil war and a long dictatorship separated Spain from the path most western European countries followed after 1945. Spain, of course, was not directly involved in the Second World War; and it was isolated after Nazi Germany's defeat. It was expelled from international institutions, and both its diplomatic and commercial foreign relations were interrupted. At the onset of the Cold War, however, the strategic importance of the Iberian Peninsula, already noted by the US Pentagon and the British High Command at the end of 1944, led to a new American policy toward Spain, and as a consequence trade relations were gradually normalized and a period of greater cooperation began. Spain in this way was partially re-admitted into the international community, and even had something like its own Marshall Plan.[2] Spain overcame ostracism, therefore, thanks to US foreign policy realism within the general approach of containment. Franco's regime consolidated its position after having nearly capsized in the immediate postwar years. Nevertheless it was an incomplete and temporary consolidation: the Spanish economy had sunk as a result of autarky; Franco had secured his personal power but the regime was still little more than that, a military dictatorship.

Uncertainty was one of the dictatorship's most important and enduring features. Franco was supported by a complex coalition of political and social forces, which were kept under control by his undisputed personal leadership and his victory in the Civil War. All of these various forces had much to lose should instability return. During the first ten years of dictatorship none of them managed decisively to prevail.[3] For example, one of the most powerful groups, the fascist party *Falange*, had great prominence from 1939 to 1942 due to its Germanophilia and totalitarian plans for the Spanish state. The European context in these years, with the incredible Nazi expansion and the French defeat, was broadly favorable to the fascist elements in Franco's new regime. For the *Falange*'s founders and most faithful followers the Spanish fascist project represented a revolutionary and totalitarian discourse, but as a matter of fact this placed it in tension with the outlook, style, and ideas held by traditional conservatives. After 1943, however, the *Falange*'s influence waned as a result of two crucial circumstances: the Nazi defeat and the need to present a friendlier face toward Atlantic partners, especially the United States. As a result, the balance of power now tilted toward Catholic traditionalists—a group that in itself was also quite complex.[4]

The spectrum of conservative groups within the regime was even richer and more varied than is conveyed in the brief sketch earlier. The *Falange*'s political weight and the symbolic concessions to the

Nazis before 1942 were in some respects misleading. Most conservatives who supported Franco's rebellion wanted an authoritarian state, not a fascist one. The Spanish right, therefore was heterogeneous. There was general agreement, however, on the need for a corporative state in which pluralism was restricted socially and politically, and in which Catholicism was the state religion with the church control of education. Rightists wanted fundamental (constitutional) laws inspired by political traditionalism. Not all of them were supporters of the monarchy, and those who were royalists had for the most part abandoned liberal-democratic positions, now preferring instead for another model of the Crown: a king or queen with real executive powers and a system of corporative representation. As this suggests, French integrism still weighed like a millstone on Spanish monarchical conservatism.[5]

However, from the mid-1940s onward, and following the decline of *Falange*, some Spanish conservatives began to discuss their own future and that of Spanish politics differently, and in ways more susceptible to wider transnational and transatlantic influence. In so doing they drew on an older debate among traditional conservative elements, the origins of which lay in the period before the Civil War. These conservatives, most of them royalists, maintained a frontal rejection of political liberalism and pluralism because for them parliamentarism and political parties connoted "political chaos." They thought the liberal regime had led to the "division of the united national consciousness," which should be grounded on the "unity of religious belief."[6] They were determined, therefore, to build a traditionalist, corporate, and Catholic state. But at the same time they noted developments elsewhere in the postwar world, recognizing that modern states—whether democratic or otherwise—needed to be efficient. In other words, they rejected liberal democracy while accepting the assumptions of economic modernization (capitalism, private property, free enterprise). Their quest was to combine paternalistic authoritarianism with modernization and their particular vision of social justice.

Fascism had been defeated in Europe, but the Communist threat remained, and this fact was of crucial importance to Franco's supporters. Voices on the Spanish right perceived the need to modernize the ideas so far used to legitimize the dictatorship, but without a turn toward democracy. The technocrats were especially important in this process. This group, which was composed of highly qualified university professors and professional economists, had been assuming positions of high responsibility within the Franco regime since the mid-1950s.[7] Their rise to power and prominence owed much to the increasing weight of a key figure in the politics of the dictatorship, Luis Carrero Blanco, who was one of Franco's closest *confidants*. His influence on the dictator was constant for many years and would eventually prove decisive in preparing the royal succession. From the late 1950s onwards, Carrero worked hard to persuade Franco to make changes in the government staff. He played a major role in assisting the rise of some technocrat ministers.

Carrero was a conservative traditionalist, completely loyal to Franco, and with fixed undemocratic convictions. He thought succession should be carefully prepared for before Franco's demise and for that purpose it was imperative, he believed, to establish in law Spain's status as a monarchy in law in order to pave the way for the selection of a future monarch. Carrero favored a traditional and representative monarchy, consistent with conservative opinion of the time. Along with other conservatives he developed a conception of a post-Franco regime designed to reconcile social and economic change with political stability through the role of the Crown. But Carrero's conservatism was matched by a pragmatism, which meant that above all he was concerned about the stability of the dictatorship. His support for the technocrats rested on two basic assumptions: first that the state should be prepared for a new era in which it was necessary to facilitate the economic and administrative modernization of Spain; second that this would involve the formation of a new powerful group within the Spanish politics. Over the course of time, this group would gain a controlling political influence, enabling them to displace other political groupings so as to secure the monarchical succession.[8]

Unlike their conservative predecessors, the technocrats had developed a project for economic and administrative modernization, which was connected with changes that had been taking place across the Atlantic world since the late 1940s. They were neither a homogeneous group, nor could they be considered a school of thought, but certain common elements did unite them: some shared similar intellectual backgrounds and pursuits, whereas others had been prominent in their professional careers in government; and many of the most important among them were members of the Opus Dei, a Catholic religious association that became increasingly influential from the late 1950s. Two people in Opus Dei circles played especially important roles in the evolution of the non-democratic Spanish right between 1950 and 1970: Laureano López Rodó and Gonzalo Fernández de la Mora.

Both López Rodó and Fernández de la Mora were interested in the relationship between the new Spanish technocratic conservatism and the intellectual concerns of other writers and politicians in the Western world—not only fellow Europeans but also Americans. Both men were outstanding personalities within Spanish conservatism during the 1950s and 1960s, and both had major political responsibilities, holding portfolios in the executive branch. They had benefited from strong humanistic training and could communicate and read in more than two languages. What is more, they maintained important contacts abroad, and they had a firm grasp of international politics, albeit somewhat distorted by visceral anti-communism and deep contempt for the mechanisms of liberal democracy. In these ways they had very much in common, but their role in the evolution of the Spanish right during those years was not identical. In fact in some important respects their personal profiles were different. López Rodó was a professor of administrative law. He had a deep understanding of the management and functioning of the modern administrative state and enjoyed a long career in the government service. He was not to any great extent concerned with political thought or sociological analysis. Fernández de la Mora, in contrast, held a highly technical set of responsibilities as an official in the ministry of Public Works, but his main activity was related to intellectual work. He was a thoughtful person and a compulsive writer and his chief interest was in providing post-Franco Spain with its own theory of the state. If López Rodó fits better the description of a political technocrat, Fernández de la Mora could be considered something of an intellectual.

Laureano López Rodó was born in November 1920, at the end of the reign of Alfonso XIII. His adolescence and early adulthood coincided therefore with the crisis of the constitutional monarchy, the first military dictatorship of the 1920s, and finally the arrival of the Second Republic in 1931. Like many other Catholic conservative figures of his generation, López Rodó was deeply scarred by his experiences during the 1930s. As he recalled in his memoirs, he and his family regarded the first months of 1936, just before the outbreak of the Civil War, as a "revolutionary" period that could end only in the worst way: "We are all in a big trouble!" ("¡Aquí va a ocurrir algo gordo!"), his father would frequently say in the early summer days of 1936. During the war, the family home in Barcelona was attacked and seized by militiamen (*milicianos*), and the factory his father ran was collectivized. After the war, López Rodó joined the army for military service. Soon he was able to finish his law studies in Barcelona and at the same time—in 1940—he made his first contact with the Opus

Dei. He specialized in administrative law and had passed his doctorate in that subject by the middle of 1943. Just two years later he secured a chair at the university in Santiago de Compostela (Galicia). Yet the academic life, though fundamentally important to him, was only a prologue to a new stage. Thanks to his studies of administrative reform, by the mid-1950s he was being consulted for advice by figures with key political responsibilities within the state apparatus. His professional profile was tremendously appealing in this new political phase of the dictatorship in which government was being opened up: he possessed a good knowledge of management and its complexities, and he was a tireless worker with numerous overseas academic contacts. During a period in which administrative efficiency, rather than ideological disputation, was being emphasized in internal debates about the nature of the dictatorship, his expertise was in high demand. In addition, López Rodó was close to the royalist cause, and this helped him considerably as it was consistent with the constitutional plans Carrero Blanco was developing, which were designed to establish a legal pathway to facilitate an orderly transition toward a new monarchy after Franco's death.[9]

The basis of López Rodó's political and economic thought was the notion that "political issues never arose in the same way or with the same violence" in rich countries as in poor ones, and that a "certain degree of well-being" changes "the tone of relations between individuals." In other words he believed that affluence helped to suppress conflict and so it was logical for him to think that not even a democracy could succeed without it. For López Rodó, public investment was a requirement to widen government action in order to implement social justice.[10] One of his central theses was that economic development would bring greater social justice, and consequently a less politicized and polarized society: "All policies to raise the standard of living," he wrote during the transition period in the 1970s, "contribute to a more cohesive society." With the aid of those policies, the regime could reduce the risk of social discomfort and tension.[11]

By the time López Rodó took up an important political position in the Technical Secretariat of the Presidency of the Government he was convinced that a new "architecture of the State" had to be created in order to modernize the country. Modernization in these terms required that the government, acting under the law, had both orderly institutions and a booming economy so as to allow the implementation of appropriate social policies. The task consisted of developing a discourse of modernization and social justice that was useful for the new stage of the Franco regime. The building of a new Right was at stake.[12]

However, López Rodó did not think that the "horizon of development" was limited to the economic order.[13] Rather, he thought that there was a clear linkage between administrative and economic modernization and the role of the dictatorship in the social sphere. "At the same time we are driving development," he said in Parliament on February 7, 1969, during the session in which the Second Development Plan was being approved, "an institutional order must be designed, a concept of State must be thought of. (...) This Plan is a way of conceiving the State. It reaches its full significance from the point of view of politics."[14] However he believed that a modernized and wealthy country did not need to adopt a democratic system.

In López Rodó's view, economic and political development was quite compatible with the maintenance of the dictatorship. Basing his observation of political developments in the Atlantic world, he believed that representative democracy, political parties, and the division of powers...were all part of a past era.[15] In adopting this position, he was following a line of reasoning theorized more completely by his fellow technocrat Gonzalo Fernandez de la Mora, who argued that once a high level of economic development was achieved, political participation would surely diminish in tandem with secularization and a greater technical complexity in government management, and that as a result, a "convergence" of previously antagonistic old ideologies was to be expected. The legitimacy derived from the state's newfound effectiveness would be more powerful than any democratic participation.[16] Like his friend Fernández de la Mora, López Rodó thought that liberalism and socialism would lose all their strength as society became more prosperous, and that the state, properly reformed and subjected to the logic of legal language and technical direction, would facilitate the path of prosperity. That is, the greater the modernization and the wealth redistribution, the more muted would be the old ideologies and the social and political struggles of the contemporary era. In this reading, ideological and class struggle would, over time, lose their *raison d'être*. Under these conditions the nondemocratic political system would be effective in meeting citizens' needs. A wealthier and more satisfied society, one in which citizens had access to good education and health care, and possessing levels of consumption comparable to those enjoyed in other Western nations, would not consider a return to democracy, which in any case was, for him, a political system doomed to social confrontation.

This approach rested substantially upon ideas circulating among Western conservatives—some democratic, others anti-democratic—during the 1950s and 1960s. These ideas were derived chiefly from the work of North American and European sociologists and political scientists. The influence of postwar North American political sociology on the Franco regime deserves greater scholarly recognition from historians of transatlantic political exchange than it has attracted to date.

In terms of circulation and impact, Daniel Bell's *The End of Ideology: On the Exhaustion of Political Ideas in the Fifties* was the most prominent manifestation of these exchanges.[17] Bell's book, written and originally published in the United States in 1960 by The Free Press, was one of the most important works of nonfiction to emerge in the generation after the end of Second World War.[18] But there were, of course, a number of US social scientists writing along similar lines in this period. For example, the political sociologist Seymour Martin Lipset argued in a similar vein that the success of the democratization process was linked to high income levels and to socioeconomic modernization. He did so first of all in his prizewinning book *The Political Man: The Social Bases of Politics*, which, like *The End of Ideology* was published in 1960, and then again in his later essays, which in broad terms reaffirmed the end of ideology thesis.[19]

The end of ideology debate was distinctly transnational in its character and trajectory. As early as 1951, the historian of culture H. Stuart Hughes wrote about "the end of political ideology," explaining that many in the West realized ideological confrontation could be overcome only when "strong governments" implemented appropriate "social policies."[20] In the context of Western defense against totalitarianism, ideological differences were less relevant. Scholars and commentators on both sides of the Atlantic such as Raymond Aron, Michael Polanyi, Edward Shils, and Anthony Crosland participated in the exchange of ideas. In fact, from 1950 onward, these figures met at meetings of the Congress for Cultural Freedom, and it was at one of these meetings—at Milan in 1955—that the end of ideology first emerged as a popular term among intellectuals attracted by various degrees to the idea of a post-capitalist order capable of transcending the poles of socialism and communism.[21] One of the most important issues discussed in Milan was the extent to which the ideological divisions of the pre-Second World War were disappearing.[22] The debate could have been entitled: "The End of an Ideological Era?" for that had been the title used by Raymond Aron in one of the chapters of *The Opium of the Intellectuals*, published the same year.[23]

Daniel Bell's thesis has led to a protracted debate. It is true that in the 1980s Bell himself said that his words had been twisted and that as a result his argument had frequently been misrepresented, but the issue at the heart of the debate was always clear. According to Bell "the ideology that once was the driving force of action" had become "a dead term."[24] The main ideologies playing a role in Western political life from the first half of the nineteenth century onward were "exhausted" but not dead. Communism had not passed away, but "one thing seems clear: for the radical intelligentsia old ideologies have lost their truth and power of persuasion."[25]

Bell's thesis did not, as some people thought, imply a prediction. He did not say that ideologies were disappearing. He also recognized that the force of utopian visions was growing in the Third World. Bell clarified what he meant in 1988 when he said that in the "ideological vision of the nineteenth century"—whose origins went back to the French Revolution—the main question was the "total transformation of society." Nevertheless, under the "normative consensus" of the postwar era "civilian politics" could replace "ideological politics." In other words, socialist and conservative parties had been able—partly thanks to the experience of the interwar years—to reach a basic consensus about the rules of the game. This consensus was based on a combination of liberal constitutionalism and the defense of the welfare state. As part of that consensus, Bell considered that "ideological politics," understood as "the dream of organizing a society based on a previously designed project" was doomed to failure. At that moment, he wrote in the late 1950s, few believed it was possible to launch a "new utopia of social harmony" through *social engineering*. But in the same way, he added, few people—Hayek notwithstanding— insisted upon "the absolute non-intervention of Government in the economy." He also said that no serious conservative could maintain, at least in England and the continent, that the welfare state was "a road to serfdom." "In Western countries," he concluded, "there was a general agreement on political issues such as the acceptance of the welfare state, the desire for decentralized power, a mixed economy and political pluralism. Thus the era of ideologies is over."[26] Like many other contributors to the end of ideology debate, Daniel Bell identified the end of ideologies with the irreversible union between democracy and a type of capitalism modified by government action.

Unsurprisingly perhaps, Spanish technocrats such as López Rodó and Fernández de la Mora interpreted the end of ideologies debate differently. For them, economic development and effective management would necessarily lead to the end of representative democracy. In this interpretation, democracy would be overtaken by a new framework of limited freedom and traditional monarchy—or something similar to an authoritarian state. The liberal representative dimensions of the debate were thus downplayed in favor of a version that emphasized the strengthening of the executive branch and abolition of needless and corrupt political parties. The experience of De Gaulle in France from 1958 onward, they believed, vindicated their position.

Our second technocrat, Gonzalo Fernández de la Mora, also spread ideas in Spain, which resonated with the debate about the end of ideologies. His mode of conservative thought was extremely hostile to the core precepts of political liberalism, placing him in the mainstream of the traditionalist and royalist Spanish right wing. His perspective was in many ways similar to that of those members of the French Right close to Charles Maurras in the 1930s. Fernández de la Mora has been called the philosopher of *inmovilismo* (nothing must change), perhaps because his main concern was how to configure the post-Franco era according to the central aspects of a traditional political system, without being either liberal or representative.[27] He was Minister of Public Works between 1970 and 1973, but his most important role in the Spanish right was in the field of ideas and intellectual debate. He was heir to the conservative Spanish tradition that admired anti-liberal thinkers and writers such as Donoso Cortés and Ramiro de Maeztu. Fernández de la Mora's political thought evolved in a very complex way, however. He adapted a new conservatism by bringing about an accommodation between tradition and the new industrial and secularized society. Finally, in the last years of Franco's regime, he thought the best way to keep the essence of the dictatorship was to establish a new monarchy based on the political framework of Francoism.[28]

Fernández de la Mora also participated in other intellectual endeavors whose basic aim was to renovate Catholic conservatism in the new era opened by the defeat of European fascism after 1945. An important activity connected with this was the emergence, in the late 1940s, of the intellectual magazine *Arbor*. Several authors collaborated in this project, many of them members of the Opus Dei, among them Rafael Calvo Serer, Florentino Pérez Embid, Ángel López Amor, and Antonio Fontán. Together they formed a group known as the *Tercera Fuerza* ("Third Force" or "Third Way").[29] Calvo Serer had used this label in his book *Theory of Restoration* to convey the idea of a "third force" referring to a "third way" or a "third position" in domestic politics, an attempt to "build something" located "between left and right." For him, the restoration of the monarchy should allow them to transcend "the antithesis between conservatism and liberalism, since a Christian person is both conservative and liberal, giving this word the meaning of desire for progress, which is one of the characteristics of liberalism."[30]*Arbor* was the "heir" to *Acción Española*, a magazine that promoted authoritarian conservativism during the Second Republic of 1931–1936, and which, as López Rodó acknowledged, was an important guide for the Spanish Catholic intelligentsia. Unlike other Catholic currents of the moment, the *Arbor* group was far from liberal in its views and supported a traditionalist approach. Its main purpose nevertheless was to merge the traditional and authoritarian views of the monarchist right with the new ideas of economic and administrative modernization. It aimed at "a synthesis between tradition and progress" that would achieve, through the action of highly qualified directors of minorities, a "neo-capitalism compatible with the traditional Catholic view of the world."[31]

In 1965, Fernández de la Mora published a book entitled *El Crepúsculo de las Ideologías* ("The Twilight—or decline—of Ideologies"), which won the National Essay Award. He did not win this prize by a fluke. The book presented an important political question: the defense of technocracy, something crucial for the dictatorship at that time. Despite its title, the author always argued that it was not a mere copy of Bell's work. In fact, there were significant differences.[32] The core thesis of Fernández de la Mora was as follows: Politics must be solidly grounded on "rigorous and accurate ideas." Ideas were important, but not ideology. Ideologies were "beliefs," "conventional common places," "clichés of which the believer is not aware of." By their own nature, ideologies "crystallize" in "dogmatic slogans and intangibles hypothesis." They led to Manichean views: one has to be in favor of them or against them, according to Fernández de la Mora.[33]

Ideologies, along with "material interests," Fernández de la Mora thought, were primarily responsible for the social tensions the Western world suffered in the twentieth century. Yet the situation was changing as a result of the spread of welfare and the development of more efficient governments. Raising standards of living produced political "inhibition" and the citizens' disregard for ideology. Thus, the major contemporary ideologies, such as liberalism and socialism, were disappearing. Politics had become more rational and less passionate. People wanted results, not conflict. Thence, socialism and liberalism were converging: Whereas liberalism was accepting socialist premises, Marxism was becoming bourgeois. In De la Mora's own words, from 1945 onward "socialism understands that its ideal of social justice is being incorporated into the programs of all major parties. They also notice that Marxism, being convicted because of serious errors and having failed in all its prophecies, has been overcome in its doctrines."[34]

This convergence implied the rejection of the idea that socialism was morally superior to liberalism, and *vice versa*. It also implied, in the words of the authoritarian conservative Rafael Calvo Serer, a logical corollary: both liberalism and socialism were the problem.[35] Despite opposition to liberalism and democracy, then, Fernández de la Mora shared much common ground with other European and North American advocates of technocratic conservatism; but the difference in his case was that he was writing about a country, and on behalf of a state, in which the Franco dictatorship bragged about being victorious not only against communism but also against the so-called decadent liberalism.[36] Accordingly, Fernández de la Mora quoted from both Keynes and Von Mises. He described the former as "the great Keynes," regarding him as the father of the new economic theory and the main destroyer of economic liberalism, and he used the work of Von Mises to bolster his criticism of socialism.[37]

As an authoritarian conservative and devoted defender of the traditional monarchy, Fernández de la Mora thought the convergence of ideologies did not lead to the union of democracy and capitalism, but rather to the overcoming of the former. To his mind, liberal democracy was at odds with efficiency because it led inevitably to the imprisonment of government by political clientelism. Political parties, he believed, disregarded the public interest and played with the state at will, and as such they were capable of representing the citizenry; instead they used state power for the benefit of a few.[38] Liberal democracy was thus inappropriate for the new era of economic development and welfare.[39]

Fernández de la Mora was familiar with and knowledgeable about the work of the scholars who participated in the international debate about the end of ideologies. His writings in the 1950s and 1960s contained references to, among others, Jean Barets' *La Fin des Politiques*, Jeanne Hersch's *Idéologies et Realité*, Wladimir Weidlé's, *Les Idéologies et Leurs Applications au Vingtième Siècle,* and to Hans Barth's *Warheit un Ideologie.*[40] *El Crepúsculo de las Ideologías* also mentions Karl Mannheim's seminal 1956 work *Idéologie et Utopie* and a number his other publications that Fernández de la Mora would have read in French such as *Man and Society in an Age of Reconstruction*— originally published in German 1935 but only translated into Spanish in 1942—and *Freedom, Power and Democratic planning*, a posthumous work translated in 1953.[41]

In 1960s Spain the major influence of these international debates came mainly through translations of French authors. As a point of reference, France's position as a leading agent in planning and policy development in postwar Europe was crucial. Moreover, there was the example of the amazing actions carried out by General De Gaulle. The near coup by De Gaulle, and its role in tackling the problems of the Fourth Republic, had notable effects in other European countries. In the eyes of many Spaniards, De Gaulle had led an offensive against a weak parliamentary system. He had defended the French general interest against a corrupt democracy. In other words, the French example showed how parliamentary politics only produced paralysis and corruption. The solution was in a strong presidential authority and firm policy of economic development.

One French author in particular was followed closely in Spain: Jean Meynaud. His books were read intently by this generation of Spanish technocrats, including by Fernández de la Mora, who quoted them often. Meynaud was a leading political scientist who first came to prominence as the author of a dissertation on pressure groups in Europe. In 1963 he published *Planification et Politique*, a small book which addressed the key questions on which the technocratic shift at that time rested.[42] Perhaps Meynaud's most important work for the question at hand, however, was his 1961 work, *Destin des idéologies*.[43] Most of Meynaud's major books—many of which addressed themes pertinent to the Spanish debate on technocracy and the decline of ideologies—were translated into Spanish soon after they were first published.[44] Jean Meynaud's writings did not address the end of ideologies debate in quite the same way as did Daniel Bell. Meynaud placed stress on what he termed the rise of "ideological appeasement" in an age when the authority of technocratic politics and technical management in the ascendancy. The French thesis was more amenable to the Spanish situation, because it was closer to what the Spanish technocrats were looking for. Meynaud's proposals reinforced their idea that technology and efficiency should increasingly prevail over politics.[45]

There is no question that López Rodó and other leaders of technocratic politics such as the minister of Treasury, Alberto Ullastres, knew Meynaud's works. Spanish government officials kept a close eye on the French political scene and on the whole had a favorable view of French planning. Similarly, they were keen observers of US politics. López Rodó had made an important trip to the United States at the beginning of his period as head of the Technical Secretariat of the Spanish government at the invitation of the Department of State. He spent the period from April 18 to May 13, 1959 in the United States where he met and spoke with many key figures in the Eisenhower administration, the economic policymaking world, and university academics. The information López Rodó gathered about how US politics operated was very important to him, and he absorbed it at a crucial time just as he was preparing his project on administrative reforms in Spain.[46] In this context it is not surprising that the Spanish technocrats' thinking was influenced by US intellectual currents. What is more, López Rodó was operating in a period when diplomatic relations between Spain and the United States were becoming more intimate and fluid. Conservatives such as López Rodó were however also strongly influenced by their early training in the French tradition of administrative law, and this had the effect of checking, or delimiting, their openness to American political and social thought. This explains why López Rodó's model for understanding the role of technocratic leadership in the postwar world more closely resembled an updated Bonapartism rather than any American alternative.

Furthermore, under the umbrella of this French connection, the dissemination in Spain of the work of another French thinker, Gabriel Ardant, was also essential in the discussions regarding the relationship among modernization, ideological renovation, and technocracy. In 1953 Ardant published an important work on government reform and economic change, *Technique de l'Etat: De la Productivité au Service Public.*[47] It is significant that this little book was translated into Spanish in the early 1960s and published by a government department both closely linked to López Rodó and intimately related to his plans for government modernization: the Center for Learning and Improvement of Civil Servants (*Centro de Formación y Perfeccionamiento de Funcionarios*). Its headquarters were in the city of Alcalá de Henares in Madrid.[48]

Ardant argued that the state should be managed along the same lines as a private company. This vision of state management made efficiency a key component in government administration. This approach greatly interested López Rodó and the technocrats who were leading the modernization of the Spanish economy. It appealed greatly to their post-ideological understanding of how a modern technocratic state should function. From the point of view of authoritarian technocrats such as López Rodó, the goal was to transcend the ostensibly futile division of contemporary ideologies, and to work toward the modernization of a state so as to simultaneously promote economic growth and consolidate the political regime.[49]

On the other hand, despite this French connection, there are other significant details. López Rodó was not a specialist in political theory. He did not have an intellectual profile. He was very good at law, but he was also versatile. Actually his knowledge about economic theory and planning was fairly good. This aspect may explain why López Rodó paid more attention to economic theory than to sociological studies, such as those by Daniel Bell. This is also the reason he wrote the foreword to the Spanish edition Walt Whitman Rostow's enourmously influential book *The Stages of Economic Growth: A Non-Communist Manifesto*, which was published in Spain in 1972.[50]

The First Economic Development Plan approved by the Spanish government in 1963, managed by López Rodó, was partially inspired by the input from economists who had argued that the state should act as a force of change, and had contributed ideas to the theoretical debates on world development. Arthur Lewis was one of the most important economists in this regard. His *Theory of Economic Development* was published in Spain in the mid-1950s, and his other shorter work on economic planning was also published and widely circulated in Spanish at about the same time, and was reprinted several times.[51] Lewis advocated a model of economic development based on the impetus of the state and the action of an efficient and "awakened" minority. He proposed that in a country such as Spain, which was not yet fully industrialized, the important factor was "the fortune of having a good leader" who could "guess the will and the spiritual capacities of his people." That is, development was tied to strong executive leadership and political authority. This approach is essential for understanding the ideological orientation of the technocrat group, and its relationship to Spanish decision-making.[52] It also helps to contextualize and illuminate some dynamics of the intellectual transatlantic connections of the Spanish technocratic right in the 1960s.

Rostow's book famously proposed five separate stages through which all nations must pass to progress in their economic growth. The first stage was that of traditional society; the second was that in which the preconditions for takeoff developed; the third was the takeoff of sustained economic growth itself; the fourth was the road to technological maturity; and the fifth, the age of high mass consumption. The fundamental and controversial idea, of course, was that of takeoff. This process occurred, according to Rostow, thanks to the interaction of three factors: productive investment exceeding 5 percent of national income; one or more manufacturing sectors developed to a high growth rate; and the acceleration of the industrial sector growth as a whole. Rostow's analysis achieved great fame and was arguably the dominant model of societal development in economics until the early 1980s.[53]

López Rodó wrote the preface to Rostow's Spanish edition because he was convinced that his theory of economic growth was pertinent to the Spanish case in that it offered a powerful theoretical model for the possibility of the authoritarian modernization of Spain. Rostow's arguments before the chairman of the Policy Planning Council in the United States were a source of inspiration for López Rodó, who often alluded to them at the beginning of his speeches.[54] López Rodó met Rostow during his visit to Washington in March 1962, on the occasion of the report on the Spanish economy being prepared by the World Bank. Rostow, who was president of the Political Committee of the Department of State, praised the new direction of the Spanish economy during a meeting López Rodó attended. He offered US aid to the Spanish Minister to prepare a development plan for Spain.[55]

These contacts reinforced López Rodó's conviction that a development plan was requried to increase the productivity of Spanish agriculture, as well as to foster the capital accumulation required for industrial expansion, so that surplus labor in the primary sector might be absorbed. The Spanish economy, he surmised, would progressively come into a new "stage of maturity" that would facilitate a consumption increase. At the same time, as Rostow had also noted, it was necessary to modernize the government, creating a new, more efficient administration that would promote modernization.

We can see therefore that the Spanish technocrats discussed here elaborated an approach to economic and administrative modernization, which shared much with the end of ideology thesis, and indeed was clearly informed by the transatlantic debates surrounding these questions in the 1950s and 1960s. The technocrats, of course, were motivated by a clear political purpose. That is why López Rodó and Fernández de la Mora endorsed it. The thesis—or at least their adaptation of it—allowed them to envision the legitimization of the Franco dictatorship from a new perspective. It provided a means for them to discard the discourse of the Civil War as a religious Crusade, although without dissociating themselves from it entirely. In addition, the end of ideology debate contributed to the formation of a political environment in which the replacement of Falangists by a new wave of technocratic politicians and supporters of the free market was justified. Ultimately the future of the dictatorship after Franco's death was at stake.

The Spanish technocrats deployed Bell's thesis and new theories of economic development such as Rostow's in order to demonstrate that the time of the ideological struggles characteristic of the Spanish Civil War and the immediate postwar period was over. Under this rationale, there was no sense in the Falange Party continuing to retain great power within the regime. Once economic development was in progress, the technocrats argued, the policy of the dictatorship was best shaped by technicians and specialists, that is, by people not unlike themselves. At the same time, according to this narrative, the struggle for democracy was of minor importance. Spaniards, they believed, wanted wealth and prosperity, which the technocrats themselves could provide by means of efficient policy implementation and administration. An era free of ideology was at hand, and as a consequence, the dictatorship could endure, even in the wider context of a democratic Europe. Socioeconomic modernization was from this point of view quite compatible with the absence of democracy. In fact, progress and technocratic authoritarianism in the service of dictatorship were mutually self-reinforcing.

Notes

1. Daniel Bell, *The End of Ideology: On the Exhaustion of Political Ideas in the Fifties* (Glencoe, IL: Free Press, 1960).
2. On Spanish foreign relations after the Second World War see Enrique Moradiellos, *Franco Frente a Churchill. España y Gran Bretaña en la Segunda Guerra Mundial* (Barcelona: Península, 2005); Juliá X. Moreno, *Hitler y Franco: Diplomacia en Tiempos de Guerra (1936–1945)* (Barcelona, Planeta, 2007); Florentino Portero, *Franco Aislado. La Cuestión Española (1945–1950)* (Madrid: Aguilar, 1989) and Qasim Ahmad. *Britain, Franco's Spain and the Cold War*, 1945–1951 (New York: Garland, 1992).
3. For summaries of the political history of the Franco dictatorship, see Stanley Payne, *The Franco Regime, 1936–1975* (Madison: University of Wisconsin Press, 1987) and Javier Tusell, *La España de Franco* (Madrid: Historia 16, 1989). For the debate about the nature of Francoism, see J. J. Linz, "An Authoritarian Regime: Spain", in *Cleavages, Ideologies and Party Systems: Contributions to Comparative Political Sociology*, eds Erik Allardt and Yrjö Littunen (Helsinki: Transactions of the Westermarck Society, 1964). On the evolving position of Catholics within the regime, see Javier Tusell, *Franco y los Católicos: La Política Interior Española entre 1945 y 1957* (Madrid: Alianza Editorial, 1984). Debates among political minorities and intellectuals contending for leadership within the regime of the new state are examined in Gonzalo Redondo, *Política, Cultura y Sociedad en la España de Franco (1939–1975)*, 2 vols (Pamplona: Universidad de Navarra, 2005).
4. On the evolution of Spanish Fascist Party (*Falange*) and its role in the first years of Franco regime, see Stanley Payne, *Falange: A History of Spanish Fascism* (Stanford, CA: Stanford University Press, 1961); Joan Maria Thomàs, *Lo que fue la Falange: La Falange y los Falangistas de José Antonio, Hedilla y la Unificación. Franco y el fin*

de la Falange Española de las JONS (Barcelona: Plaza & Janés, 1999); and J. A. Parejo Fernández, *Las Piezas Perdidas de la Falange: el Sur de España* (Sevilla: Universidad de Sevilla, 2008).

5. The Spanish right had been mindful of the possibilities of corporatism even before the Civil War. In fact, since 1923 the liberal conservative majority had been losing influence in favor of a new authoritarian thinking. Catholic traditionalists glorified the old regime, perhaps because they longed for a society in which hierarchies and social order were more clearly valued. The Spanish right before 1936 had been strongly influenced by the rise of the corporate and authoritarian right in France. The failures of the democratic experience during the Second Republic of 1931–1936, and the Republicans' identification between democracy and revolution, served to alienate conservatives from liberal and constitutional ideas. On the various sectors of the Spanish right during the 1930s, see Richard A. H. Robinson, *The Origins of Franco's Spain: The Right, the Republic and Revolution, 1931–1936* (Newton Abbot, UK: David & Charles, 1970); Javier Tusell, *Historia de la Democracia Cristiana en España*, 2 vols (Madrid: Sarpe, 1986); Martin Blinkhorn, *Carlism and Crisis in Spain*, 1931–1939 (Cambridge: Cambridge University Press, 1975); and Manuel Álvarez Tardío, "CEDA: Threat or Opportunity," in Manuel Álvarez Tardío and Fernando del Rey Reguillo, eds, *The Spanish Second Republic Revisited. From Democratic Hopes to Civil War (1931–1939)* (Eastbourne, UK: Sussex Academic Press, 2011).

6. These are the words of Florentino Pérez Embid, an important Spanish intellectual within the Franco regime. See Florentino Pérez Embid, *En la Brecha* (Madrid: Rialp, 1956), 48. See also Cañellas Mas, *Laureano López Rodó: Biografía Política de un Ministro de Franco (1920–2000)* (Madrid, Biblioteca Nueva, 2011), 102.

7. On the decisive evolution of politics within the Franco regime between 1957 and 1962 see Pablo Hispán, *La Política en el Régimen de Franco entre 1957 y 1969: Proyectos, Conflictos y Luchas por el Poder* (Madrid: Centro de Estudios Políticos y Constitucionales, 2006), chapters 1 and 2.

8. On Carrero see Javier Tusell, *Carrero: La Eminencia Gris del Régimen de Franco* (Madrid: Temas de Hoy, 1993) and Carlos Fernández, *El Almirante Carrero* (Barcelona: Plaza & Janés, 1985). For Carrero's major writings and political ideas see Luis Carrero Blanco, *Discursos y Escritos, 1943–1973*, (Madrid: Instituto de Estudios Políticos, 1974).

9. On the type of monarchy that López Rodó wanted, and his role in defending it, see Laureano López Rodó, *La Larga Marcha hacia la Monarquía* (Barcelona: Plaza & Janés, 1978).

10. Interview by Eugenio Mannoni, editor of *France-Soir*, February 9, 1971 in Laureano López Rodó, *Política y Desarrollo* (Madrid: Aguilar, 1971), 449.

11. López Rodó, *La Larga Marcha*, 199.

12. This type of discourse, influenced by López Rodó and Carrero, was repeatedly deployed in Franco's main speeches in the second half of the 1960s. See, for example, his speech at the opening of the IX Legislature, November 17, 1967 as quoted in López Rodó, *Memorias*, vol. II, *Años Decisivos* (Barcelona: Planeta, 1991), 239.

13. He believed that "a development plan is primary and substantially a political enterprise." It was not "make a richer state with the poorest citizens," but "a society of free men based on welfare and not coercion." See López Rodó, *Política y Desarrollo*, 77.

14. López Rodó, *Memorias*, vol. II, 391.

15. The "organic representation does not override the individual, but in contrast to the nineteenth-century verbiage, is the best way to respect and serve it." These words are from the speech to the Parliament in defense of the Right of Petition Act, December 19, 1960. Ibid., 170.

16. Gonzalo Fernández de la Mora, *El Crepúsculo de las Ideologías* (Madrid: Ediciones Rialp, 1965).

17. Bell, *The End of Ideology*.

18. For detailed studies of Bell's work see Howard Brick, *Daniel Bell and the Decline of Intellectual Radicalism* (Madison: University of Wisconsin Press, 1986) and Nathan Liebowitz, *Daniel Bell and the Agony of Modern Liberalism* (Westport, CT: Greenwood Press, 1986). For an introduction to the wider intellectual context see Howard Brick, *Transcending Capitalism: Visions of a New Society in Modern American Thought* (Ithaca, NY: Cornell University Press, 2006), chapter 5.

19. Seymour Martin Lipset, *Political Man: The Social Bases of Politics* (Baltimore: Johns Hopkins University Press, 1981), especially chapters 13 and 15; Seymour Martin Lipset, "A Concept and Its History: The End of Ideology," in Lipset, ed., *Consensus and Conflict: Essays in Political Sociology* (New Brunswick, NJ, 1990), chapter 3.

20. J. L. Dittberner, *The End of Ideology and American Social Thought: 1930–1960* (Ann Arbor, MI: UMI Research Press, 1979), 117.

21. Brick, *Transcending Capitalism*, 163.

22. Ibid., 103. For a guide to the many articles published as part of the end of ideology debate, see Chaim I. Waxman, ed., *The End of Ideology Debate* (New York: Funk & Wagnalls, 1969) and Mostafaq Rejai, ed., *Decline of Ideology?* (Chicago: Lieber-Atherton, 1971) The Anglo-American magazine *Encounter* published Edward Shils' report on this Congress, "The End of Ideology?" For a comprehensive account of the debate, see Pierre Grémion, *Intelligence de l'anticommunisme: Le Congrès pour la Liberté de la Cultura à Paris, 1950–1975* (Paris, Fayard, 1995), 317–59. For a critical perspective on Bell's thesis see Giovanni Sartori, *The Theory of Democracy Revisited* (Chatham, NJ: Chatham House Publishers, 2005), II: 583.

23. See Raymond Aron, *L'opium des Intellectuels* (Paris: Calmann-Lévy, 1955). Ten years later Aron published an major essay on this

topic: Raymond Aron "The End of Ideology and the Renaissance of Ideas," in Aron, *The Industrial Society: Three Essays on Ideology and Development* (New York, Frederik A. Praeger Publishers, 1967), 96–160.

24. Bell, *El Fin de las Ideologías: Sobre el Agotamiento de las Ideas Políticas en los Años Cincuenta* (Madrid: Ministerio de Trabajo y Seguridad Social, 1992, 440.

25. Ibid., 449.

26. Ibid., 465.

27. Jose Maria Jover Zamora, Guadalupe Gómez-Ferrer Morant and Juan Pablo Fusi, *España: Sociedad, Política y Civilización (Siglos XIX–XX)* (Madrid: Areté, 2001), 783.

28. Fernández de la Mora, *Río Arriba. Memorias* (Barcelona: Planeta,1995), 145–211.

29. Rafael Calvo Serer, *Teoría de la Restauración* (Madrid: Rialp, 1952), 40–42, 106–107.

30. Ibid.

31. Cañellas Mas, *Laureano López Rodó*, 100–103. On *Arbor* see Onesimo Díez Hernandez, *Rafael Calvo Serer y el Grupo Arbor* (Valencia: Universidad de Valencia, 2008). López Rodó was partially linked to the *Arbor* project, but he only published in it once, in the form of a 1964 article on economic development. Still, López Rodó unquestionably shared the "ideological background" of the magazine. See Cañellas Mas, *Laureano López Rodó*, 103.

32. Fernández de la Mora, *Río Arriba*, 147.

33. Fernández de la Mora (1965, 23, 34–36).

34. Fernández de la Mora (1965), 64.

35. Calvo Serer wrote: "In the field of international politics, a 'third force' or 'third place' between East and West is trying to be built." This force was situated between collectivism and Bolshevism on the one hand, and capitalism and democracy, on the other. "The last years we have witnessed several attempts in domestic politics with the purpose of building something similar between left and right." Faced with these alternatives, Calvo Serer pointed out that there were "middle forces," those that strove to search for a "new synthesis." The "third force" was attempting to surpass the "present polarization." Calvo Serer, *Teoría de la Restauración*, 106–107.

36. Fernández de la Mora wrote that the "most spectacular feature in recent decades, especially in the West, is the trend towards integration of two irreconcilable positions such as traditional liberalism and socialism." Fernandez de la Mora, *El Crepúsculo de las Ideologías* (Madrid: Rialp, 1965), 61.

37. Ibid., 64–65

38. Ibid., 84–90.

39. Fernández de la Mora's thesis encountered significant opposition from the complex and heterogeneous world of the Spanish right.

One opponent was Manuel Fraga, who belonged to the so-called aperturistas who were in favor of a gradual political liberalization and admired the British monarchy. See Manuel Fraga, El *Desarrollo Político* (Barcelona, Ediciones Grijalbo 1972).

40. Jean Barets, *La Fin des Politiques* (Paris: Calmann Levy, 1962); Jeanne Hersch, *Idéologies et Réalité: Essai d'orientation politique (Paris: Plon, 1956);* Wladimir Wiedlé, *Las Ideologicas y sus Aplicaciones en el Siglo XX* (Madrid: Instituto de Estudios Políticos, 1962); Hans Barth, *Wahrheit und Ideologie* (Zürich: Manesse-Verlag, 1945).

41. Karl Mannheim, *Idéologie et Utopie* (Paris, Librairie Marcel Rivière et Cie, 1929); *Mensch und Gesellschaft im Zeitalter des Umbaus* (Leiden: A. W. Sijthoff Uitgeversmaatschappij, 1935); *Freedom, Power, and Democratic Planning* (New York: Oxford University Press, 1950). Mannheim's publications had an important role at the beginning of the Spanish debate on economic planning in the second half of the 1940s. See Jordi Gracia, *"La idea del Estado en la Revista de Estudios Políticos (1945–1958)"* in Tusell, Javier *et al.,* eds, *El Régimen de Franco, 1939–1975: Política y Relaciones Exteriores* (Madrid: UNED, 1993), I: 581–92.

42. Jean Meynaud, *Planification et Politique* (Lausanne: Études Science Politique, 1963).

43. Jean Meynaud, *Destin des Ideologies* (Lausanne: Études Science Politique, 1961).

44. In addition to those works of Meynaud already cited earlier see Meynaud, *La Technocratie: Mythe ou Réalité?* (Paris: Les Éditions Payot, 1964); and Jean Meynaud and Alain Lancelot, *Les Attitudes Politiques* (Paris: Les Presses Universitaires de France, 1964). In 1960 the influential publisher Tecnos published Meynaud's: *Introduction à la Science Politique* (Paris: Armand Colin, 1960) in Spanish. The key Spanish translations of Meynaud published on this subject in the Spanish market were Meynaud, *Problemas Ideológicos del Siglo XX.* (Barcelona: Ariel, 1964) and *La Tecnocracia. ¿Mito o realidad?* (Madrid: Tecnos,1968).

45. Jean Meynaud, *La Tecnocracia. ¿Mito o realidad?* 381. See also A. Valencia Saiz "La teoría política en la era de la tecnocracia," in Vallespín, F., ed., *Historia de la Teoría Política, 6. La Reestructuración Contemporánea del Pensamiento Político* (Madrid: Alianza, (1995), 433.

46. On details of the second visit see López Rodó (1990, 173–80). There is also a document entitled "Report on the Trip to U.S. of Six Employees of the General Secretariat of the Presidency of the Government" in the Archives of the University of Navarra (López Rodó Fund, Box 156). Quoted in Cañellas Mas (2011, 154).

47. Gabriel Ardant, *Technique de l'Etat: De la Productivité au Service Public* (Paris: Presses Universitaires de France, 1953).

48. *Técnica del Estado (Sobre la Productividad del Sector Público)*, Serie Estudios Administrativos, vol. 17, Madrid, Imprenta del BOE, 1962.

49. On Armand approach and his relation to López Rodó, see Cañellas
    Mas, *Laureano López Rodó*, 114.
50. Laureano López Rodó's "Foreword," in W. W. Rostow, *Política y
    Etapas de Crecimiento* (Barcelona: Dopesa, 1972).
51. Arthur Lewis, *La Planeación Económica* (México City: Fondo de
    Cultura Económica, 1957); Arthur Lewis, *Teoría del Desarrollo
    Económico* (México City: Fondo de Cultura Económica, 1958). The
    fact that new editions of the former text were published in 1963 and
    1964 indicates the great impact of Lewis's work in Spain.
52. Cañellas Mas, *Laureano López Rodó*, 192–93.
53. See Albert Carreras, "La industrialización Española en el Marco de
    la Historia Económica Europea: Ritmos y Caracteres Comparados,"
    in J. L. García Delgado, ed., *España. Economía* (Madrid: Espasa-
    Calpe,1988): 108.
54. Cañellas Mas, *Laureano López Rodó* 194.
55. López Rodó *Memorias*, vol. I (Barcelona: Planeta, 1990), I: 320. On
    that trip, López Rodó talked with several World Bank economists
    and his vice president. He also attended a meeting with the direc-
    tor of the International Monetary Fund and discussed other matters
    with the vice director of the Agency for International Development.

Chapter 8

"We Are All Europeans": Toward a Cosmopolitan Understanding of the American Traditionalist Right*

David Sarias Rodríguez

In 1961, an interoffice memo circulated to senior editors of the US conservative journal *National Review* recommended, based on a suggestion made by James Burnham, that the magazine "should be distributed overseas" because "it is needed" and "acceptable there."² International distribution, the memo continued, would "have a strong beneficial effect" upon the journal's "influence."³ At the time the memo was sent *National Review* conservatives already possessed a significant transatlantic network, which in itself is not surprising given that the journal was the brainchild of Willy Schlamm, a central European émigré to the United States. In fact, most *National Review* senior staffers and regular contributors cultivated a peculiar form of cosmopolitan conservatism in the sense that their backgrounds, ideas, and political identities were informed by study in European educational institutions as well as considerable interaction with European rightwing thinking, activists, and organizations. Conservative theorist Russell Kirk, for example, took his PhD at the University of St Andrews in Scotland, foreign-policy expert James Burnham attended Oxford, the influential writer and opinion-maker Frank Meyer studied at the London School of Economics, and William F. Buckley Jr, the magazine's editor-at-large and main stockholder, spent part of his early education in British boarding schools. Virtually all American conservatives retained extensive networks of European friendships and acquaintances. Buckley's brother-in-law L. Brent Bozell and

Frederick Wilhelmsen, two conservative Catholics, both engaged in doctoral study in Spain.

In 1957, two years after the inception of *National Review*, Russell Kirk established *Modern Age*—another new conservative magazine designed to complement *National Review* by providing more literary and academic-minded articles as well as information about "the cause of conservatism in foreign lands."[4] Well over a third of its first number was devoted to introducing its readers to "the importance of recent Spanish thought" through translations of and comments on the "clairvoyant" work of philosopher José Ortega y Gasset. The journal promised to showcase the work of "other European philosophers and men of letters" in future issues.[5] The first issue also included essays authored by Ortega's disciple, the Catholic conservative Julian Marias, who introduced readers to the delights of "the fields of Castile" and how to understand the world "as a Spaniard [and] a European in the twentieth century."[6] The transatlantic contents of *Modern Age*'s first number were completed by "Recuperating Spain," written by the Austrian conservative Catholic author Erik von Kuehnelt-Leddihn, who was a regular contributor to *National Review*—and then by contributions from American poet Anthony Kerrigan, who had been raised in Cuba and was at the time of publication living in the Balearics, from a Yugoslav émigré then living in Chicago, a Bulgarian resident in London, two British writers (a Scot and an Englishman), an American graduate from St Andrews (two if we count Kirk himself), and a German who had fought, the journal made sure to state, with the Deutsches Heer in the First World War and the US Army in the Second World War.[7] These various contributions illuminate the extent to which, by the late 1950s and early 1960s, the world of the *National Review*—and of traditionalist conservatism more broadly— was distinctly transnational in character and substance.

From the late 1940s onward, US traditionalist conservatives established an international network that was articulated through organizations that possessed an independent life of their own. Out of this emerged a cohesive community that was more or less insulated and largely autonomous from those formed by other conservative intellectual families. Russell Kirk explained that by 1961 there existed a significant international epistemic community made up of individuals based on both sides of the Atlantic. In this community, European intellectuals such as British Colm Brogan and Spanish Rafael Calvo Serer figured as prominently as their American, German, and Italian counterparts. This group was held together by shared ideological premises, and its members tended to be at odds with those of other significant intellectual communities, such as progressive cold warriors and neoclassical liberals, with whom traditionalists of all national backgrounds were often associated in the domestic realm.[8]

The international dimension of the early American conservative movement has thus far received scratchy, scattered, and unsystematic attention. This is the case despite the abundant academic literature on conservatism and the willingness of conservatives themselves to publish their own in-house reflections and recollections. The cosmopolitan educational background of many early postwar conservatives—from Buckley protégée Garry Wills to first-generation neoconservatives such as Irving Kristol and Norman Podhoretz—has been acknowledged by both biographers and in conservative autobiographies.[9] And there have been major studies of the influence of European thought on US conservatism, for example in works on Russell Kirk, William F. Buckley, Frank Meyer, and L. Brent Bozell, and on the importance of Spaniards such as José Ortega y Gasset, other writers of Spanish origin such as George Santayana, and British thinkers such as Edmund Burke and Lord Acton.[10] However, no consistent, in-depth analysis of this cosmopolitan dimension has been undertaken.

In part, traditionalist conservatives themselves are responsible for neglect of the transnational dimension of their movement. The English philosopher Roger Scruton, for example, suggests that "there is no universal conservative policy," arguing that conservatism is deeply rooted in national tradition and custom, which in turn makes it difficult to establish a solid international community.[11] Scruton contrasts the relative parochialism of traditionalism with the socialist and liberal capacity to offer universal models of universal applicability.[12] Similarly, is the case that American traditionalist conservatives were on occasion met with hostility when they attempted to incorporate European thinking. Writing in 1967, for instance, the conservative publisher and activist Neil McCaffrey, apparently suffering an acute attack of exasperation, told L. Brent Bozell that the "Spanish Catholicism," which was the inspiring force behind Bozell's new journal *Triumph*, was "fine, for Spaniards" but not for the American public.[13]

At around the same time, in the mid-1960s, a number of disgruntled New York liberals who were in the process of making a shift to the right, reached similar conclusions about a US conservative movement whose "basic principles," according to Irving Kristol, possessed "limited force" and "little relevance to American realities."[14] Another prominent neoconservative, Norman Podhoretz, stated that Russell Kirk's writings "applied Burkean conservatism almost mechanically to the United States" and as such were based on ideas that did not "shape the American experience."[15] Given the origins of neoconservatism in the progressive left, it is not perhaps surprising that Kristol and Podhoretz's perspectives were mirrored by liberal intellectuals such as Louis Hartz, who judged that the European undertones of the early American conservative movement were strong enough to make it "un-American," a view shared by the idiosyncratic conservative poet Peter Viereck, who believed the work of Russell Kirk to be "unhistorical" and "traditionless" in the American context. The historian and political scientist Clinton Rossiter concluded that Kirk simply "sound[ed] like a man born...in the wrong country."[16]

Despite this hostility on the part of both conservatives and liberals, historians' neglect of conservatism's transnational dimension remains noteworthy. To some extent, this oversight can be explained by the fact that historians have devoted so much attention to the transnational efforts undertaken by liberal-progressive and left-wing intellectuals in the 1950s and 1960s, the same postwar years that saw the birth of modern American conservatism.[17] Two factors may help account for this discrepancy between historians' attention to the left on the one hand, and their inattention to the right on the other. First, it was liberal and left-of-center intellectuals who set the dominant political and ideological postwar discourse. The liberal canon that proposed to deal with the Soviet threat through containment abroad and the combination of mixed economies, liberal democracy, and a redistributive state at home reached its zenith in these years. This dominance manifested itself in the considerable efforts undertaken by the US federal government to propel, finance, and sustain postwar liberal internationalism in order to both legitimate its own foreign policy and to counter the intellectual influence of the Soviet Union. In this context, right-wing international networks and the traffic of ideas they carried could not hope to match their liberal-progressive rivals in either volume or public impact. Generally speaking, there was nothing on the right comparable to the combined influence of initiatives carried under the auspices of, for example, the Fulbright Program or the Ford Foundation, never mind the more scandalous and better known Congress for Cultural Freedom.[18]

Second, conservative cosmopolitanism developed, by and large, in frontal opposition to and in near-complete isolation from its liberal counterpart. To be sure, Willy Schlamm could be found at an early gathering of the CCF, whereas other prominent *National Review* intellectuals such as Will Herberg and James Burnham had been deeply involved with the New York left-wing intellectuals that populated the same organization. Both Buckley and Burnham regularly attended the seminar run at Harvard by Henry Kissinger, the quintessential "organic intellectual"—even if quite a maverick and not necessarily a *bona fide* member of the establishment—of the 1950s and 1960s.[19] Yet although conservatives were on occasion happy to adopt and make use of liberal progressive logistics, the cosmopolitan network they built was largely impervious to, and almost entirely segregated from, the liberal international apparatus. If one considers the case of Spanish-American international networks, for example, not one of the international intellectuals involved in the Ford Foundation's rather lengthy program in Spain ever corresponded with, or, it seems, was aware of, the existence of either *National Review* or the intellectuals associated with it. The same applies to Spanish right-of-center émigré intellectuals such as Salvador de Madariaga, a man who could be found in the pages of *New York Times*, was a member of the right-of-center Liberal International and, more tellingly, was listed as speaker for a gathering of the Mont Pelerin Society. [20]

Madariaga's case points to a more surprising issue: the relationship between traditionalist conservatives of the *National Review* variety and their classical liberal counterparts. Both epistemic communities could be found so deeply intertwined at the national level that they are perhaps best approached as belonging to a single intellectual and political movement.[21] Thus, in the United States, *National Review* became a venue in which both communities gathered—with varying degrees of unhappiness—under one umbrella organization. On the other side of the Atlantic, there was a similar state of affairs in Great Britain. *National Review*'s role was played there by the London-based Institute of Economic Affairs, where one could find classical liberals such as Milton Friedman and Friedrich Hayek together with distinctly authoritarian and traditionalist authors, such as Roger Scruton or Rhodes Boyson.[22] Like their *National Review* counterparts, these British figures seemed less worried by monetary deregulation and individual freedom than by a range of social and moral issues. Informed by a general view that Britain was subject to "attempts by subversion to destroy our society" they worried about the deterioration of educational standards and discipline, proposing the reintroduction of corporal punishment and the use of school vouchers as remedies, as well as by what they considered to be rampant homosexuality, which should in their view have been dealt with by changing the law.[23] In the international sphere, however, the uncomfortable but strong link between classical liberals and traditionalists in the domestic arena evaporated. It is true that some traditionalists attended meetings of the Mont Pelerin Society, the most important organization of the transnational classical liberal community and that the proceedings of these gatherings were described in *NR*. The presence of each one of these traditionalists at the MPS, however, was never a regular, long-lasting affair. For instance, although they both attended MPS gatherings, Buckley and Kirk hardly knew either Ralph Harris or Arthur Seldon, the founders of the IEA who essentially ran the society during the 1960s and were on intimate terms with Friedrich Hayek and Milton Friedman.[24]

Of course, this is not very surprising if one bears in mind the main characteristic of traditionalism both at home and in the international sphere. Traditionalism's *raison d'être*, in the international arena as in the domestic sphere, was outright opposition to what they saw as the regnant liberal-progressive hegemony. Their views of classical liberals ranged from the polite but limited interest of Buckley, to the deep irritations and disdain of Russell Kirk.[25] Domestically, as some scholars have already noted, the need to influence right-of-center political parties, together with the shared adversarial attitude toward liberal progressivism and certain common values compelled traditionalists and classical liberals to cooperate, or at the very least to work within the same umbrella organizations. The work of Friedrich von Hayek provides a case in point of the powerful ideological coincidences between classical liberals and traditionalists, and of the limits of these same coincidences. Hayek made the threat of "collectivism by stealth" the heart of his popular *The Road to Serfdom* and accorded considerable stock to the positive effects of religious prescription and traditional habits, but still this neoliberal narrative placed more emphasis on individual autonomy and market freedom than most traditionalists could stomach.[26] Tellingly, Buckley and Irving Kristol, two prominent traditionalists who belonged to different epistemic subcommunities as "godfathers" of, respectively, the *National Review* and neoconservatism, either fell out with Hayek or never got around to properly reading *The Road to Serfdom*.[27] And of course in the international arena the pressure to influence particular political parties was absent.[28]

In contrast to neoliberals and liberal progressives, traditionalists were held together by their defense of European empires, their lack of faith in democratic institutions, and their strong attachment to a peculiar right-wing reading of Christian, and particularly Catholic, communitarian values, which they in turn set against growing secularization. At heart, these views led traditionalists to believe that the real threat to the survival of the "free world" against the Soviet onslaught did not rest in the Soviets' strength. Conservatives ridiculed the obvious lies in official Soviet statistics, noting the military "backwardness" of the Eastern bloc and identifying the Unites States' superior "skill and technological plant."[29] They saw danger, instead, in the "complacency" and "intellectual flabbiness" of Western societies, and in what the Scottish journalist and political writer Colm Brogan described as the "plain, unadulterated funk" of "nearly all progressives."[30]

In its approach to imperialism, therefore, *National Review* saw decolonization as "a rout" fast on the way to becoming a "catastrophe" that was provoked by the West's "folly" and its refusal to accept that "most Africans were indifferent or favourable to continuing European predominance."[31] It consistently came down on the side of flagging European empires, supporting the desperate rearguard actions of, for example, the French in Algeria and the Spanish in the Western Sahara, and they did so in a way that was diametrically opposed to both the official Cold War rhetoric of the United States and the views of most liberal intellectuals. Frank Meyer, to quote a typical view, denounced the "mirage" of "liberal concepts" such as "the abstract equality of nations" and the "abstract evil of the pre-war regime of Western domination of the world."[32] He recommended that the United States develop "an imperial policy of full responsibility" towards the Third World.[33] The Middle East and North Africa were cases in point. According to the traditionalists, Arab nationalist groups such as the Palestinian Fedayeen or the Algerian National Liberation Front were "analogous to the Vietnamese Vietcong-NLF."[34] Accordingly, when confronted with the Suez Crisis, Burnham deplored Eisenhower's abandonment of the Anglo-French initiative.[35]

In their heart of hearts, traditionalists understood that even if "the world was well served" by the "notable contribution to human development and welfare" of imperialism, the collapse of the European empires was "irreversible."[36] But where possible, the cause of Western civilization was best defended, in their view, by the various remnants of white settlement. Thus, Peter Duignan, an American-born, Stanford-educated scholar who spent a three-year spell at Jesus College, Cambridge, and Lewis Henry Gann, a British-educated former imperial civil servant, did not hesitate to use *National Review* as a platform for denouncing the "untenable" liberal "mythology" of African exploitation by the European powers, writing that "wherever white settlement occurred, there was economic progress" and therefore "more—not less—economic advance[ment] for Africans." There was evidence for this in the much maligned but, to them at least, shining example of "the Union of South Africa."[37] However they look now, most readers of *National Review* would not have found such arguments odd. The journal consistently reproduced such views, incorporated into its outlook the perceptions of the developing world put across by right-wing European, die-hard imperialist authors such as Erik von Kuehnelt-Leddihn, Anthony Lejeune, and Elspeth Huxley. Leddihn was an Austrian Catholic aristocrat who reported for *National Review* for four decades, celebrating, for instance, the "cultural and artistic explosion" unleashed by Spanish imperial rule in Latin America.[38] Lejeune, a British traditionalist, believed Rhodesian white settlers to be equivalent to the "pioneers" in the "American west"; he also thought that the Congo's future would have been best served by "twenty years of firm rule" by "some civilized power"—not specifying whether King Leopold's heirs might fit such a bill. This was a man who said he "refused to applaud when I see introduced into Africa everything I most dislike in the politics of modern Europe and America."[39] For her part, Huxley, who was raised in East Africa as a child of the British Empire, was the *Review*'s African correspondent for the greater part of the 1960s. She defended imperial rule and the views of the beleaguered white minorities, even as the tempo of African decolonization accelerated.

   National Review traditionalists did more than merely reproduce European pro-imperial views for the benefit of their readers. These perspectives also powerfully influenced the journal's approach to the racial tensions within the United States during the 1960s. In a tantalizing mirror image of the pan-African anti-imperialism of those radicalized civil rights activists who argued that "ghettoes were analogous to colonies," the Buckleyites articulated a view of African-Americans in the South that was astonishingly close to the one that was applied by die-hard imperialists to the black majorities in African nations struggling for independence during the 1950s and 1960s.[40] According to this view, African-Americans deserved the same treatment that the British had dispensed to the Kenyans and the French to the Algerians, all in the name of preserving a superior "European" culture. The political enfranchisement of black Rhodesians was undesirable, it was argued, because white Rhodesians saw the one man one vote principle as "a form of reverse racism," which "would destroy the white community completely and deprive the country of all the techniques of a modern society." Hence, "the franchise should call for a high degree of education and other qualifications." Just as black Rhodesians should expect the advent of full political equality "gradually" so segregation in the United States should last "for whatever period it takes to effect a genuine equality between the races," or in other words, according to conservatives, for as long as it took blacks both in the United States and in Africa to be "westernized"—that is, to become socially and culturally "white." Subsequently, the editors of *National Review* reached the "sobering" conclusion that Southern whites were "entitled to prevail" because "for the time being" they were "the advanced race," like the Rhodesian whites who had created a "western, parliamentary and democratic society" in parallel to a black "tribal society." According to *National Review*, both in the Southern US states and in Africa "the claims of civilization supersede those of universal suffrage." By this reasoning, Jim Crow in the United States, like white rule in Africa, should only last "so long as" it contributed to the enlightenment of African-Americans "by humane charitable means," just as white Rhodesians ought to "tamper with the tribal society" only through "example and persuasion."[41]

Over time, traditionalists' views did evolve toward somewhat milder positions. The magazine remained sympathetic to white South Africans, but by the late 1960s it had accepted the need to reform Apartheid, albeit gradually and without the pressure of international economic sanctions. Huxley, for instance, and even Lejeune, deplored the reality of segregation in Rhodesia and South Africa, calling for an improvement of black civil and economic status parallel to increasing assimilation of European cultural mores.[42] William Rusher adopted these views when he defended South African economic paternalism and economic controls, for he believed that "free enterprise could not reasonably be expected to bring . . . a middle-class society of happy Africans" given that "virtually all wealth, know-how and enterprise [were] in one small set of [white] hands."[43] Perpetrators of the most extreme cases of outright racism were summarily excommunicated from the traditionalist transatlantic community. The case of A. K. Chesterton and his racist League of Imperial Loyalists was a case in point. After a brief and friendly initial correspondence between Chesterton and *NR* circles, Buckley, probably acting on the advice of his numerous British friends, abruptly ended all contacts, telling the Loyalists that *NR* was "not in sympathy with [their] racial views" and therefore did "not feel free to make common cause."[44]

Burnham's analogy between Arab nationalists and the Vietcong reveals the extent to which pro-imperial discourse was heavily informed by Cold Warriorism, in this way mirroring conservative views of the Civil Rights Movement, which was consistently associated with communist infiltration.[45] Ultimately, however, this was a secondary issue. Anticommunism was politically useful, for it allowed American traditionalist spokesmen to translate views closer to old-style European imperialism into a language understandable to the American public. Barry Goldwater, for instance, used the Soviet threat to justify taking his cue from *NR* when he suggested that "Algerian freedom be postponed" even if "self determination is a worthy objective." He denounced "the childish myth" that the "the evil of European power" led "to national and international disaster."[46] The crucial element separating the traditionalist community from their liberal counterparts, therefore, was the former's positive view of direct European and/or "white" rule over supposedly lesser peoples as compared to the latter's defense of democracy as the best tool with which to confront the Soviets. As Lejeune put it, traditionalists saw the "winds of change" in Africa as a case of liberal progressives trying to impose on the developing world the same policies conservatives abhorred in Europe and in the United States. Liberal iniquity was certainly compounded by the fact that, according to conservatives, these policies were failing miserably in their objective to bring freedom to Africans, and were in fact aiding Soviet expansionism. Yet, the root of the difference was not Communism. The absence of Communism would not have substantially changed conservative views of decolonization—when it came to domestic race relations, US traditionalists had no trouble inventing a red menace where there was none—any more than it would have dampened liberal enthusiasm for spreading democracy and liquidating European empires.

The pattern we have observed in relation to decolonization and race occurred in relation to almost every other aspect of the cosmopolitan traditionalist narrative. In 1963, for instance, Buckley and a group of intellectuals close to the *NR* circles traveled to a conservative meeting in Rome organized by the Centro di Vita Italiana. The *NR*'s report on the gathering focused chiefly on Cold War developments, but Buckley stressed that it was "not in the least likely that the Russian armies will swarm down the Po." Rather, Italy was "threatened from within" by the same "welfarist sloth" then staining the whole continent and the United States. Italian conservatives recommended not just confronting Communists (whether Italians or Russians), but that "'the West" should "arm itself against the prodigious hypocrisies of our time" produced by the progressive intelligentsia, among them opposition to South African Apartheid.[47] Over ten years later, in 1975, Henry Regnery, the book publisher and close acquaintance of Buckley, also traveled to Italy for a similar gathering, this time organized by the International Association of Western Culture. His report for the *National Review* emphasized the "eternal truths of Christianity" the impossibility of an alliance between progressives and "those who generally draw their values from our religious and classical past," and, predictably, "the myth of imperialism."[48] In 1970, midway between Regnery and Buckley's articles, the British economist Arthur Shenfield exposed the American readership of *Modern Age* to a comprehensive overview of traditionalist views. In a lengthy article devoted to analyzing the "ideological war against Western society" waged by "academics, journalists and get-with-it clergymen" such as Yale president Kingman Brewster Jr and Swedish economist Gunnar Myrdal, Shenfield concluded that liberalism was a "far more dangerous and effective" foe than Communism.[49] Shenfield downplayed the shortcomings of General Franco, the Greek Colonels, and Rhodesia, also noting that the racial limitations of the South African franchise were "positively desirable in the interest of all races," whereas "the principle of Apartheid" he judged "neither dishonourable nor, in the bad sense, racist."[50] In his analysis, the less than universal acceptance of his view was a consequence of a conspiratorial attack against, among other things, the legacy of empire calculated to "undermine [the Western nations'] post-imperial position" in order to "deprive [Western] society of its defenses against its inner enemies."[51] In another neat association between international politics and the domestic troubles of the United States, he identified "American whites" as perpetrators of "the most striking case" of anti-Western campaigning in their willingness to both accept the claims of the Civil Rights Movement and to identify "America's role in Vietnam [as] an expression of imperialism [and the] general sickness of American society."[52]

Nearly a decade earlier Buckley had noticed "a great deal of resentment in [conservative] Italy against America" provoked, according to the Italians, by "the decline of values in America, a nation which has become feminized and impotent." Buckley, amid much patriotic anguish, was forced to "understand...the point insofar as America's leadership is concerned," and to acknowledge that the United States had "not provided adequate leadership." In a move consistent with the dominant US conservative narrative of the period, he tried to separate the American liberal intelligentsia from the rest of the nation, noting at the same time how the American delegation, "though enjoying the spectacle hugely," occasionally "felt rather like voyeurs."[53] It is, however, difficult to understand why Buckley and his fellow Americans would have felt anything but at home. John Dos Passos, who led the delegation, ecstatically noted that he felt he had "really encountered Europe" and Buckley enthusiastically described how Italian conservatives were seeking, just as he was in the United States, "a modern reformulation of traditional mores." Articles blasting the shortcomings of a notionally feminized and valueless postwar American society were, despite Buckley's outburst of patriotic defensiveness, rather common in the *National Review*. On the next page to Buckley's European report, for instance, one could find Frank Meyer demanding "a *deep-going* renewal of American life in the spirit of the Western and American tradition—a renewal at *every level*, of existence: social, intellectual, philosophical, spiritual, as well as political."[54]

A couple of weeks after the first Italian get-together, *NR*'s British correspondents also informed their American readership that exactly the same process of moral deterioration was affecting their nation. Britain had become a place, in their view, dominated by the "whole pack of leftists, liberals, satirists, fellow-travellers and fashionable commentators"—notice how "liberals" and "fashionable commentators" are put on a par with actual "fellow travellers'"—who had been consistently "leading the country to pure socialism," with the exception of the "splendid" Suez expedition or, in other words, except for the last imperial initiative undertaken by Whitehall and the Quai D'Orsay independently from the White House and Foggy Bottom.[55] A few months later, it was the turn of the British-educated American, Russell Kirk, to note how progressive ideas "exert power in Britain today, at least as great as in America," and how liberals in Britain were as enthusiastically engaged in the "degradation of the democratic dogma" as were their counterparts in the United States.[56]

Ultimately, the various elements that sustained the transatlantic traditionalist dialog are best understood from the viewpoint described by Willmoore Kendall, who believed that "Americans are Europeans." Kendall's views were reproduced in the pages of *National Review* by Rafael Calvo Serer, a Spanish traditionalist then operating in right-wing Catholic circles. Serer led a gathering of American and European conservative intellectuals organized by the Centro Europeo de Documentación e Información (CEDI), a peculiar organization run and financed by the Franco regime with the object of garnering foreign intellectual support.[57] Like Kendall, Serer was impressed by the "profoundly European consciousness and sense of responsibility of the American participants." This feeling was no doubt reinforced by James Burnham's paper, which had deplored the "Afro-Asiatic tendencies in the White House," as well as the views of those who "speak as if the better world the US must build must wait upon America's freeing himself from decadent old Europe." Burnham was critical of how "Eisenhower and Dulles joined with the Communists and the Afro-Asiatics to denounce the two courageous European nations who were defending, at Suez, the interests of the entire West." To be sure, that defense was related to Communism and the Soviet menace. Serer, for one, defined the meeting as a "rallying point of serious European anti-communists." A closer look, however, reveals a lot more than mere cold-warrior fervor. The main threat to the West, as *National Review* contributor Frederick "Fritz" Wilhelmsen assuredly maintained, was not simply Communism, but "post-modern man, the mass man."[58] Against modernity, traditionalists "venerated" both "classical antiquity" and "the cross."[59] It was also to that shared pre-liberal, pre-democratic heritage that Kendall and Serer referred when they spoke of the "European-ness" of Americans.

Some 20 years later, when another contingent of American Catholics gathered in the same location—the Royal Palace of El Escorial—a number of them came to an arresting conclusion, voiced most clearly by the occasional *National Review* contributor and right-wing Catholic Regis Martin Jr. He wondered whether "America was utterly vile" because of its "decision to displace God and His Church as sovereign centrepiece."[60] A rather large number of European conservatives, and not only of the traditionalist variety, wholeheartedly agreed.[61] Among them was Spanish former-Falangist Rodrigo Royo, who was sufficiently close to Buckley to send him, to the American's apparent horror, the proofs of a book-length blistering attack on the American way of life. Royo, it seems, was completely oblivious to the fact that Buckley might object to a European blasting his own country, however close the criticism was to that reproduced in *National Review*.[62]

Most American traditionalists could never fully accept such a statement. Regis Martin, for instance, wrote *against* that conclusion, and L. Brent Bozell, who embraced it and went on to establish *Triumph*, a magazine that consistently defended that position and reached a circulation of about 30,000 readers at its peak, was eventually excommunicated from the movement in spite of the fact that he was Buckley's brother-in-law.[63] Yet *National Review* conservatives still managed to became embedded in a broader transatlantic community because they were rather closely attuned to the basic tenets of the European right. In fact, they were arguably closer to those tenets than American progressives were to their European counterparts. They were skeptical toward egalitarian impulses, disdained democracy, and defended the civilizational value of empire. In addition, they were critical of both American culture and the so-called Americanization of Europe. At a time when, as Daniel T. Rodgers's *Atlantic Crossings* states, Americans had ceased looking toward Europe for answers to social and political ills, and were engaged in trying to adjust Europeans to American habits and ways, American traditionalists reversed the trend.[64] Some, like Russell Kirk, believed that the basis of conservative thought was provided by an assortment of European thinkers ranging from Burke to George Santayana.[65] Others, such as Willmoore Kendall, addressed the issue head on. In a literary conversation with a liberal interested in remodeling Spain in a more American way, he declared that "instead of dreaming up" contraptions such as "cultural exchanges, that would bring American social scientists to Spain, to instruct, to persuade, and of course, to patronize," Americans "should themselves *come* to Spain to *learn*."[66] Together with other Catholics involved with the CEDI such as Wilhelmsen and Brent Bozell, Kendall took up this dictum himself by attempting a transplantation of Spanish ultra-conservative Carlist Catholicism in the United States. There was of course, the rather depressing, pessimistic message of *Triumph*, but to the astonishment (and sometimes the embarrassment) of most Buckleyites, the Bozell group led the charge toward the culture wars, which at that time were just starting to get into gear.[67] It is perhaps no surprise that their efforts, which antedated and heralded the later exploits of the evangelical Protestant right, found more support among British Catholic conservatives such as Malcolm Muggeridge than among their fellow Americans.[68]

Although admittedly marginalized by his radicalism (and propensity to mental breakdown) Bozell was by no means alone. He was joined, for example, by the University of Illinois political scientist Francis G. Wilson, a Catholic convert, "practicing conservative" and student of Spanish affairs.[69] Wilson belonged to an earlier conservative generation than the *National Review* crowd, but he influenced the development of postwar traditionalism, and indeed had acted as Kendall's doctoral advisor, a role in which he took his protégée along on his intellectual trips "traversing broad expanses of Western culture" that went well beyond the American tradition. As a result, Wilson also helped to pave the way toward Russell Kirk's decidedly transatlantic reformulation of conservative thought, and by the late 1950s had joined *Modern Age*'s staff as an editorial adviser.[70] Like his former student, Wilson did not see the need to send Americans to Spain, but unlike Kendall, he did not believe these programs were completely counterproductive. In his view, "the Anglo-American political proposition" was in fact already "similar to what a Spanish conservative would hold."[71] From Wilson's perspective, which was largely oblivious to the centralized Jacobin practices of the Spanish government, the US systems of governance at university, municipal, and state levels would have been understandable to a Spaniard as an example of "corporate liberty which is in accordance with Catholic principles of the organization of a free society."[72] In the end, however, following similar reasoning to Kendall's, Wilson reached opposite conclusions. He approved of "American foreign aid" which, he hoped, would help Spaniards to "employ the economic, technical and scientific means available generally in Europe for the ends of Spain." This optimistic conclusion was supported by the belief, similar to Kendall's, that Spanish traditionalism was "more real, more lucid in philosophical commitment" than that of its "Anglo-American" counterpart.[73]

In the short run, US traditionalist conservatives failed to change of American foreign policy or, for that matter, American attitudes toward Europe.[74] For nearly three decades, however, from the late 1940s to the late 1970s, there was an intense traffic of ideas and of people across the Atlantic that resulted, at the very least, in the consolidation and the strengthening of the American right and of its convictions. Roger Scruton was correct to emphasize the force of national habits for traditionalist conservatism, just as Irving Kristol and Norman Podhoretz, who themselves went on to become important figures in the conservative movement, were right to point toward the distinctiveness of the European traditionalist right. These intellectuals, however, had it backward when they concluded that cosmopolitanism either lacked significance or was something utterly negative for the development of American conservatism.

Scruton, in fact, spent some considerable time in the United States and developed strong links with the American conservative movement, whereas the neoconservatives themselves were just as strongly attracted to a certain, romanticized British tradition as the *National Review* crowd.[75] Based on the contents of conservative media such as *National Review*, *Modern Age*, and *Triumph*, it seems clear that, whatever Roger Scruton may have thought about conservatism in general, mid-century American conservatives were anything but parochial in their origins, interests, and acquaintances. The abrupt shift away from the prewar, near-nativist isolationism of the American right propelled by the likes of Buckley and Burnham during the early 1950s had a lot to do with political calculus and plain opportunism, but the presence of a large number of European émigrés and the thorough acquaintance of most American conservatives with like-minded activists and events of European origin helped to lubricate the slide toward a Cold Warrior perspective. Most importantly, as some conservatives themselves acknowledged, the particulars of right-wing Catholicism and the determined defense of European imperialism were direct imports from the other side of the Atlantic.

Notes

* Research for this chapter has been conducted with the assitance of the Proyecto de Investigación HAR2010–21694/HIST, del Plan Nacional de I+D+I (2011), Ministerio de Economía y Competitividad, the History Department, University of Sheffield, the Gerald R. Ford Foundation, the Royal Historical Society and the Gilder Lehrman Institute for American History.

1. Unauthored memo to William F. Buckley, William Rusher, and Jim McFadden, July 11, 1961, f. IOM box 14, William F. Buckley Jr papers, Manuscripts and Archives, Yale University Library (hereafter WFB papers).
2. Ibid.
3. "This and Other Issues," *Modern Age*, vol. 4 no., 1 (Winter 1959–1960): 2.
4. "The Achievement of Ortega y Gasset," *Modern Age*, vol. 1, no. 1 (Summer 1957): 50 and "Apology for a New Review," 3.
5. Julian Marias, "José Ortega y Gasseti," *Modern Age*, vol. 1, no. 1: 50–53.
6. "Contents" and "Notes on Contributors," *Modern Age*, vol. 1, no. 1: 108–109. "Anthony Kerrigan: Translator of Works in Spanish was 72," *New York Times*, March 9, 1991.
7. Russell Kirk, "Conservatism, Reaction and Fascism," *Modern Age*, vol. 5 no. 2 (Spring 1961): 114–16.
8. See Russell Kirk, *The Sword of Imagination: Memoirs of a Half-Century of Literary Conflict* (Grand Rapids, MI: William B. Eerdmans Publishing Co., 1995) and John B. Judis, *William F. Buckley: Patron Saint of the Conservatives* (New York: Simon & Schuster, 1988).
9. George H. Nash, *The Conservative Intellectual Movement in America Since 1945* (Wilmington DE: Intercollegiate Studies Institute, 1998), 133–35.
10. Roger Scruton, *The Meaning of Conservatism* (South Bend, IN: St Augustine Press, 2002), 1.
11. Ibid.
12. Neil McCaffrey to L. Brent Bozell, November 28, 1967, f. McCaffrey, Neil, box 43, WFB papers.
13. Irving Kristol, *Neoconservatism: The Autobiography of an Idea* (New York: The Free Press, 1995), 378.
14. Author interview with Norman Podhoretz, July 30, 2004, telephone.
15. As quoted in Nash, *Conservative Intellectual Movement*, 173, see also 172–204; Peter Vierek, "The Philosophical 'New Conservatism'" in Daniel Bell, ed., *The Radical Right* (New York: Doubleday, 1963), 158, 163–64.
16. For a recent overview of the literature published in Spanish, see José Antonio Montero Jiménez, "Diplomacia Pública, Debate Político e

Historiografía en La Política Exterior de los Estados Unidos (1938–2008)," *Ayer*, 75 (2009): 63–95.

17. Sidney Hook, *Out of Step: An Unquiet Life in the 20th Century* (New York: Harper & Row, 1987), 254–56, 263; Gary Dorrien, *The Neoconservative Mind: Politics, Culture, and the War of Ideology* (Philadelphia: Temple University Press, 1993), 19–67; Nash, *Conservative Intellectual Movement*, 105–106. For a detailed evaluation of the Ford Foundation's program in Spain, see Fabiola de Santisteban Fernández, "El Desembarco de la Fundación Ford en España," *Ayer*, 75 (2009), 159–91.

18. Henry Kissinger to William F. Buckley, February 7, 1956, f. Kirk–Kissinger (1956), box 3, WFB papers; Kissinger to Buckley, June 1, 1961, f. Kissinger, box 15, WFB papers; Frank Meyer to Buckley, February 27, 1963, f. IOM, box 26, WFB papers; Kissinger to Buckley, April 17, 1967, Gertrude E. Voigt to Linda Baker, June 26, 1967, f. Kirby, J. Lewis–Kissinger, Henry A., box 44, WFB papers. The observation regarding Kissinger's status as an outsider vis-à-vis the foreign policy establishment is taken from Godfrey Hodgson, "The Foreign Policy Establishment," in Steve Fraser and Gary Gerstle, eds., *Ruling America: A History of Wealth and Power in a Democracy* (Cambridge, MA: Harvard University Press, 2005), 245–46. Hodgson rightly notes that Kissinger's ascendancy coincided with the rise of a new group of conservative-minded foreign-policy makers. Yet, Kissinger, who managed to combine a close friendship with Buckley with membership of Nelson Rockefeller's inner circle, was no more part of the conservative movement than he was of the foreign policy establishment. Like his main *partenaire*, Richard Nixon, Kissinger belonged to (and had in mind the interests of) a community of one: himself.

19. See for instance Salvador de Madariaga, "Franco Agreements Opposed; Grave Consequences Predicted if Pact with Spain Is Signed," *New York Times*, September 16, 1953; Salvador de Madariaga, "Agreements with Spain," *New York Times*, October 12, 1953; "The Mont Pelerin Society. Main Speakers at the Meeting of September 1961 (Turín-Italy)," f. 3, box 86, Mont Pelerin Society papers, Hoover Institution, Palo Alto, CA.

20. Nash, *Conservative Intellectual Movement*, xv. Nash was an "insider" within the *National Review* group, and his book was very much focused on the evolution of *National Review* conservatism. Nash's view of a three-pronged (libertarians, traditionalists, and anticommunists) conservative movement held together by anticommunism is repeated in every book surveying the postwar conservative movement in the United States. See for instance Godfrey Hodgson, *The World Turned Right Side Up: A History of the Conservative Ascendancy in America* (Boston: Houghton Mifflin, 1996), 44–45, 51; Jerome L. Himmelstein, *To the Right: The Transformation of American*

Conservatism (Berkeley: University of California Press, 1990), 49–60; Sarah Diamond, *Roads to Dominion: Right-Wing Movements and Political Power in the United* States (New York: Guilford Publications, 1995), 29–35; John Micklethwait and Adrian Wooldridge, *The Right Nation: Conservative Power in America* (New York: Penguin, 2004), 51; Michael Schaller, *Right Turn: American Life in the Reagan–Bush Era* (New York: Oxford University Press, 2007), 4–6; Jean Hardisty, *Mobilizing Resentment: Conservative Resurgence from the John Birch Society to the Promise Keepers* (Boston: Beacon Press, 1999), 39–40; Lee Edwards, *The Conservative Revolution: The Movement that Remade America* (New York: Free Press, 1999), 78–79. This view has been persuasively challenged along lines not entirely dissimilar from those expressed here, in James A. Hijiya, "The Conservative 1960s," *Journal of American Studies*, 37, no. 2 (August 2003): 201–27, especially 214–18. Hijiya's analysis has been partially answered according to more orthodox assumptions in Sandra Scanlon, "The Conservative Lobby and Nixon's 'Peace with Honor' in Vietnam," *Journal of American Studies*, 43, no. 2 (August 2009): 255–76, particularly 259, footnote 6.

21. Rhodes Boyson, ed., *Down with the Poor* (Enfield, UK: Churchill Press, 1971), 131; Boyson, "Standards and Choice in Education" in Rhodes Boyson, ed., *1985: An Escape From Orwell's 1984* (Enfield, UK: Churchill Press, 1975), 64–70, 64.

22. Richard Crockett, *Thinking the Unthinkable: Think Tanks and the Economic Counter-Revolution* (London: Harper Collins, 1994), 177–78; Boyson, "Standards and Choice," 66, 68; Anthony Lejeune, "Controversy over the Wolfenden Report: Can Morality Be Legislated," *National Review*, September 28, 1957 (hereafter *NR*).

23. Author interview with William F. Buckley, July 25, 2005, New York City.

24. See Russell Kirk to William F. Buckley, April 8, 1961, f. Russell Kirk, box 14, WFB papers.

25. For a perceptive analysis of Hayekian thought, see Andrew Gamble, *Hayek: The Iron Cage of Liberty* (Cambridge, UK: Polity Press, 1996), particularly 102–107.

26. Interview with William F. Buckley; Friedrich von Hayek to William F. Buckley Jr, December 8, 1961, f. Hayek Controversy, box 14, WFB papers; Kristol, *Autobiography of an Idea*, 102–103, 378.

27. Hijiya, "Conservative 1960s,": 214–18.

28. See James Burnham, "The Burnt Child Jumps into the Fire," *NR*, October 5, 1957; Frank Meyer, "Moving to a Showdown," *NR*, November 1957; Gary North, "The Crisis in Soviet Economic Planning," *Modern Age*, 14, no. 1 (Winter 1960), 49–56.

29. Richard M. Weaver, "Roots of the Liberal Complacency," *NR*, June 8, 1957; Colm Brogan, "Mr. K's Quick Comeback," *NR*, July 2, 1960.

30. James Burnham, "The African Shambles," *NR*, January 28, 1961.
31. Frank Meyer, "The Mirage-World of Liberal Ideology," *NR*, July 2, 1960.
32. Ibid.
33. James Burnham, "A Middle East Vietcong?" *NR*, March 25, 1969.
34. As quoted in Rafael Calvo Serer, "They Spoke for Christian Europe," *NR*, July 27, 1957.
35. George Schwartz, "The Future of Britain," *Modern Age* 4, no. 4 (Fall 1960), 371–80, 372; H. G. Nicholas, "Britain After Labour's First Year," *NR*, vol. 10 no. 1 (Winter 1965–66): 21–30, 29; John Dreijmanis, "The Rhodesian Question: Where Britain and the UN Went Wrong," *NR* 12, no 4 (Fall 1968): 371–78.
36. Peter Duignan and Lewis Henry Gann, "White and Black in Africa," *NR*, January 28, 1961.
37. Erik von Kuehnelt-Leddihn, "Socialism Sí, Communism No," *NR*, January 28, 1961.
38. Anthony Lejeune, "The Day Lumumba Died," *NR*, March 25, 1961; Antony Lejeune. "No Surrender in Rhodesia," *NR*, May 6, 1961.
39. Allen J. Matusow, *The Unraveling of America: A History of Liberalism in the 1960s* (New York: Harper & Row, 1984), 358.
40. "A Clarification," *NR*, August 31, 1957, 199; "The South's Travail," *National Review Bulletin*, March 14, 1960; John Ashbrook, Max Yergan, and Ralph de Toledano, "Report from Rhodesia: Pointing the way to a Multi-Racial Africa?" undated, *c.* July 1966, f. ACU, box 58, Marvin Liebman papers, Hoover Institution. This pamphlet was published by the American-African Affairs Committee, Thomas Molnar, "South Africa Reconsidered," *Modern Age*, Winter 1966.
41. See for instance Tom Stacey, "An Englishman Looks at Apartheid," *NR*, June 1, 1971; Elspeth Huxley, "The Castle of Apartheid," *NR*, August 28, 1968; Huxley, "To Crush a Mouse," *NR*, April 9, 1968; Duignan and Gann, "White and Black in Africa," "Letter from Congo," *NR*, March 25, 1961.
42. William A. Rusher to the Editors, April 12, 1966, f. IOM, box 39, WFB papers.
43. W. F. Buckley to A. K. Chesterton, January 21, 1963, f. Chamber of Commerce—Chesterton, box 24, WFB papers.
44. For the association between Civil Rights activism and Communism, see "Summer, 1968—Riot or Rebellion?" *Washington Report*, April 15, 1967; Paul D. Bethel, "Black Power and Red Cuba," *NR*, September 2, 1968.
45. Barry Goldwater, "A Foreign Policy for America," *NR*, March 25, 1961.
46. William F. Buckley, "Conservatives in Europe Too," *NR*, November 5, 1963.
47. Henry Regnery, "The Post-Communist World," *NR*, October 24, 1975.

48. Arthur A. Shenfield, "The Ideological War Against Western Society," *Modern Age* (Spring 1970): 158–59, 164–65.
49. Ibid., 169.
50. Ibid., 170.
51. Ibid., 172.
52. Buckley, "Conservatives in Europe Too."
53. Ibid.; Frank S. Meyer, "Conservatism and the Goldwater Consensus," *NR*, November 5, 1963.
54. Anthony Lejeune, "Lord Home Got the Job," *NR*, November 19, 1963; Auberon Waugh, "But He Won't Keep It Long," *NR*, November 19, 1963.
55. Russell Kirk, "Expansion and Decay in British Education," *NR*, January 1964.
56. See Antonio Moreno Juste, "El Centro Europeo de Documentación e Información. Un Intento Fallido de Aproximación a Europa," in Javier Tusell, ed., *El Régimen de Franco, 1936–1975: Política y Relaciones Exteriores* vol. 2 (Madrid: UNED, 1993), 459–74.
57. Serer, "They Spoke for Christian Europe."
58. Ibid.
59. Regis Martin Jr, "Idabel Is Well, Thank You," *NR*, March 31, 1972.
60. In the Spanish case see the notorious Blas Piñar, "Hipócritas," *ABC*, January 19, 1962, as well as Rodrigo Royo, *El Paraiso del Proletariado (Biografía de Norteamérica)* (Madrid: SP, 1959).
61. Rodrigo Royo to William F. Buckley, November 5, 1958; Buckley to Royo, November 26, 1958, f. Roberts–Royo, box 6, WFB papers; Buckley to José María de Areilza, December 16, 1958, f. Areilza, box 5, WFB papers.
62. Judis, *William F. Buckley*, 319–22.
63. Daniel T. Rodgers, *Atlantic Crossings. Social Politics in a Progressive Era* (Cambridge, MA: Harvard University Press, 1998), 504–505.
64. See Russell Kirk, *The Conservative Mind: From Burke to Elliot* (Washington DC: Regnery, 1983), 3–12.
65. Willmoore Kendall, manuscript of book review of Arthur Whitaker, *Spain and the Defense of the West* (Washington, 1961), undated, f. Kendall, Willmoore, box 14, WFB papers.
66. See Patricia Bozell to Neal McCaffrey, December 14, 1967, f. Bozell, Patricia and Brent, box 42, ibid.; Patrick Allitt, *Catholic Intellectuals and Conservative Politics in America 1950–1985* (Ithaca, NY: Cornell University Press, 1993), 141–42.
67. Malcolm Muggeridge to Patricia Bozell, March 22, 1971, f. Malcolm Muggeridge, box. 208, WFB papers.
68. Robert L. Paquette, "A Pioneer Conservative," *Intercollegiate Review*, vol. 38 no. 21 (Fall 2002): 56–59.
69. Ibid.; Nash, *Conservative Intellectual Movement*, 212.

70. Francis G. Wilson, "The New Conservatives in Spain," *Modern Age*, vol. 5 no. 2 (Spring 1961): 149–60, 158.
71. Ibid.
72. Ibid., 160.
73. In the case of Spain, see Daniel Fernández de Miguel, "La Erosión del Antiamericanismo Conservador durante El Franquismo," *Ayer*, 75 (2009): 193–221.
74. Jacob Heilbrunn, *They Knew They Were Right: The Rise of the Neocons* (New York: Anchor Books, 2009), 57–60; Norman Podhoretz, *Breaking Ranks: A Political Memoir* (New York: Harper & Row, 1979), 22–23; Interview with Norman Podhoretz, June 28, 2004, telephone.

Chapter 9

Transnational Social Politics after the 1960s: *New Left Review*, Verso Books, and the Politics of Central American Solidarity

Nick Witham

Daniel Rodgers's pathbreaking *Atlantic Crossings* (1998) refocused the lens of Progressive and New Deal era historiography, bringing the period's transatlantic social politics into sharp relief. In the wake of this achievement, and with similar goals in mind, several historians have conducted research into the development of what Joel Pfister has termed a "New Left Atlantic" originating in late 1950s European and American thought and culture, and laying foundations for the radical student and anti-war movements of the "long sixties."[1] The more recent history of this Anglo-American radical social thought, however, has yet to garner the scholarly attention it deserves. What then became of the transatlantic links between the United States and British New Lefts after the 1960s?

This study addresses that question by examining two publishing initiatives established in 1985 by Verso Books (the publishing imprint of British radical journal *New Left Review*) to deal specifically with American topics: *The Year Left* and *The Haymarket Series*. Brainchildren of scholar-activists Mike Davis and Michael Sprinker, these projects featured the work of notable leftist authors, among them Manning Marable, Robert Brenner, and Alexander Cockburn. Those involved were drawn into the shared undertaking of developing a concept of intercontinental solidarity that would both underpin and promote the practical and material linkages that had developed between Trotskyist intellectuals in the United Kingdom (UK), the United States (US), and those struggling for independence and equality in Central America. An intricate transnational triangle therefore developed out of reciprocal relationships among the British publishing house, its American editors, and various Central American radicals contributing to the initiatives. Utilizing the methodologies of intellectual and cultural history, this essay reconstructs the contexts in which this radical print culture developed, with the aim of complicating extant narratives of the 1980s that stress the "declension" of the American left in the face of a hegemonic conservative movement. In fact, *The Year Left* and *The Haymarket Series* were important zones of engagement that enabled a transnational community of radical intellectuals to contribute to an alternative and vibrant critical public sphere, thereby negotiating the complex and variegated legacies of New Left anti-interventionism.

One of the "new social movements" that materialized in the two decades after the 1960s, the US Central America solidarity movement comprised a loose coalition of leftist, peace, and religious groups united around a commonly held opposition to US foreign policy toward Nicaragua, El Salvador, Guatemala, and Honduras during the late 1970s and 1980s.[2] Throughout this period, the movement responded vigorously to calls to stand in "solidarity" with the region's revolutionary movements. However, it was often the case that no attempt was made precisely to define the term. Did it merely connote gathering knowledge about the struggles of revolutionary groups such as the Salvadoran *Frente Farabundo Martí para la Liberación Nacional* (FMLN) and the Sandinistas, and contributing financial and material aid to them? Or, did it imply a more expansive, transnational aspiration to learn from these struggles, and thereby conceptualize Central America's revolutions as somehow interlinked with the struggle of the North American left? These were questions asked by many of the authors involved in *The Year Left* and *The Haymarket Series* projects.

Verso, which was originally established as New Left Books (NLB) in London in 1970, came to the forefront of Anglophone radical publishing during the 1980s, with its catalog bridging the divide between scholarly and activist readerships. By examining the company's first attempts to deal directly with US politics, this chapter highlights a specific context in which a group of radical intellectuals sought to relate their work unambiguously to the activism of the Central American solidarity movement. Furthermore, although the authors who grouped themselves under the banners of *The Year Left* and *The Haymarket Series* did not all identify with a single political project, Verso provided them with a heterodox platform that encouraged a specific type of intellectual and political engagement based on the politics of solidarity.

As such, this chapter explores the transatlantic development of a publishing venture that represents one of the most influential intellectual
currents in recent Anglo-American radical politics.

To trace the history of Verso Books, it is necessary to look back to
1960, and the founding in London of *New Left Review* (*NLR*). An
unofficial organ of the British New Left, and initially under the edi-
torship of Stuart Hall, *NLR* was formed from the merger of two older
journals: *The New Reasoner* (*NR*) and *Universities and Left Review*
(*ULR*). Based in Yorkshire, *NR* was edited by historians John Saville
and E. P. Thompson and emerged from a split in the Communist
Party of Great Britain (CPGB) over its response to the repression of
the Hungarian revolution by the USSR in 1956. Although techni-
cally independent from the CPGB, the journal entertained the hope
of reforming the party in the name of "communist humanism."[3]
ULR, on the other hand, was established by a younger generation of
leftists with fewer formal ties to the British Communist movement.
Edited by four recent graduates of Oxford University (Hall, Charles
Taylor, Raphael Samuel, and Gabriel Pearson), the publication represented what Hall has since described as an "independent socialist
tradition": it was more cosmopolitan in focus than *NR*, and keener
to pay further attention to popular culture, as well as to movement
building initiatives that were independent of the CPGB.[4]

The merger between the two publications in 1960 resulted in
NLR, which attempted to fuse the separate outlooks represented by
NR and *ULR* through journalistic explorations of the cultural and
social, as well as economic and political, dimensions of a "humanist
socialism."[5] Also vital to the journal's mission was the provision of
"education" to the British socialist movement through the publication of various books and pamphlets, and the organization of summer schools, conferences, and discussion groups. A project that drew
inspiration from Victor Gollancz's Left Book Club of the 1930s and
1940s,[6] this intellectual and cultural nexus was intended to form a
"spearhead of the New Left," which would radicalize previously apa-
thetic or apolitical social groupings.[7] In such a vein, *Out of Apathy*
(1960), a collection of essays edited by E. P. Thompson and published
by Stevens & Company, became the first text to be loosely named a
"New Left Book."[8] This eventually led to the formal foundation of
New Left Books (NLB) in 1970, and the independent publishing
company began trading under the moniker of its paperback imprint,
Verso Books, in the early 1980s.

Even before *NLR* was created, its parent journals received crucial
transatlantic support from US leftist publications. For example, *NR*

gained its only commercial revenue from the regular full-page adver-
tisements taken out by Paul Sweezy and Leo Huberman's *Monthly
Review*, and *ULR* editor Raphael Samuel regarded Irving Howe's
Dissent as his journal's "sister publication."[9] Further to this, radical
American sociologist C. Wright Mills first published his now famous
"Letter to the New Left" in the pages of *NLR*.[10] These links highlight the manner in which many of the ideas that shaped nascent
New Lefts in the United States and the United Kingdom crisscrossed
the Atlantic before developing political coherence. It is therefore
possible to conceive of a "New Left Atlantic" that developed during
the late 1950s and early 1960s; a transnational intellectual space in
which a political sensibility emerged that saw the goals of the British
and American New Lefts as essentially intertwined, thereby forcing
those involved to "transnationalize... [their] scope of critique and
concern."[11] This was a process in which *NLR* played a central role.
However, as this study will demonstrate, the transatlantic dimension
in Anglophone leftist thought was not contained within the gesta-
tional period of the British and American New Lefts. Indeed, Verso's
focused engagement with North American topics during the 1980s
indicates the continued importance of transatlantic exchange to the
intellectual culture of late Cold War anti-interventionism.

In the decade between the founding of *NLR* and the formal emergence of NLB, however, a significant shift in the journal's political
orientation took place, one that would influence the eventual constitution of the imprint, and draw certain key intellectuals into its
sphere of influence. In its first three years, *NLR* had struggled to
survive due to its oversized, fractious editorial board and a constant
lack of funds. In 1963, in a bid to save the journal, legal, financial,
and editorial control transferred to a new editorial team headed by
Perry Anderson. *NLR* was kept alive through an injection of personal funds from Anderson, his brother Benedict, and Ronald Fraser,
all of whom were independently wealthy.[12] The takeover saw Robin
Blackburn and Tom Nairn become the new editor's key advisors, and
is now thought of by historians as one of the signal events dividing
the "first" generation of the British New Left from the "second."[13]

For the next two decades, a significant number of those involved
with the journal and its publishing imprint also played significant
roles in the British Trotskyist movement. During the late 1960s and
throughout the 1970s, for example, Robin Blackburn and Quintin
Hoare were members of the International Marxist Group (IMG), the
British section of the Fourth International, as was Tariq Ali, who was
not an official member of either editorial board until 1983, but was an

influential interlocutor nonetheless.[14] Furthermore, Perry Anderson explicitly addressed this political orientation in print in 1976, when he ended his book *Considerations on Western Marxism* by arguing for a Trotskyist strategy of fostering solidarity between the struggles of leftists throughout the world as the only means by which radical change could be achieved. In his view, the movement needed to look beyond the spatial confines of Western Europe in order to avoid political pessimism: "Western Marxism," he argued, "is necessarily less than Marxism to the extent that it is Western."[15]

As a consequence of these internationalist political proclivities, Anderson, Blackburn, and Ali had all been centrally concerned with the potential of Latin America's various revolutionary struggles since at least 1967, when they traveled to Bolivia on behalf of the Bertrand Russell Peace Foundation in order to meet with French leftist Régis Debray. Debray had been imprisoned by the Bolivian government after making contact with Che Guevara—then participating in a guerrilla war in the country—and the British trio hoped that their presence would ensure that he received a fair trial.[16] Upon their return, Anderson and Blackburn published a short essay in *NLR*, entitled "The Marxism of Régis Debray," a preface to two extended contributions to the journal by the Frenchman himself.[17] The piece praised Debray's "Leninist focus on *making the revolution*, as a political, technical and military problem," as well as his insistence that "electoral illusions are the death of any revolutionary movement." Both of these formulations, which Anderson and Blackburn argued were "universally valid," led them to the conclusion that it was essential for any revolutionary movement to confront the bourgeois state rather than attempt to coopt its political processes, an observation that they believed could be used and developed by the British left.[18]

Tariq Ali's most significant engagement with Latin American politics in the period came several years later, when, in the aftermath of the 1973 coup against Salvador Allende's socialist government in Chile, he contributed to an IMG pamphlet analyzing the topic. He began by praising Allende's Popular Unity (UP) movement for having been both Marxist and anti-Stalinist, before describing its route to electoral victory in 1970 and subsequent period in power. Ali's intention was to use the historical record to demonstrate the inherent inaccuracy of Allende's suggestion that there was a "Chilean Road" to socialism that ran via elections and engagement with the bourgeois state.[19] Nonetheless, the author played up the dead president's heroism, arguing that when it became clear that the army was unstoppable after launching its coup in September 1973, Allende "could have resigned and left the country in comparative safety, but he chose to go down with a gun in his hand." From this assertion, Ali concluded with a hypothetical question: "could it be that in his last hours Salvador Allende decided to symbolically demonstrate the futility of the 'peaceful road' and point the way to the future?"[20]

In its inherent opposition to the bourgeois state, then, Ali's analysis shared a common core with Anderson and Blackburn's engagement with Debray's political thought. But Ali also moved beyond this point to elaborate the importance of the formation of a Chile solidarity movement within the British left, and is therefore worth quoting at length:

> Solidarity means...agitating on the relevance of Chile for the struggle of the working class in this country as well as in Western Europe as a whole. Chile may be a faraway Latin American country, but what has happened there has had a deep impact on the advanced sections of the working class throughout Europe. A solidarity movement should therefore see as one of its main tasks the linking up of Chile with the real problems that confront workers and other oppressed layers in Britain. This is something that was very difficult to do at the time of the Vietnam mobilisations. Today, it is not only possible, but also vital, as the class struggle enters a new phase.[21]

With this type of discourse, Ali essentially presaged the arguments made by various sectors of the 1980s Central America solidarity movement on both sides of the Atlantic by suggesting that enacting the concept of solidarity involved something more expansive than simply supporting Latin American revolutionaries: Western radicals had a political responsibility to learn the lessons of the Chilean left's failures, and envisage their separate national struggles as essentially interconnected.

In line with the preoccupations of Anderson, Blackburn, and Ali, *NLR* and NLB/Verso published a significant body of work on Latin American politics during the 1970s and 1980s, thereby highlighting the manner in which the two publishing ventures operated as platforms for radical discussion of the continent by authors from all over the world.[22] Further to this, Anderson himself published two short book reviews of titles relating to the continent in US publications during the same period, thereby indicating a continued personal engagement with the region, and, most notably, with the role played by US foreign policy in the continuing Central American crisis.[23] Overall, then, it is possible to see the gradual development of an institutional culture within *NLR* and NLB/Verso that was strongly influenced by Trotskyist political ideals, acutely aware of developments within Latin American radicalism, and keen to see the Trotskyist left stand in solidarity with the continent's revolutionary movements.

This was an institutional culture that Mike Davis became intimately involved in upon moving to London in 1980 to take up work at *NLR*. Davis, a Californian by birth, first became involved in left-wing politics when he worked on civil rights campaigns with the Congress of Racial Equality (CORE) in the South, before becoming a full-time Students for a Democratic Society (SDS) organizer between 1964 and 1967, working in Oakland, Los Angeles, and Austin. He then spent a brief spell in the Southern California Communist Party, at that point led by Dorothy Healey, who attracted Davis's sympathies by breaking with party orthodoxy and supporting Dubcek rather than Brezhnev in the aftermath of the 1968 Prague Spring.[24] After completing an undergraduate degree at UCLA, during which time he came under the influence of economic historian Robert Brenner, Davis traveled to the United Kingdom in 1975 to study at the University of Edinburgh. In Scotland, his Trotskyist politics brought him into the sphere of the "docks faction" of the IMG in Edinburgh, which in turn led him to his first contact with members of the *NLR* editorial committee who were also involved with the group. Indeed, Perry Anderson was so impressed by Davis's knowledge of the history of the US left that NLB/Verso offered the American a $2,000 advance to write the book that would eventually become *Prisoners of the American Dream* (1986).[25] In 1980, he moved to London to work full time for *NLR*.[26]

Davis—who lived permanently in the UK until 1986—was employed by the journal to expand its coverage of US politics, a task at which he proved adept: as historian Duncan Thompson has calculated, articles emanating from North America accounted for 25 percent of the journal's output by 1983 alone, when in 1979 they had accounted for less than 6 percent.[27] After achieving this breakthrough at *NLR*, Davis set to work establishing *The Year Left* and *The Haymarket Series*, initiatives that he and co-editor Michael Sprinker hoped would fill a similar gap in Verso's publishing catalog. Sprinker—who received a PhD in English from Princeton aged 25 and moved straight into a career as a literary theorist and critic working at Oregon State University and subsequently SUNY Stony Brook—was more of a *bona fide* academic than Davis. Nonetheless, he had a no less radical set of political credentials, forging a reputation as an Althusserian Marxist in his scholarly work, and playing a role as an activist in the New American Movement, a socialist-feminist group founded in 1971 that traced its roots back to SDS but merged in 1982 with Michael Harrington's Democratic Socialist Organizing Group to form Democratic Socialists of America. Much like Davis, he forged links with the *NLR* and Verso editorial collectives during an extended visit to London in 1982–1983, and it was out of this transatlantic nexus of relationships that *The Year Left* and *The Haymarket Series* ultimately developed.[28]

The first volume of *The Year Left*, published in 1985, was subtitled "An American Socialist Yearbook" and its editors (Davis, Sprinker, and Fred Pfeil) laid out their intentions in a "Statement of Purpose":

> We are launching this first instalment of *The Year Left* with a sense of the overriding and immediate necessity for new analyses by and for the American left—analyses and initiatives shaped by the specificity of the historical moment that North America has now definitively entered.[29]

The "historical moment" referred to was one defined by Ronald Reagan's triumphant election to a second presidential term. Reagan's malevolent influence was, the editors argued, not *only* a problem for the US Left, as they made clear in reminding their readers of words uttered by a Salvadoran activist soon after his election: "Your President is our President, too."[30] The complex, interconnected nature of the late Cold War demanded that *The Year Left* be "genuinely 'North American' in both a geographical and conceptual sense."[31] The yearbook was therefore designed as a forum in which leftists throughout the Americas could bring the specificities of their own national struggles into dialog to produce a shared political outlook.

The Haymarket Series was established soon after *The Year Left* to offer "original studies of politics, history and culture focused on North America." The introductory notes for each volume in the series suggested that it would "present innovative but representative views from across the American left on a wide range of topics of current and continuing interest to socialists in North America and throughout the world." Named to commemorate the deaths of the "martyrs" who died in the Haymarket massacre of 1886, the studies in the series would "testify to the living legacy of activism and political commitment for which they gave their lives."[32]

Although no specific mention of solidarity was made in the rationale for the Haymarket Series, its references to "North America" should be interpreted as broadly as those in *The Year Left*. This becomes clear upon brief examination of the first title released in the series: Davis's own *Prisoners of the American Dream*. As its subtitle suggested the book's main focus was "politics and economy in the history of the US working class." However, Davis peppered his analysis of US industrial and social history with the language and discourse of internationalism. "It is a central thesis of this book," he argued in its foreword, "that the future of the left in the United States is more than ever before bound up with its ability to organise solidarity with revolutionary struggles against American imperialism."[33] Davis also argued that "democracy in present-day Central America has become an essentially *revolutionary* goal,"[34] before concluding:

> If socialism is to arrive one day in North America, it is much more probable that it will be by virtue of a combined, hemispheric process of revolt that overlaps boundaries and interlaces movements...It is necessary to begin to imagine more audacious projects of coordinated action and political cooperation among the popular lefts in all the countries of the Americas. We are all, finally, prisoners of the same malign "American Dream."[35]

Davis's approach to internationalism therefore meshed with those articulated by his British comrades, and helps to highlight the transatlantic dimensions of the Trotskyist politics that developed around the issue of solidarity with Latin American revolutionary struggles. It also shows the vital importance of anti-interventionism to Verso's US projects. Davis's text was not centrally concerned with US involvement in Central America, but it formed a key issue in his analysis nonetheless.[36] Indeed, he has since suggested that one of the immediate priorities in setting up the series was "to recover the CISPES experience," referring to a key US solidarity organization, Committee in Solidarity with the People of El Salvador.[37] This helps to demonstrate that although discourses of solidarity were by no means the only ideas dealt with in the essays and books published under the aegis of *The Year Left* and *The Haymarket Series*, they were some of the most significant.

In order to examine the discussions of solidarity that took place within the pages of *The Year Left* and *The Haymarket Series*, this chapter will now focus on a single example of Verso's output during the Reagan era: Roger Burbach and Orlando Nuñéz's book *Fire in the Americas: Forging a Revolutionary Agenda*, which was published in 1987 as a part of *The Haymarket Series*. As well as seeking to reconstruct the context in which the book was written, it will illuminate how the ideas contained within it intersected with those expressed elsewhere in the two series, so as to more accurately map the coordinates of the brand of internationalism articulated by Verso's US projects.

Roger Burbach gained a PhD in Latin American history at Indiana University in 1975. By the time of the *Fire in the America*'s publication, he was employed at the Center for the Study of the Americas at the University of California, Berkeley, and had published a number of articles on Central American politics in the Third Worldist political journal, *Monthly Review*.[38] Nuñéz, on the other hand, was a Nicaraguan national involved with the study and implementation of agrarian reform in the aftermath of the Sandinista revolution. *Fire in the Americas* was, then, a product of transnational collaboration. Originally published in Spanish, it received the Carlos Fonseca Prize in 1987, Nicaragua's highest social science award. The authors quickly translated the text into English, with Mike Davis playing an integral role in helping to arrange its publication in the United States as the seventh instalment in *The Haymarket Series*.

At little over 100 pages, *Fire in the Americas* was not intended as a scholarly monograph. Instead, it formed an attempt to concisely set the agenda for debate among leftists in Central and North America. In his foreword for the book's English translation, for example, Pablo González Casanova argued (perhaps somewhat hyperbolically) that it took its place "within…a revolution in thought," a "great epistemological break" in which leftists throughout the Americas were moving away from the doctrinaire discussions of "correct" or "incorrect" revolutionary lines that dominated the 1970s, and toward a more constructive engagement with political struggle in Central America.[39] As Gopal Balakrishnan has recently pointed out, one of the distinguishing features of the political manifesto as a literary genre is the manner in which it mobilizes "a de-linking from the present, from the status quo," and thereby offers up a singular rhetorical form that is capable of expressing "the conditions of possibility in bringing forth 'the new.'"[40] Considered as such, *Fire in the Americas* can itself be read as a type of manifesto that laid out a set of theoretical suppositions and practical proposals for a transnational social movement that centered its attention on forging solidarity with the struggles of the Central American left.

But how did Burbach and Nuñéz's text fit within the context provided by Verso's two US series, and what does this context tell us about the intellectual underpinnings of the solidarity movement? Section three of the second volume of *The Year Left*, entitled "Crisis in the Hemisphere," was designed, according to its editors, to "survey" the conjuncture in Central America so as to aid "the long labour of understanding and ultimately transforming the major structures of oppression in the heartlands of the American imperium."[41] This brief reference signals a broad concern throughout Verso's US initiatives with the development of an explanatory framework that could offer a detailed understanding of the crisis in the Isthmus, even if the series were primarily concerned with theorizing a political praxis that would help to transform hemispheric politics. An examination of the economic and political underpinnings of the approaches developed in *The Year Left* and *The Haymarket Series* is therefore essential.

The first major analytical foundation of the two series was a keen understanding of the differences between politics and culture in Central and North America. For example, in an essay in *The Year Left*, anthropologist Carol A. Smith sought to destabilize what she saw as the left's over-reliance on class as an explanatory category by suggesting that, in the case of Guatemala, *ethnicity* was in fact the structuring dynamic in political life. Such a situation arose because the state was governed by a predominantly Ladino grouping that took a racially inflected and uniformly repressive approach to Guatemala's indigenous population.[42] However, rather than rejecting a Marxist logic altogether, Smith argued that an analysis of Guatemalan politics needed to understand the nature of its civil society as one in which class struggle *did* exist, but not necessarily between classes whose interests could be defined purely in economic terms.[43]

This was an approach echoed by Roger Burbach and Orlando Nuñéz. The pair argued that a "third force" existed within Central American oppositional politics that consisted of "distinctive constituencies" that could not necessarily be defined in strict class terms. Again, in such an analysis "ethnic Others," as well as radicalized Christians and other social movements, were regarded as vitally important groups whose politics were not yet fully understood by many activists in the United States.[44] The key implication of such arguments was that any radical political alternative to US imperialism could not be realistically considered without an engagement with the numerous complexities of the region's various social and political make-ups.

Burbach and Nuñéz signaled another major analytic theme of the two series when they questioned the logic of the dependency theory that held sway in many left-wing academic circles during the 1960s and 1970s. They suggested that the inter-American debate over dependency theory had focused on "issues relating to the political economy of capitalism," but had contributed very little to the understanding of "concrete political processes."[45] Indeed, this was a criticism that had already made in the pages of *The Year Left*.[46] In the yearbook's second volume, economists Marc W. Herold and Nicholas Kozlov had attacked the influential "New International Division of Labour" (NIDL) theory, which had been developed during the early 1980s. They suggested that the theory's problem, one it shared with the dependency theories it sought to replace, was its "neglect of internal class relations" in Central American economies.[47] "Our approach," the authors argued,

> seeks to affirm the effectivity of contradictions and developments *internal* to social formations, as opposed to the dependency and NIDL perspectives, which stress determination by *external* forces. Whereas for the dependency school, the relevant external factor was the state of dependency imposed by one *nation* on another, the NIDL theoreticians believe they have found a new "dependence" rooted in the activities of *multinational corporations*.[48]

This focus on external determination conferred on dependency and NIDL theories "a nationalist character and a longing for a frustrated autonomous development."[49] Third World economies should instead, Herold and Lozlov argued, be understood as part of a *global* system of class-based capitalist expansion that was never confined within national boundaries.[50] This lack of faith in contemporary economic theory actually signaled a move in the opposite direction to the stress on Central American difference noted earlier. In this case, a class-based, traditionally Marxist approach was deemed more, rather than less, important than in previous scholarship. However, the overall lesson was the same: the American left needed to learn more, and in more detail, about the configuration of forces any politics of solidarity would have to resist.

The final structural dynamic regularly highlighted in *The Year Left* and *The Haymarket Series* was that of Reaganism itself. Aline Frambes-Buxeda, for example, argued in *The Year Left* that Puerto Rico, often overlooked in analyses of Central American politics, was being used as a "staging ground" for what she saw as the four main elements of the Reaganite project. She suggested that "a new and more extreme social polarisation" was combining with "venal entrepreneurialism," a militaristic "Rambo stridency" and "creeping state terrorism" on the island, and that these were the main building blocks of the Puerto Rican "model" Reagan was hoping to export throughout the Isthmus with his interventionist foreign policy.[51]

These points can be closely linked to Mike Davis's earlier suggestion, in *Prisoners of the American Dream*, that a "New Cold War"
had been initiated by the Reagan administration, which had "called
forth an overarching program of geomilitary expansion" with the
aim of creating "nothing less than omnicompetent US interventionism."[52] Indeed, the genesis of this position can be traced even further
back through Verso's history to the publication of Fred Halliday's
The Making of the Second Cold War in 1983, in which the prominent
international relations scholar suggested that a new era had emerged
in postwar history after the election of Reagan. This "second Cold
War" was characterized by mounting tension and confrontation
between the superpowers, justified on both sides by "threat and
challenge, self-justification and vilification of the other."[53] The anti-
interventionist print culture established through Verso's engagement
with American topics was therefore based on a view of Reaganism as a
world political force that, although not without precedent in the history of American empire, represented a new and more extreme form
of expansionism, one that was intent on asserting its neoconservative
agenda throughout Central America.

But how were such structures of imperial domination to be resisted?
This was the most important question that *The Year Left* and *The
Haymarket Series* sought to answer. The first problem was to establish
whether or not an engagement with US electoral politics could form a
fruitful oppositional strategy. Volume one of *The Year Left* was published soon after Ronald Reagan's second inauguration in 1985, and
the issue of electoralism was placed front and center. In the volume's
opening essay, Manning Marable suggested that electoralism *could*
play a significant role for the US left, if they were able to build "a
permanent coalition of social groups" that would remain independent
from the Democratic Party.[54] The essay, as well as his *Haymarket
Series* book *Black American Politics* (1985), drew inspiration from the
1984 campaign of Jesse Jackson, which had united certain groups on
the left in his challenge for the Democratic Presidential nomination.
Marable argued that in drawing together his "Rainbow Coalition,"
Jackson had proved that "when Black political movements express
their own objective interests, they speak not only for the masses of
Afro-Americans, but for all of the oppressed."[55] In this view, then,
the popular force of Jackson's campaign, which was mounted within
the boundaries of official Democratic politics, easily had the potential
to transcend narrow electoralism and become a mass movement.

This was a position with which Robert Brenner, author of the
volume's second essay, strongly disagreed. He suggested that the

"paradox of American social democracy" had led to a situation in which,

> On the one hand…the expansion of working-class self-organisation, power and political consciousness…has provided *the* critical condition for the success of reformism as well as of the far left. On the other hand…its core representatives…have invariably sought to implement policies reflecting *their own* distinctive social positions and interest— positions which are *separate from* and interests which are…*opposed to* those of the working class.[56]

This complex conjuncture, which Brenner argued the US left did not fully understand, deemed any electoralist strategy essentially null and void, as those who were elected to represent the interests of oppressed groups would always end up contradicting that goal. As a consequence, Marable's characterization of Jackson's coalition as a "vanguard of the left" was, in Brenner's view, entirely misplaced.[57] "By conflating electoralism and program mongering with movement building," he argued, "Marable perpetuates the myth that winning office is winning power, and that there is a shortcut to the long, hard and daunting task of rebuilding the movements."[58] Put simply, the essential question was whether or not the left should have any faith in the ability of America's existing democratic institutions to usher in new, emancipatory political forms.

Fire in the Americas contributed a hemispheric perspective to this debate by arguing against the Marxist-Leninist orthodoxy that suggested democracy to be an inherently bourgeois form of government. Instead, Burbach and Nuñéz maintained that democratic ideals and aspirations were at the center of the "ideological battle" between capitalism and socialism.[59] "There will be few easy targets like Batista, Somoza, or Duvalier," they averred, as

> in many parts of the Third World the struggle will be fought over democracy, over whether the United States and its reformist allies—be they Duarte in El Salvador or Aquino in the Philippines—can contain the democratic aspirations of the masses and prevent revolutionary alternatives from developing. And the left, to meet this new challenge, will have to take up the democratic banner in a way that it never has before.[60]

In this formulation, then, there was a certain type of democracy that was essentially imperialist in nature, "managed" by US intervention to ensure results that were pleasing to Washington. This was the type of sham democracy to which the left could provide an alternative, but not by attempting to establish a "dictatorship of the proletariat." Rather, what was needed was a revolutionary "pluralism" that recognized the vital importance of competing voices within a framework that sought to challenge the damaging influence of American intervention.[61] Indeed, it was precisely this formulation that won the book wider praise in the form of a review in the *Guardian*, a radical New York weekly newspaper that was dedicated to building the Central American solidarity movement, which suggested that the text's primary value resided in its promotion of democratic pluralism from *within* the Marxist fold.[62]

Another important theme in both Verso series was the continuing utility of the work of Régis Debray. In 1967, at the behest of Fidel Castro, Debray published a short work entitled *Revolution in the Revolution?* that collected his thoughts on the importance of the Cuban Revolution for those oppositional groups throughout Latin America, which were seeking to recreate its anti-imperialist achievements.[63] The book, which rapidly became an influential manual of guerrilla warfare, asserted that there were certain "truths, of a technical, tactical and even of a strategic order" that could be learnt from a detailed study of Castro's overthrow of the Batista regime.[64] Perhaps the most important of these was Debray's argument that "in Latin America today, a political line, which, in terms of its consequences, is not susceptible to expression as a precise and consistent military line, cannot be considered revolutionary."[65] This necessitated the establishment of military *focos* (small, highly trained revolutionary cadres), which would fulfil the role of vanguard by "confronting imperialism with acts and not merely with words."[66] Debray's close links with Castro, as well as with Che Guevara, gave the Frenchman's theories a currency they perhaps would not have otherwise garnered. But, as Burbach and Nuñéz were keen to point out, "the defeat in the 1960s of guerrilla movements in Guatemala, Venezuela, Nicaragua, and Brazil...demonstrates that it requires much more than a small band of guerrillas to overthrow an established order buttressed by the USA." This meant that, in a changed political climate, new tactics were needed to resist Central America's *ancien régime*.[67]

One of the main underpinnings of these new tactics was a commonly held scepticism toward political and theoretical dogma. This approach resisted strict adherence not only to theories such as Debray's, but also those of more traditional Marxism-Leninism. As Paul Buhle put it in his history of Marxism in the United States, which was published as a part of *The Haymarket Series*, this new approach was based on an

ecumenical understanding that "Marxism is as Marxism does," and
that those groups in Central America who embraced various strands
of revolutionary thought had "just as much claim to the mantle as
Trotsky, Mao or Marx himself."[68] This line was reinforced by Carol
A. Smith in *The Year Left*. Concluding her essay on indigenous communities in Guatemala, she suggested that, "if Marxism is to become
truly the theory of liberation in Latin America it must break free of
the dogmatism that reduces age-old cultures of resistance to mere
epiphenomena of objectivized class struggles."[69] In making the case
for a Marxist praxis that was responsive to local conditions and not
ridden by the intense factionalism of the past, both Buhle and Smith
were clearly singing from similar hymn sheets.

Burbach and Nuñéz furthered this argument, but shifted the
emphasis to a more constructive engagement with the topic of political praxis. The authors suggested, again *contra* Debray, that the key
lesson to be learnt from the Cuban and Nicaraguan revolutions did
not relate to the use of explicitly military tactics. Rather, it was that
success came about in each case because revolutionary leaders were
able to draw on the "radical political traditions of their own countries
to come up with successful strategies for seizing power."[70] Castro and
his followers often referred to the example of nineteenth-century theorist of Cuban independence Jose Marti, and in Nicaragua, the revolutionary movement drew its name from that of Augusto Sandino,
the leader of resistance to US imperial presence in the country during
the late 1920s and early 1930s. These distinctly *national* examples of
revolutionary praxis needed to be borne in mind so that anti-inter-
ventionist movements could remain "constantly on guard," and again
avoiding turning potentially valuable theory into dogma.[71]

But perhaps the most important contribution made by Burbach
and Nuñéz was the concept of the "fourth force." The authors' theoretical division of the left into various forces has already been briefly
referenced, but a fuller examination of its implications is worthwhile.
The schema set forth in *Fire in the Americas* originated in a conventional Marxist observation: that the primary revolutionary force in any
society was the working class. Burbach and Nuñéz supplemented this
starting point with a dose of Leninism, suggesting that the second
revolutionary force was formed by the peasant classes, which, although
often retained some structural similarities with the working class, had a
fundamentally divergent experience of capitalism, and, in almost every
Latin American society, constituted the "largest social force." This fact
consequently necessitated the formation of "a worker–peasant alliance
as the central axis for revolutionary struggle."[72] Such a bloc was defined

as the "*historic subject* of all popular revolutions," consisting as it did of the social groupings that were "destined by history to form the antithesis of capitalism while that system exists."[73] Building on this theoretical foundation, though, Burbach and Nuñéz introduced the concept of the third force, which was derived from an essentially New Leftist view of social change. The third force consisted of an amorphous amalgamation of intellectuals, students, ethnic others, and religious communities that cohered together to shape the "*social subject* of all revolutions," or those groups that, although not inherently opposed to capital because of their social status, were, for various reasons, compelled to "incorporate themselves into any revolutionary project."[74]

Up until this point, then, Burbach and Nuñéz had done little more than ventriloquize the arguments of the Old and New lefts. In articulating their concept of the fourth force, however, they went a step further and sought to make an original contribution to socialist strategy. The fourth force, they argued, was formed by the international solidarity movements that had grown out of the Cuban Revolution and developed full coherence in response to the 1973 coup in Chile and the success of the Nicaraguan revolution in 1979. Indeed, Burbach and Nuñéz went as far as suggesting that the very success of the Sandinista revolution "owed almost as much to the mobilisation of international forces and pressures against the Somoza regime as it did to the internal upheaval within Nicaragua."[75] Operating at the grass roots, then, and with networks that were all but unimpeded by national boundaries, the Central American solidarity movement was theorized as a core force within the international left, one that was essentially independent from the struggles of workers, peasants, and the third force, but that helped to establish a concretely internationalist sensibility amongst activists throughout the Americas.

This was a point that was furthered in a *Year Left* essay discussing the history of United States-based solidarity activism. The piece, which was written by CISPES activist Van Gosse, again detailed the roots of the 1980s movement in earlier struggles against US involvement in Cuba and Chile. Gosse went on to suggest that, rather than being enmeshed in the sectarian rivalries of the US left, solidarity activism distinguished itself by

> responding directly to the immediate conjunctures and long-term dynamics of revolutionary processes as defined by the organisations representing the people that (individual activist groups) support. The solidarity group itself was defined ultimately as another sector in the war, and the United States as another front, no more and no less.[76]

In this formulation, then, the solidarity enacted by disparate activist groups such as CISPES and Witness for Peace was conceptualized as a pragmatic opposition to the specific political circumstances engendered by US policymaking in Central America, rather than an abstract and holistic opposition to imperialism or capitalism as global structures. This approach did not ignore the fact that many of those involved in the movement were firmly rooted in the political traditions of the anti-capitalist left, but it did maintain that the goal of solidarity could not stand in as a substitute for broader struggles for social change.[77]

It seems clear, then, that the authors involved with *The Year Left* and *The Haymarket Series* were drawn together around a group of key political and economic issues. A concrete analysis of the structures of domination used to enforce the imperial status quo was, in almost all cases, fused with the proposition of a left-wing praxis that was anti-dogmatic and democratic in spirit. These assertions formed the economic and political foundations for the concept of solidarity that developed out of the two series. A specific focus on the role played by the writing of Roger Burbach and Orlando Nuñéz within this context also provides an insight into the manner in which these ideas intersected with the goals of the solidarity movement. Throughout the 1980s, there existed the potential for contradiction between those espousing solidarity as a means of ending US intervention in Central America and those who believed it implied a much broader, revolutionary project. But Burbach and Nuñéz's argument that it was necessary to fan the flames of "fire in the Americas" aimed to bridge the divide between these two positions. In their formulation, sweeping internationalist theory could not be understood without active engagement in political praxis. But the reverse was also true: the single issues attended to by traditional methods of activism needed to be related to broader struggles against the status quo, both North and South.

For those involved in the US Central American solidarity movement, the very term "solidarity" was a multifaceted and slippery one. In certain circumstances, this versatility united activists espousing disparate and potentially contradictory political philosophies around a common cause. Nonetheless, during the latter half of the Reagan era, it became increasingly obvious that debate was needed over the intellectual underpinnings of the relationship between US leftists and the revolutionary movements of Central America. Verso's *The Year Left* and *The Haymarket Series* were designed as forums in which such a discussion could take place, and therefore aimed to provide significant intellectual underpinning for the solidarity movement. The origins of the two series in the transatlantic history of the New Left also highlight the importance of transnational exchange within this context, whether it was between leftists in the United Kingdom and the United States (in the case of Verso's relationship with its series' editors), or between those in the United States and Central America (in the case of the authorship of *Fire in the Americas*). Ultimately, then, the issue of solidarity with revolutionary struggle in Central America during the 1980s concretized debates about Latin American politics that had been crisscrossing the Atlantic since the emergence of the 1960s New Left.

The Progressive era reformers discussed by Daniel Rodgers in *Atlantic Crossings* were primarily concerned with the development of a "welfare state," rooted in measures such as unemployment insurance and social security that sought to expand the role of government in the economic sphere. On the other hand, the transatlantic leftist community brought together by *New Left Review* and Verso Books through engagement with the politics of Central America solidarity was more radical in its emphasis on an internationalist, revolutionary sensibility that would unite a variety of activist forces in their opposition to US interventionism. These constituted very different definitions of "social politics": whereas the former focused primarily on *domestic* reform, the latter demonstrated the importance of *international* politics, arguing that social change was impossible without an end to US funding of repressive regimes in the name of "anticommunism." These differences aside, the existence of such an intellectual and political community during the 1980s points to the fact that the transnational focus exemplified in *Atlantic Crossings* remains essential to any understanding of the history of the British and American lefts during the latter half of the twentieth century.

Notes

1. Joel Pfister, *Critique for What? Cultural Studies, American Studies, Left Studies* (Boulder: Paradigm Publishers, 2006), 63–69.
2. The following book-length studies of the US Central American solidarity movement use the methodologies of "social movement studies" to examine its development: Christian Smith, *Resisting Reagan: The US Central America Peace Movement* (Chicago: University of Chicago Press, 1996); Sharon Erickson Nepstad, *Convictions of the Soul: Religion, Culture and Agency in the Central America Solidarity Movement* (Oxford: Oxford University Press, 2004); and Clare Weber, *Visions of Solidarity: US Peace Activists in Nicaragua from War to*

Women's Activism and Globalization (Lanham, MD: Lexington Books, 2006). Significant book chapters and articles covering the movement include Van Gosse, "'El Salvador Is Spanish for Vietnam': A New Immigrant Left and the Politics of Solidarity," in *The Immigrant Left in the United States*, Paul Buhle and Dan Georgakas, eds (Albany: State University of New York Press, 1996), 302–30; Roger Peace, "The Anti-Contra-War Campaign: Organizational Dynamics of a Decentralized Movement," *International Journal of Peace Studies* 13, no. 1 (Spring/Summer 2008): 63–83; Héctor Perla Jr, "Si Nicaragua Venció, El Salvador Vencerá: Central American Agency in the Creation of the US-Central American Peace and Solidarity Movement," *Latin American Research Review* 43, no. 2 (2008): 136–58; and Roger Peace, "Winning Hearts and Minds: The Debate over US Intervention in Nicaragua in the 1980s," *Peace and Change* 35, no. 1 (January 2010): 1–38.

3. For an entertaining first-hand account of the conjuncture out of which *NLR* emerged, see Stuart Hall, "Life and Times of the First New Left," *New Left Review*, 2nd ser., 61 (January–February 2010): 177–96. The founding of the journal is covered in more detail in Duncan Thompson, *Pessimism of the Intellect? A History of* New Left Review (Monmouth, UK: Merlin Press, 2007), 1–42 and Lin Chun, *The British New Left* (Edinburgh: Edinburgh University Press, 1993), 10–15.

4. Hall, "Life and Times," 178–80.

5. Editorial, *New Left Review*, 1st ser., 1 (January–February 1960): 1.

6. Between 1936 and 1948, the Left Book Club published hundreds of broad-ranging and cheap political paperbacks, by fiction and nonfiction authors such as George Orwell, André Malraux, Arthur Koestler, Clifford Odets, G. D. H. Cole, Harold Laski, and Sidney and Beatrice Webb. It combined this publication project with the nationwide organization of study groups that sought to develop cultural and social links between those groups in British society interested in Left politics, but not actively engaged in government. See John Lewis, *The Left Book Club: An Historical Record* (London: Victor Gollancz, 1970).

7. Ibid., 2.

8. E. P. Thompson, ed., *Out of Apathy* (London: Stevens & Company, 1960).

9. Chun, *British New Left*, 125.

10. C. Wright Mills, "Letter to the New Left," *New Left Review*, 1st ser., 5 (September–October 1960): 18–23. For an illuminating discussion of the transatlantic contexts of Mills's work, see Daniel Geary, *Radical Ambition: C. Wright Mills, the Left, and American Social Thought* (Berkeley: University of California Press, 2009), 179–215.

11. Pfister, *Critique for What?* 63–69.

12. Duncan Thompson, *Pessimism of the Intellect?* 8–9.

13. Ibid., 10.
14. Ibid., 66.
15. Perry Anderson, *Considerations on Western Marxism* (London: New Left Books, 1976), 94.
16. Duncan Thompson, *Pessimism of the Intellect?* 37.
17. Régis Debray, "Latin America: The Long March," *New Left Review*, 1st ser., 33 (September–October 1965): 17–58; Régis Debray, "Problems of Revolutionary Strategy in Latin America," *New Left Review*, 1st ser., 45 (September–October 1967): 13–41.
18. Perry Anderson and Robin Blackburn, "The Marxism of Régis Debray," *New Left Review*, 1st ser., 45 (September–October 1967): 8–10. The piece was republished a year later in a *Monthly Review* collection on Debray, once again demonstrating the transatlantic flow of ideas between the British and American lefts during the 1960s. See Leo Huberman and Paul Sweezy, eds, *Regis Debray and the Latin American Revolution* (New York: Monthly Review Press, 1968), 63–69.
19. Tariq Ali, "Lessons of the Coup," in *Chile: Lessons of the Coup, Which Way to Workers Power?* Tariq Ali and Gerry Hedley, 4–12 (London: IMG Publications, 1974).
20. Ibid., 18.
21. Ibid., 23.
22. From *NLR*: Ernesto Laclau, "Feudalism and Capitalism in Latin America," *New Left Review*, 1st ser., 67 (May–June 1971): 19–38; Jose Carlos Mariátegui, "The Anti-Imperialist Perspective," *New Left Review*, 1st ser., 70 (November–December 1971): 67–72; Fernando Henrique Cardoso, "Dependency and Development in Latin America," *New Left Review*, 1st ser., 74 (July–August 1972): 83–95; Göran Therborn, "The Travail of Latin American Democracy," *New Left Review*, 1st ser., 97 (May–June 1976): 71–109; Atilio A. Borón, "Latin America: Between Hobbes and Friedman," *New Left Review*, 1st ser., 130 (November–December 1981): 45–66; George Black, "Central America: Crisis in the Backyard," *New Left Review*, 1st ser., 135 (September–October 1982): 5–34; Fred Halliday, "Cold War in the Caribbean," *New Left Review*, 1st ser., 141 (September–October 1983): 5–22; Edward S. Herman and James Petras, "Resurgent Democracy: Rhetoric and Reality," *New Left Review*, 1st ser., 154 (November–December 1985): 83–98; Paul Cammack, "Resurgent Democracy: Threat and Promise," *New Left Review*, 1st ser., 157 (May–June 1986), 121–28; Carlos M. Vilas, "Revolutionary Unevenness in Central America," *New Left Review*, 1st ser., 175 (May–June 1989): 111–25. From NLB/Verso: Régis Debray, *Conversations with Allende: Socialism in Chile* (London: New Left Books, 1971); Henri Weber, *Nicaragua: The Sandinist Revolution* (London: Verso, 1981); Adolfo Gilly, *The Mexican Revolution* (London: Verso, 1983).

23. Perry Anderson, "Contraband," *The Nation*, June 20, 1987, 855–57; Perry Anderson, "Laboring Under Various Pretenses in Latin America," *In These Times*, April 6–12, 1988, 19.

24. Victor Cohen, "The Left Coast: An Interview with Mike Davis," *The Minnesota Review* 73–74 (Fall 2009–Spring 2010): 22–24. For more information on Healey, see Dorothy Ray Healey and Maurice Isserman, *California Red: A Life in the American Communist Party* (Urbana: University of Illinois Press, 1993).

25. Mike Davis, *Prisoners of the American Dream: Politics and Economy in the History of the US Working Class* (London: Verso, 1986).

26. Ibid., 28–29.

27. Duncan Thompson, *Pessimism of the Intellect?* 214n.

28. See Alan Wald, "Committed to the End: Michael Sprinker, 1950–1999," in *Cultural Logic: An Electronic Journal of Marxist Theory and Practice* 3, no. 1 (Fall 1999) http://clogic.eserver.org/3-1&2/3-1%262.html. For a brief overview of the early history of the New American Movement, see Max Elbaum, *Revolution in the Air: Sixties Radicals Turn to Lenin, Mao and Che* (London: Verso, 2006), 118–21.

29. Mike Davis, Fred Pfeil, and Michael Sprinker, eds, *The Year Left: An American Socialist Yearbook* (London: Verso, 1985), vii.

30. Ibid., viii.

31. Ibid.

32. All of the quotations in this paragraph are taken from the introductory notes that appeared in every volume published as a part of *The Haymarket Series*.

33. Davis, *Prisoners of the American Dream*, ix.

34. Ibid., 205.

35. Ibid., 314.

36. Indeed, it was even dedicated to "the combatants of the FMLN." See ibid., vi.

37. Mike Davis, e-mail message to author, December 14, 2010.

38. See Roger Burbach, "Nicaragua: The Course of the Revolution," *Monthly Review*, February 1980, 28–39; Burbach, "Central America: The End of US Hegemony?" *Monthly Review*, January 1982, 1–18; Burbach, "Revolution and Reaction: US Policy in Central America," *Monthly Review*, June 1984, 1–20.

39. Roger Burbach and Orlando Nuñéz, *Fire in the Americas: Forging a Revolutionary Agenda* (London: Verso, 1987), ix–x.

40. Gopal Balakrishnan, *Antagonistics* (London: Verso, 2009), 268–69.

41. Davis et al., *The Year Left 2: An American Socialist Yearbook: Towards a Rainbow Socialism* (London: Verso, 1987), xiii.

42. Carol A. Smith, "Culture and Community: The Language of Class in Guatemala," in *The Year Left* 2, Davis et al., 205.

43. Ibid., 214.

44. Burbach and Nuñéz, *Fire in the Americas*, 64–67.

45. Ibid., 37.
46. Indeed, lengthy discussion of the relevance/utility of dependency theory had also taken place in the pages of *NLR* during the 1970s and early 1980s. See, for example, Laclau, "Feudalism and Capitalism," and Cardoso, "Dependency and Development."
47. Marc W. Herold and Nicholas Kozlov, "A New International Division of Labour? The Caribbean Example," in *The Year Left 2*, Davis et al., 219.
48. Ibid., 221.
49. Ibid., 222.
50. Ibid., 225.
51. Aline Frambes-Buxeda, "Puerto Rico Under the Reagan Doctrine," in *The Year Left 2*, Davis et al., 242–250.
52. Davis, *Prisoners of the American Dream*, 181.
53. Fred Halliday, *The Making of the Second Cold War* (London: Verso, 1983), 1.
54. Manning Marable, "Race and Realignment in American Politics," in Davis et al., *The Year Left*, 24.
55. Manning Marable, *Black American Politics: From the Washington Marches to Jesse Jackson* (London: Verso, 1985), ix.
56. Robert Brenner, "The Paradox of Social Democracy: American Case," in *The Year Left*, Davis et al., 36.
57. Ibid., 71.
58. Ibid., 79.
59. Burbach and Nuñéz, *Fire in the Americas*, 41.
60. Ibid., 43.
61. Ibid., 52.
62. Peter Camejo and John Trinkl, "A Challenge: To Find a Democratic, Pluralist Marxism," review of *Fire in the Americas: Forging a Revolutionary Agenda* by Roger Burbach and Orlando Nuñéz, *Guardian* (Summer 1988 Book Supplement): S-16.
63. In his autobiography, Debray tells of the felicitous circumstances that drew him into Castro's sphere of influence. He had published a brief essay on the Cuban Revolution and its meanings for Latin America as a whole in the January 1965 issue of Jean-Paul Sartre's French journal, *Les Temps Modernes*. A copy of the piece found its way into the hands of Che Guevara, who translated it for Castro. Impressed, the Cuban leader sent for Debray because he seemed to have "a sound grasp of the difficulties of urban and the advantages of rural guerrilla warfare." He then spent a number of years in Cuba, before traveling to Bolivia with Guevara. *Revolution in the Revolution?* was, in significant part, the result of these experiences. See Régis Debray, *Praised be Our Lords: A Political Education* (London: Verso, 2007), 28–29.
64. Régis Debray, *Revolution in the Revolution?* (London: Penguin, 1967), 15.

65. Ibid., 24–25.
66. Ibid., 126.
67. Burbach and Nuñéz, *Fire in the Americas*, 3. In fact, Debray himself had reached a similar conclusion a number of years earlier. After a series of conversations with Chilean President Salvador Allende, he sounded a note of cautious optimism regarding the legal, rather than military, route to power. Electoralism, the Chilean example forced him to admit, did have the potential to give birth "to a really new society freed from exploitation and foreign domination." See Debray, *Conversations with Allende*, 15.
68. Paul Buhle, *Marxism in the United States: Remapping the History of the American Left* (London: Verso), 16.
69. Smith, "Culture and Community," 217.
70. Burbach and Nuñéz, *Fire in the Americas*, 38.
71. Ibid., 39.
72. Ibid., 7.
73. Ibid., 8.
74. Ibid., 8–9.
75. Ibid., 81–83.
76. Van Gosse, "The North American Front: Central American Solidarity in the Reagan Era," in *The Year Left 3: An American Socialist Yearbook: Reshaping the US Left: Popular Struggles in the 1980s*, Mike Davis and Michael Sprinker, eds, (London: Verso, 1988), 35.
77. Van Gosse, "Active Engagement: The Legacy of Central America Solidarity," *NACLA Report on the Americas* XXVIII, no. 5 (March/ April 1995), 28.

Contributors

Manuel Álvarez Tardío is Senior Lecturer in the History of Political Thought and Social and Political Movements at Rey Juan Carlos University of Madrid, Spain. His research focuses on the breakdown of democratic regimes during the interwar period, the Spanish transition from dictatorship to democracy, and the evolution of political thought of the Catholic Right from 1930s onward. Publications include *El camino a la democracia en España: 1931 y 1978* (2005) and *El precio de la exclusión: La política durante la Segunda República* (2010), and an edited volume, *The Spanish Second Republic Revisited: From Democratic Hopes to Civil War (1931–1936)* (2012).

Jonathan Bell is Professor in US History and Director of the Institute of the Americas at University College London. A historian of post-New Deal US politics and political culture, he is the author of *California Crucible: The Forging of Modern American Liberalism* (2012) and *The Liberal State on Trial: The Cold War and American Politics in the Truman Years* (2004), and is co-editor with Timothy Stanley of *Making Sense of American Liberalism* (2012). His current major project is a study of sexual minorities and the politics of healthcare. Jonathan is Chair of Historians of the Twentieth Century United States (HOTCUS), an international organization based in the United Kingdom for historians of the United States.

Andrew Heath is a Lecturer in American History at the University of Sheffield. Since completing his PhD at the University of Pennsylvania in 2008, he has published articles on urban history and political culture in the *Journal of Urban History*, *Civil War History*, and *American Nineteenth Century History*. He is currently finishing a book on the spatial, social, and political reconstruction of Philadelphia between 1837 and 1877.

David Komline is a PhD candidate in history at the University of Notre Dame, United States. He works on early-nineteenth-century transnational and transatlantic history and is writing a dissertation called "The Common School Awakening: Education, Religion, and Reform in Transatlantic Perspective, 1800–1848." His research for this project, which draws upon archival sources in France, Germany, and the United States, has been supported by grants from the Fulbright Commission, the Virginia Historical Society, the American Congregational Association in conjunction with the Boston Athenaeum, and several institutes at the University of Notre Dame.

Jean-Louis Marin-Lamellet is a PhD candidate at the Lumière University in Lyon, France. He works on late-nineteenth and early-twentieth-century US history, US cultural and intellectual history, and the history of the book and journalism. His doctoral thesis is an intellectual biography of the Boston reform editor Benjamin Orange Flower (1858–1918).

David Sarias Rodríguez holds a PhD in American History from the University of Sheffield, United Kingdom, and currently teaches History of Political Thought and Public Opinion at Universidad San Pablo CEU in Madrid, Spain. He is writing a book on Richard Nixon and American conservatism and a book chapter on the role of anti-communism in the postwar ascendancy of the US Right.

Axel Schäfer is Professor of American History and director of the David Bruce Centre for American Studies at Keele University. His research focuses on nineteenth- and twentieth-century US intellectual and cultural history, with a particular emphasis on religion and politics, transatlantic social thought, and public policy. He is the author of three monographs: *Piety and Public Funding: Evangelicals and the State in Modern America* (2012); *Countercultural Conservatives: American Evangelicalism from the Postwar Revival to the New Christian Right* (2011); and *American Progressives and German Social Reform, 1875–1920: Social Ethics, Moral Control, and the Regulatory State in a Transatlantic Context* (2000). He has published numerous journal articles and essays in edited volumes, including a prize-winning essay on W. E. B. Du Bois in the *Journal of American History*. In his current research he examines the nexus between immigration and welfare state building in the United States, Britain, and Germany in the decade after the First World War.

Daniel Scroop is Senior Lecturer in US History and Contemporary Citizenship at the University of Glasgow. His research examines the national and transnational contours of the US politics of reform. He is the author of *Mr. Democrat: Jim Farley, the New Deal, and the Making of Modern American Politics* (2006), and editor of *Consuming Visions: New Essays on the Politics of Consumption in Modern America* (2007). His work on the anti-chain store movement, published in *American Quarterly*, won the 2009 Constance Rourke Prize of the American Studies Association. He is currently writing a book on "the politics of scale" in US political economy from the 1890s to the present.

Nick Witham is Senior Lecturer in American Social and Cultural History at Canterbury Christ Church University, United Kingdom. His book *The Cultural Left and the Reagan Era: U.S. Protest and Central American Revolution*, will be published in 2015 by I. B. Tauris.

Index

Printed and bound by CPI Group (UK) Ltd, Croydon, CR0 4YY